The State of Economic Inclusion Report 2024

Scan the QR code to see this and prior editions of
The State of Economic Inclusion Report.

The State of Economic Inclusion Report 2024

Pathways to Scale

Inés Arévalo-Sánchez, Janet Heisey,
Sarang Chaudhary, Timothy Clay,
Victoria Strokova, Puja Vasudeva Dutta,
and Colin Andrews

WORLD BANK GROUP

ISBN: 978-1-4648-2076-2
ISBN (electronic): 978-1-4648-2077-9
DOI: 10.1596/978-1-4648-2076-2

Cover photo: Vincent Tremeau / World Bank. Further permission required for re-use.
Cover design: Will Kemp / World Bank.

Library of Congress Control Number: 2024917592

Contents

BOXES

FIGURES

MAPS

TABLES

Foreword

People living in extreme poverty have faced tremendous challenges over the past few years, with many having emerged from the global pandemic with their precarious household finances further disrupted by climate shocks or displacement. The number of people living in extreme poverty has also increased, underscoring the importance of development initiatives that are evidence-backed, scalable, and capable of building resilience to future shocks.

Economic inclusion is one such initiative that delivers on that challenge. *The State of Economic Report 2024: Pathways to Scale* reveals that millions of people have benefited from economic inclusion programs that empower participants to build skills and experience, secure better employment, provide food for their table, send children to school, and build resilience to shocks and crises. In short, these programs help those who face the greatest challenges find a pathway out of poverty.

The report reveals that the number of economic inclusion programs has grown, in part, because governments extended their social protection programs to help citizens build resilience to multiple shocks. More people were included in these programs, and their geographic footprint has grown. However, as the report highlights, the current scale of these efforts falls short of the need, and there is significant potential to scale up proven economic inclusion models to get back on track to reach the Sustainable Development Goals.

This report documents the progress made in global economic inclusion efforts and builds on the foundation laid by the first report in this series, *The State of Economic Inclusion Report 2021: The Potential to Scale*. While the first report explored the *potential* to scale, this latest report identifies those programs that have *achieved* scale, both government- and nongovernment-led, and highlights the progress and challenges of scaling up. The report also explores the vital roles governments, nongovernment organizations (NGOs), and the private sector are playing to achieve scale and how these institutions are working together. This collaborative effort is vital for achieving scale and ensuring that economic inclusion programs reach their full potential.

Evidence from government-led programs in different countries and contexts shows they can be delivered at scale, cost-effectively. Governments, as the primary drivers of scaled economic inclusion programs, are increasingly institutionalizing these initiatives, integrating them into policies, and are exploring ways to expand coverage, broaden scope, and expand functions. The report summarizes new findings from government-led programs, complementing the extensive evidence presented in the 2021 report; identifies remaining knowledge gaps; and provides insights for future programmatic approaches.

Among the most-pressing priorities shaping the future of economic inclusion are two critical areas: women's economic empowerment and climate resilience. The report provides examples of programs that prioritize gender equality and ensure that women and girls are integral to program scale-up. A Special Focus section on climate-resilient economic inclusion examines the emerging agenda of integrating climate resilience into program design and the need for targeted support to poor and vulnerable communities facing climate-induced challenges.

As members of the Steering Committee for the Partnership for Economic Inclusion (PEI), we are encouraged by the progress toward scale that economic inclusion programs are making and the critical lessons on good practice that have emerged. PEI's work to support the adoption and scale-up of government-led economic inclusion programs, working with governments, bilateral and multilateral organizations, NGOs, research institutions, and the private sector, remains critical. This partnership network provides an opportunity for all stakeholders to share cutting-edge knowledge on economic inclusion and contribute to evidence-based best practices. It also invests in innovations in government-led economic inclusion to further expand our understanding of how to effectively scale up these programs.

Protecting people living in extreme poverty is at the heart of the World Bank's vision of creating a world free of poverty on a livable planet. The World Bank aims to scale up social protection programs, working alongside partners to support at least 500 million people in developing countries by 2030—aiming for half of those to be women and girls. Economic inclusion is a key component of this ambitious goal, and *The State of Economic Inclusion Report 2024* represents a significant milestone in our ongoing efforts to scale up sustainable economic inclusion programs for the poorest populations.

We look forward to continued and successful collaboration.

Gregory Chen
Managing Director
Ultra-Poor Graduation Initiative
BRAC International

Michael Gaffey
Director General
Irish Aid

Olivia Leland
Co-Founder and CEO
Co-Impact

Iffath Sharif
Global Director, Social Protection
World Bank

Dr. Ariane Hildebrandt
Director General, Global Health, Equality
of Opportunity, Digital Technologies,
and Food Security
Federal Ministry for Economic
Cooperation and Development (BMZ)

Acknowledgments

The report was prepared by an authoring team from the Partnership for Economic Inclusion (PEI) in the World Bank's Social Protection Global Practice, including Inés Arévalo-Sánchez, Janet Heisey, Sarang Chaudhary, Timothy Clay, Victoria Strokova, Puja Vasudeva Dutta, and Colin Andrews. Shilohni Sumanthiran and Yetimwork Habte provided extensive support to the authors and editors during the research, drafting, and editing stages of the report.

The team is grateful for the overall strategic guidance and support from Iffath Sharif, Loli Arribas-Banos, and Jamele Rigolini, as well as to Michal Rutkowski (all with the World Bank) during the report's conceptualization. The team further appreciates guidance from PEI's Steering Committee members Greg Chen (BRAC International), Doris King (Co-Impact), Susanne Lein (Deutsche Gesellschaft für Internationale Zusammenarbeit), and Paula Nolan (Irish Aid).

We are grateful for the thorough guidance and direction from peer reviewers Thomas Bossuroy (World Bank), Aline Coudouel (World Bank), Felipe F. Dizon (World Bank), Ugo Gentilini (World Bank), Keetie Roelen (Open University, UK), Klas Sander (World Bank), and Joana Silva (World Bank). In addition, we appreciate the detailed suggestions on the preliminary draft provided by PEI Advisory Council members Frank DeGiovanni (Ford Foundation, retired), Nathanael Goldberg (Innovations for Poverty Action), Rita Larok (AVSI), Nana Oye Lithur (former cabinet minister, Ghana), Marvi Memon (former minister, Pakistan), and Carolina Trivelli (Peruvian Studies Institute).

This report would not have been possible without the detailed survey contributions from nearly 100 organizations, including governments, nongovernmental organizations, United Nations agencies, and development organizations, as well as from World Bank operational staff. A special thanks goes to PEI's technical partners for providing program data and inputs: BOMA, CARE, Concern Worldwide, the Food and Agriculture Organization, Fundación Capital, ideas42, Innovations for Poverty Action, Trickle Up, the United Nations High Commissioner for Refugees, Village Enterprise, and World Vision International. Appendix C documents the contributing programs in full.

Several individuals generously provided time and resources for background interviews, including Paul Carr and Dermot Hegarty (Concern Worldwide); Kajal Chatterjee (United Nations Development Programme [UNDP], Bangladesh); Sandrine Chetail (Mercy Corps); Carolina de Miranda and Victor Ortiz Mangano (Fundación Capital); Theara Khoun and Mao Meas (UNDP, Cambodia); Anna Mecagni (BOMA); and Harry Edmund Moroz, Alreena Renita Pinto, Claudia Zambra Taibo, and Michele Zini (all of the World Bank).

We thank the following World Bank colleagues who provided valuable contributions, ideas, and feedback during the consultation and report-writing processes: Afrah Alawi Al-Ahmadi, Thomas Bossuroy, Helle Buchhave, Hugo Brousset Chaman, Sarah Coll-Black, Wendy Cunningham, Tracy Hart, Alex Kamurase, Matteo Morgandi, Edmundo Murrugarra, Ashesh Prasann, Patrick Premand, Claudia P. Rodriguez Alas,

Luz Stella Rodriguez, Solenne Rougeaux, Nian Sadiq, Klas Sander, Emil Tesliuc, Margaux Vinez, and Stephen Joseph Winkler.

John Felton and Sabra Ledent edited the report. Tyler McClelland (World Bank) coordinated the publication process and oversaw design. The team also appreciates all the administrative support provided by Adriana Cecilia Espinal and Yolaina Montoya (both of the World Bank) during the various stages of the report's preparation. Finally, we are grateful to the team at the World Bank's Publications Office, particularly the close guidance and support provided by Cindy A. Fisher, Jewel McFadden, and Christina Ann Davis.

About the Authors

Colin Andrews is global lead for social assistance in the World Bank's Social Protection Global Practice. He has more than 15 years of social protection experience in Africa and South Asia and in global policy. His current work focuses on social protection financing, food and nutrition security, and disaster risk reduction. From 2019 to 2023, Colin led the Partnership for Economic Inclusion (PEI). Previously, Colin managed lending operations on safety nets and service delivery in Africa. He has published widely on safety net impacts, crisis response, and financing. He also has worked for the Food and Agriculture Organization of the United Nations, the European Commission, and nongovernmental organizations (NGOs). Colin holds a master's degree in economics from Trinity College, Dublin.

Inés Arévalo-Sánchez is a consultant with the World Bank's PEI and Social Protection Global Practice. She is an economist with more than 15 years of experience in economic and financial inclusion, rural development, and social protection in various countries in Africa, Asia, Latin America, and the Middle East. Inés has extensive experience in conducting evaluative and operational research, designing monitoring and evaluation systems, and working with operations to build the capacity of local teams and to translate research and evaluation results into insights for program implementation. She has coauthored several publications on economic inclusion, including *The State of Economic Inclusion Report 2021*. Previously, Inés worked as a consultant with private philanthropical organizations and NGOs, including the Aga Khan Agency for Microfinance and Trickle Up. She holds an MA in development economics from the University of Sussex, England.

Sarang Chaudhary is an advisor with the Deutsche Gesellschaft für Internationale Zusammenarbeit GmbH, where he focuses on the digital transformation of social protection systems and building global consensus on interoperability standards. Previously, he served as an economist with the World Bank's PEI and Social Protection Global Practice, where he designed and supported the implementation of national social assistance and economic inclusion programs. Sarang also led a nonprofit in India focused on community-driven development and grassroots program implementation in collaboration with state and city governments. He holds a bachelor's degree in electronics and communication engineering from APJ Abdul Kalam Technical University in India and a master's degree in public policy from the University of California, Berkeley.

Timothy Clay is an economist with the World Bank's PEI and Social Protection Global Practice. He specializes in researching and designing policies and programs focused on job creation, economic inclusion, and climate resilience. Timothy has spent most of his career at the World Bank in technical and operational roles, primarily focusing on programming in Africa and South Asia. Recently, he led PEI's cross-sectoral climate resilience work program to introduce climate-resilient adaptations and innovations to improve the resilience of poor and vulnerable communities. Timothy holds an MSc in public policy from both Maastricht University and the United Nations University–MERIT.

Puja Vasudeva Dutta is an economist with expertise in social protection and economic inclusion. She was a researcher in the Poverty Research Unit at the University of Sussex in England and the National Council of Applied Economic Research in India, focusing on poverty, inequality, and labor markets research. Puja was then in the World Bank's Social Protection Global Practice in South Asia and East Asia from 2006 to 2018, where she worked on social protection policy reform, program design, and delivery systems in Afghanistan, Cambodia, India, Laos, the Maldives, Myanmar, and Viet Nam. She is now an independent consultant with global assignments with the World Bank's PEI and Social Insurance Administration Diagnostic and in the Pacific with the Partnerships for Social Protection program, funded by the Government of Australia's Department of Foreign Affairs and Trade. She holds a DPhil in economics from the University of Sussex.

Janet Heisey is a senior consultant with the World Bank's PEI, where she leads its partnership work, is the editor of the *In Practice* publication series, and supports country engagement and knowledge management workstreams. She is coauthor of *Working for Inclusion: Economic Inclusion in Contexts of Forced Displacement* and *The State of Economic Inclusion Report 2021*. She also has consulted on World Bank economic inclusion programs in Ethiopia and Kenya. She has more than 20 years of experience developing strategy and partnerships and designing economic inclusion programs for people living in poverty, including people with disabilities and displaced populations. Previously, Janet created and led a technical assistance unit at Trickle Up, working in partnership with the UN High Commissioner for Refugees to design economic inclusion programs that foster refugee self-reliance. She holds a bachelor's degree from Michigan State University.

Victoria Strokova is the program manager for the World Bank's PEI. With more than 15 years of experience in international development, she has technical expertise in social safety nets (cash transfers), building social protection systems (social registries), labor and economic inclusion programs, and cross-sectoral topics such as jobs and human capital. At the World Bank, Victoria has gained extensive experience across multiple regions and global units within the Social Protection Global Practice, as well as in cross-cutting units like the Jobs Group and the Human Capital Project, where she was co–program manager for the Human Capital Umbrella program and coled cross-sectoral analytical work on disruptive technology. Previously, she led operational and analytical work in Ethiopia and Liberia, focusing on the design, implementation, and evaluation of economic inclusion programs in rural; urban; and fragility, conflict, and violence contexts. She holds a master's degree in public policy with honors from the University of Chicago's Harris School of Public Policy.

Executive Summary

Introduction

The State of Economic Inclusion Report (SEI) is a flagship initiative under the Partnership for Economic Inclusion.[1] The first report in this series, *The State of Economic Inclusion Report 2021: The Potential to Scale* (SEI 2021; Andrews et al. 2021), established a baseline of the global landscape, reviewed the evidence on impact and costs, and introduced a framework for scaling up economic inclusion. This new report—*The State of Economic Inclusion Report 2024: Pathways to Scale* (SEI 2024)— explores efforts to scale up policy and programming, including progress and challenges around government-led programs, and the interplay with nongovernment actors and the private sector.

The SEI 2024 emerges in a context of overlapping crises, which have affected poor and vulnerable people disproportionately. For example, since 2020, the COVID-19 pandemic increased the number of people living in extreme poverty to 700 million. Additionally, the number of people experiencing severe food insecurity more than doubled during this period (UNDESA 2023), while up to 122 million more individuals may fall into extreme poverty by 2030 due to climate change (IPCC 2022). These overlapping crises have had global repercussions but have disproportionately affected poor and vulnerable people. The United Nations (UN) Sustainable Development Goal (SDG 1) of ending extreme poverty by 2030 may be missed without a concerted effort (Sachs et al. 2023).

As a result, economic inclusion programs are more relevant now than ever. Using a multidimensional approach, these programs address multiple constraints faced by poor and vulnerable individuals, households, and communities with the aim to increase their incomes and assets. As ample evidence shows, these programs can play a critical role in creating job opportunities for poor and vulnerable individuals and building their resilience to various shocks, including those exacerbated by climate change.

This report identifies the following 10 key messages with respect to the scale-up of economic inclusion programming globally.

Message 1: The Number of Economic Inclusion Programs Has Almost Doubled, and Coverage Has Increased by 50 Percent

This report surveyed 405 economic inclusion programs in 88 countries, an increase from 219 programs in 75 countries in 2021.[2] Many programs included in the 2021 report have also expanded despite, or in some cases in response to, the current context of overlapping crises. As a result, coverage of these programs has expanded from 9.8 million households in 2021 to more than 15 million households, benefiting more than 70 million individuals directly or indirectly.

FIGURE ES.1   **Distribution of Economic Inclusion Programs and Participants, by Lead Institution**

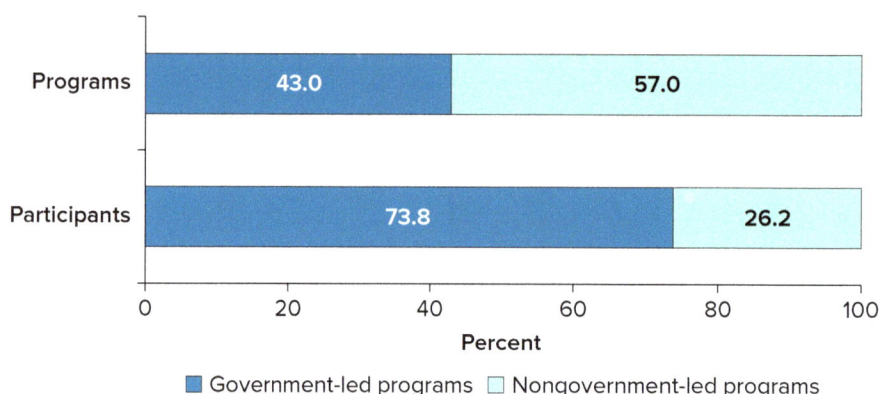

Source: Partnership for Economic Inclusion, World Bank.

Note: Data on the number of participants are missing for 72 programs (16 nongovernment-led and 56 government-led programs), most of which were in the last phases of preparation before actual delivery of support for participants began. Overall, 405 programs were surveyed (231 nongovernment-led and 174 government-led programs). The total number of participants (15,323,059) and beneficiaries (70,043,913) include direct participants and indirect beneficiaries.

Governments continue to lead the scale-up of economic inclusion programs, with 43 percent of all programs being government led, covering 74 percent of participants (refer to figure ES.1). However, nongovernment-led programs also contribute significantly to the increase in coverage, leading 57 percent of economic inclusion programs. Although their coverage is lower (26 percent of participants), nongovernment organizations (NGOs) can help pilot economic inclusion approaches in new geographic areas or with different population groups or test new methods or approaches. NGOs also play a key role in government-led programs as service providers and technical assistance providers, helping increase the capacity of government agencies to implement and scale up economic inclusion programs.

Message 2: Compelling Evidence of Impact Underpins This Surge and Scale of Programs

The growth in programs is in part a result of the strong body of evidence showing that these programs can effectively build resilience and facilitate economic opportunities for the poor population. A global review of evidence in SEI 2021 found that economic inclusion programs can significantly impact food security, consumption, income, business revenues, and asset accumulation (Andrews et al. 2021).

More-recent evidence reviewed in the current report suggests that government-led programs are cost-effective and are high-return investments (refer to box ES.1). Investing in economic inclusion programs pays off in the long run, with the benefits significantly outweighing the initial costs. A recent meta-analysis highlights evidence from studies conducted in Afghanistan, Bangladesh, the Democratic Republic of Congo, Ghana, Nepal, and Niger, revealing cost-benefit ratios between 121 percent and 379 percent and internal rates of return ranging from 16 percent to

66 percent (J-PAL 2023). For policy makers, this robust evidence from diverse settings demonstrates that economic inclusion programs consistently deliver economic benefits that surpass the initial investment, can be considered effective tools for poverty alleviation, and are wise investments with considerable returns, all leading to broader social and economic development. While this evidence is encouraging, more research is required to fill critical learning gaps on how government-led economic inclusion programs can be effectively and efficiently scaled up.

BOX ES.1   Emerging Evidence from Government-Led Programs

Government-led economic inclusion programs have demonstrated significant impacts on various economic outcomes among vulnerable populations. Evidence from programs in Afghanistan, Niger, Senegal, and Zambia highlights substantial improvements in food security, consumption, income, and business revenues (refer to figure ESB1.1). Programs not only improved economic well-being but also contributed to the resilience of rural households, particularly through diversifying women's economic activities. Moreover, these programs have demonstrated positive impacts on psychosocial well-being and women's empowerment.

Although limited to a few studies, evidence shows that, when implemented through government systems, these programs are highly cost-effective and yield high returns on investment. In Niger, for example, the program demonstrated a cost-benefit ratio of 127 percent 18 months after implementation, while in Zambia, the program broke even within 12 months, albeit with a slightly lower cost-effectiveness. Assuming sustained impacts, both Niger and Zambia show positive returns on investment, at 73 percent and 36 percent, respectively (Bossuroy et al. 2022; Botea et al. 2023).

FIGURE ESB1.1   Evidence and Cost of Select Government-Led Programs

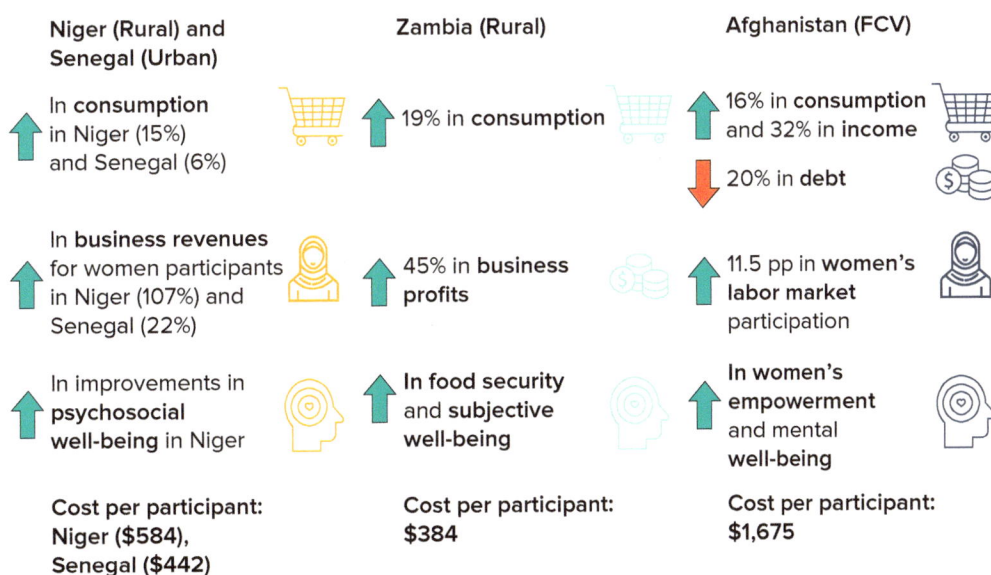

Niger (Rural) and Senegal (Urban)

- In **consumption** in Niger (15%) and Senegal (6%)
- In **business revenues** for women participants in Niger (107%) and Senegal (22%)
- In improvements in **psychosocial well-being** in Niger

Zambia (Rural)

- 19% in **consumption**
- 45% in **business profits**
- In **food security** and **subjective well-being**

Afghanistan (FCV)

- 16% in **consumption** and 32% in **income**
- 20% in **debt**
- 11.5 pp in **women's labor market** participation
- In **women's empowerment** and mental **well-being**

Cost per participant: Niger ($584), Senegal ($442)

Cost per participant: $384

Cost per participant: $1,675

Sources: Bossuroy et al. 2022, 2024; Botea et al. 2023; Bedoya et al. 2023.

Note: FCV = fragility, conflict, and violence; pp = percentage points.

(Box continues next page)

BOX ES.1   **Emerging Evidence From Government-Led Programs** *(continued)*

However, critical learning gaps still exist. First, assessing the cost-effectiveness of large-scale government-led programs in different contexts is needed. Second, researching how more-scalable program delivery methods, such as group coaching and digitally delivered training, can influence program impact and cost-effectiveness is required. Third, identifying the appropriate package that can achieve maximum impact in a given context and for targeted groups is important. By addressing these research questions, policy makers and practitioners can enhance the design and implementation of economic inclusion programs to better serve vulnerable populations and achieve sustainable impacts at scale.

Message 3: The Program Landscape Is Diverse, in Both Geographic Coverage and Program Design

The majority of economic inclusion programs (79 percent) are implemented in low-income and lower-middle-income countries. Sub-Saharan Africa hosts the largest share of these programs and the most participants (refer to figure ES.2), but these programs can be found in all regions of the world.

Rural areas remain the primary focus of operations, accounting for 84 percent of programs, with 43 percent exclusively targeting rural populations. This finding is in line with the majority of the world's extreme-poor population residing in rural areas (World Bank 2022). However, there is a notable trend of economic inclusion programs, particularly more recent ones, expanding their operations into urban areas. Approximately 38 percent of programs now serve urban or peri-urban populations. This percentage includes programs with national coverage, those designed to cater to both urban and rural areas, and those initially launched in rural areas that have since expanded to include urban and peri-urban populations.

Programs are also designed with a range of policy objectives with an emphasis on enhancing job opportunities for the poor and women's empowerment (refer to figure ES.3, panel a). These programs enhance self-employment opportunities for poor and vulnerable populations (47 percent of all programs), diversifying participants' income sources (36 percent), and increasing their productivity (31 percent). With an increased recognition of the need to address the barriers to women's economic empowerment, 33 percent of programs prioritize empowering women—a significant rise since 2021, when only 17 percent of all programs had this objective.

Programs are refining design and delivery to meet the needs of different population groups. Economic inclusion programs typically prioritize vulnerable populations at the lower end of the income distribution, targeting the ultra-poor (40 percent of programs), extreme-poor (53 percent), and poor (55 percent) populations. Many programs also focus on specific demographic groups, including women (90 percent of programs), youth (65 percent), displaced and conflict-affected populations (39 percent), and people with disabilities (39 percent) (refer to figure ES.3, panel b).

FIGURE ES.2 **Distribution of Economic Inclusion Programs and Participants, by Region**

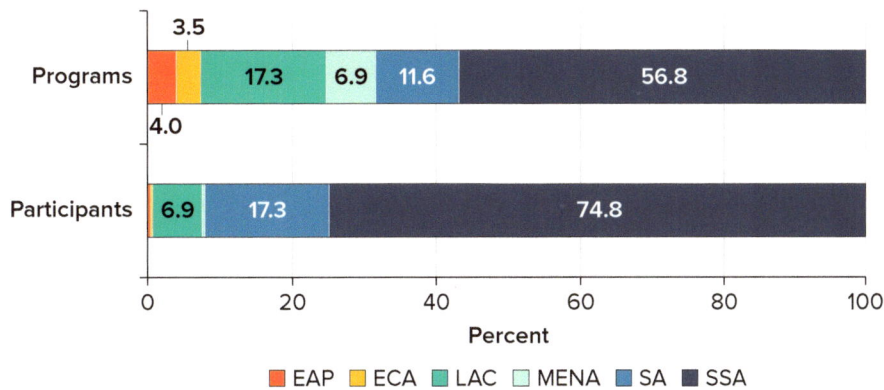

Source: Partnership for Economic Inclusion, World Bank.
Note: The figure is based on survey data for 405 programs: 16, EAP; 14, ECA; 70, LAC; 28, MENA; 47, SA; and 230, SSA. The total number of participants is 15,323,059 and beneficiaries is 70,043,913, which includes direct participants and indirect beneficiaries. Data on the number of participants are missing for 72 programs, most of which were in the last phases of preparation before actual delivery of support for participants began. EAP = East Asia and Pacific; ECA = Europe and Central Asia; LAC = Latin America and the Caribbean; MENA = Middle East and North Africa; SA = South Asia; SSA = Sub-Saharan Africa.

These multidimensional programs customize a comprehensive package based on constraints, vulnerability, and local context, often providing specific components to a subset of participants to tailor support to their needs (refer to figure ES.3, panel d). Programs seek to achieve the core objectives by providing a comprehensive package of support, and more than 81 percent of programs, both government and nongovernment led, include 5–9 components and so are very complex programs. These components may include training (96 percent), coaching (89 percent), business capital (77 percent), and market links (74 percent) (refer to figure ES.3, panel c). These components are usually delivered in a sequence, ensuring that participants receive support when they can benefit most.

Message 4: Programs Are Taking Diverse Paths to Scale

The majority (74 percent) of economic inclusion programs have scaled up along several dimensions, including and beyond coverage expansion (refer to figure ES.4). In fact, the landscape reveals an increasingly wider range of sectoral interventions that constitute the foundations on which economic inclusion packages are built, including social safety nets, jobs and livelihoods, financial inclusion, social development, and agricultural and environmental interventions.

This report identifies two diverse but often complementary strategies for economic inclusion at scale (refer to figure ES.5). SEI 2021 emphasized household-focused programs that use a "push" strategy to enable households and individuals to build the assets, income, knowledge, and confidence to access services and engage in broader systems, including market systems. In addition to these programs, SEI 2024 also identifies "area-focused" programs or community- or sector-level strategies that seek to improve the broader availability and quality of economic opportunities and services. These programs use a "pull" strategy to enroll people broadly, including those living in extreme poverty, and engage them in the community, region, market, or other systems that the program seeks to change.

FIGURE ES.3   **Key Features of Program Design**

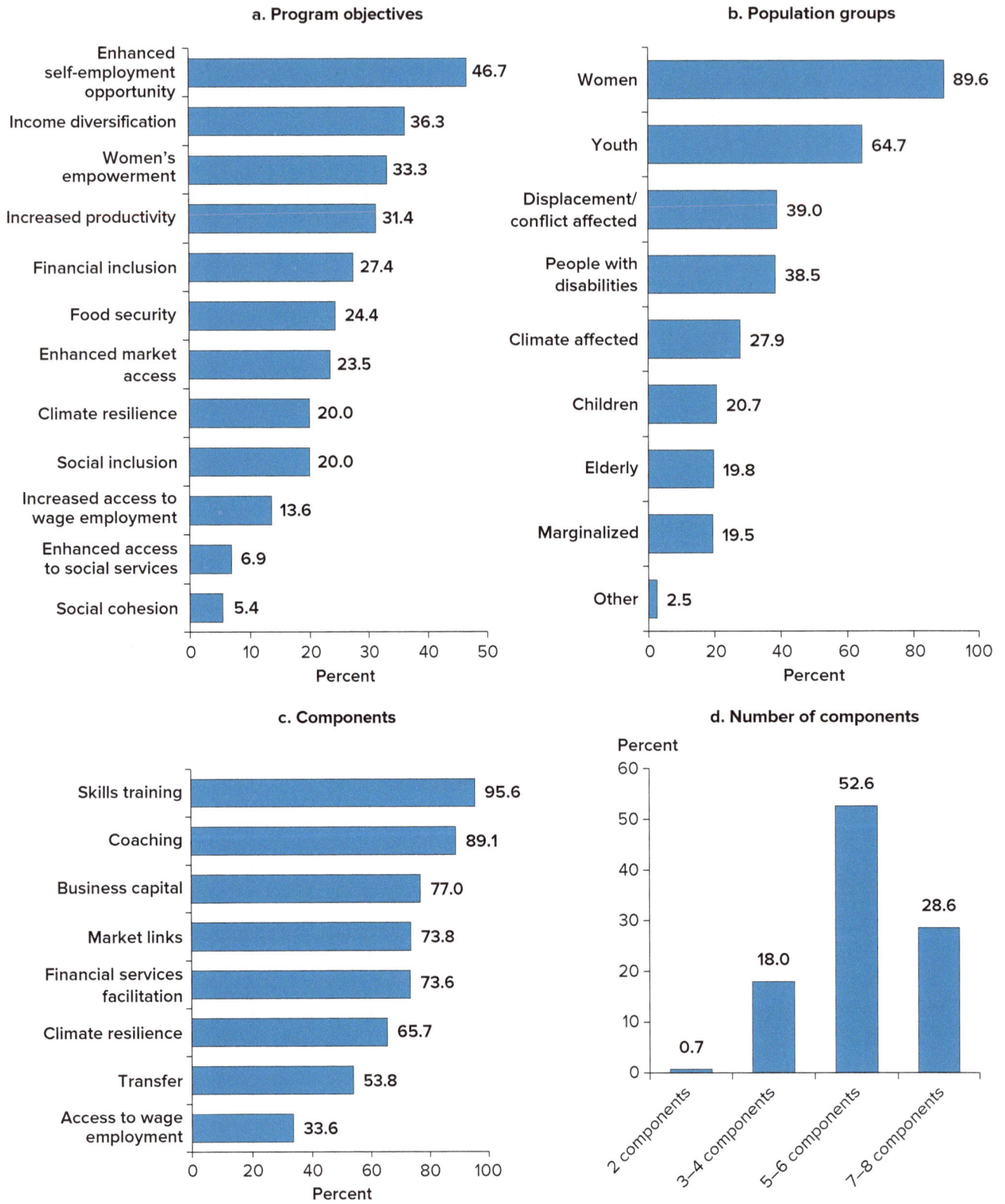

a. Program objectives

Objective	Percent
Enhanced self-employment opportunity	46.7
Income diversification	36.3
Women's empowerment	33.3
Increased productivity	31.4
Financial inclusion	27.4
Food security	24.4
Enhanced market access	23.5
Climate resilience	20.0
Social inclusion	20.0
Increased access to wage employment	13.6
Enhanced access to social services	6.9
Social cohesion	5.4

b. Population groups

Group	Percent
Women	89.6
Youth	64.7
Displacement/conflict affected	39.0
People with disabilities	38.5
Climate affected	27.9
Children	20.7
Elderly	19.8
Marginalized	19.5
Other	2.5

c. Components

Component	Percent
Skills training	95.6
Coaching	89.1
Business capital	77.0
Market links	73.8
Financial services facilitation	73.6
Climate resilience	65.7
Transfer	53.8
Access to wage employment	33.6

d. Number of components

Number of components	Percent
2 components	0.7
3–4 components	18.0
5–6 components	52.6
7–8 components	28.6

Source: Partnership for Economic Inclusion, World Bank.

Note: Figures show the percentage of all programs (*N* = 405).

FIGURE ES.4   Programs Have Scaled Up Along Core Dimensions

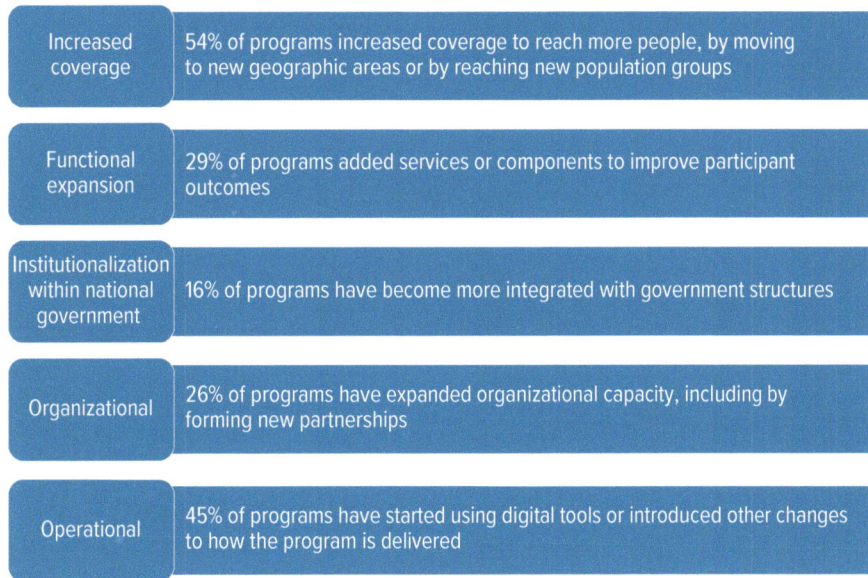

Increased coverage	54% of programs increased coverage to reach more people, by moving to new geographic areas or by reaching new population groups
Functional expansion	29% of programs added services or components to improve participant outcomes
Institutionalization within national government	16% of programs have become more integrated with government structures
Organizational	26% of programs have expanded organizational capacity, including by forming new partnerships
Operational	45% of programs have started using digital tools or introduced other changes to how the program is delivered

Source: Partnership for Economic Inclusion, World Bank.

Note: Figure shows the percentage of all programs (*N* = 405) that have scaled up along five dimensions.

FIGURE ES.5   Complementary Approaches to Economic Inclusion at the Household and Area (System) Levels

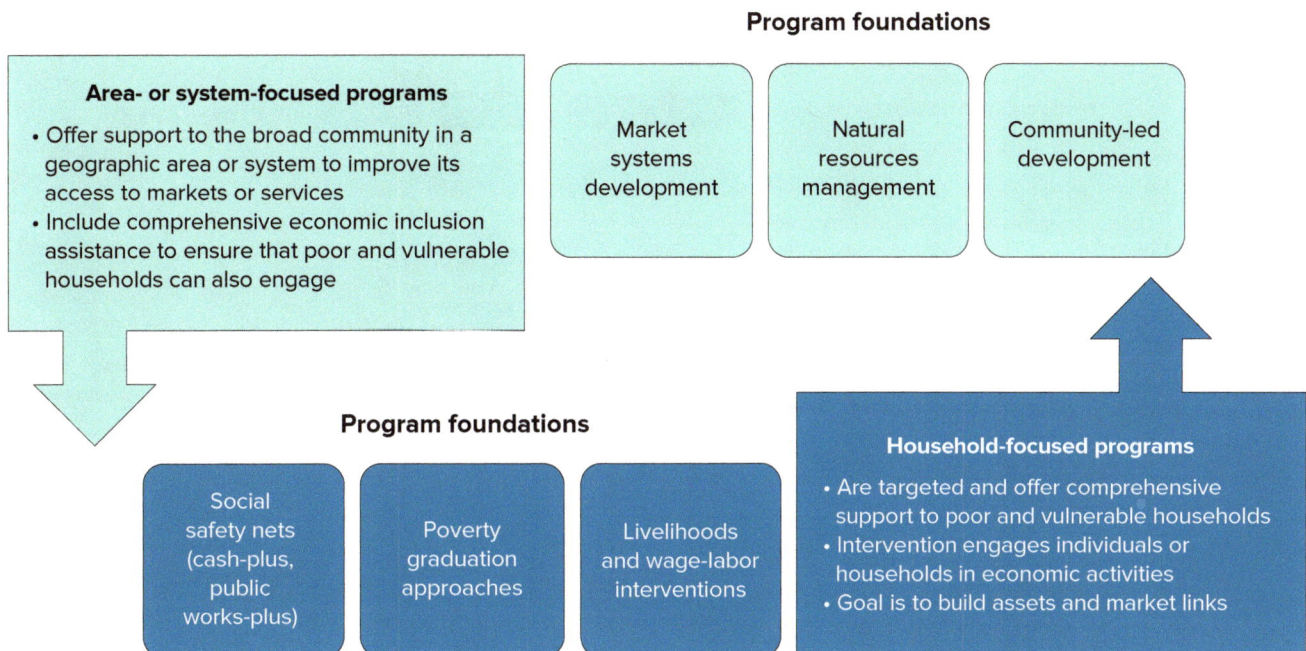

Program foundations

Area- or system-focused programs
- Offer support to the broad community in a geographic area or system to improve its access to markets or services
- Include comprehensive economic inclusion assistance to ensure that poor and vulnerable households can also engage

- Market systems development
- Natural resources management
- Community-led development

Program foundations

- Social safety nets (cash-plus, public works-plus)
- Poverty graduation approaches
- Livelihoods and wage-labor interventions

Household-focused programs
- Are targeted and offer comprehensive support to poor and vulnerable households
- Intervention engages individuals or households in economic activities
- Goal is to build assets and market links

Source: Partnership for Economic Inclusion, World Bank.

Still, significant knowledge gaps remain on how area-focused approaches are helping increase income and assets for poor and vulnerable populations. As programs move to scale, a strategic approach will also involve understanding the interplay between household-focused and area-focused interventions to catalyze sector-wide transformation.

Message 5: Ensuring Program Quality Requires Collaboration Across Stakeholders and Strong Monitoring, Evaluation, and Learning

In this evolving landscape, ensuring program quality is key for sustaining impacts. Both government-led and nongovernment-led programs rely extensively on external agencies for service delivery (refer to figure ES.6). Globally, 81 percent of programs collaborate with external agencies to deliver at least one program component. For government-led programs, this figure rises to 91 percent. Engaging NGOs as service providers can be an important strategy for scaling economic inclusion programs through government systems, especially in low-capacity contexts.

Evidence-based design and effective monitoring, evaluation, and learning can improve program quality and impact. Given the complexity of program bundles, drawing on good practices and diagnosing key constraints for various population groups and in specific contexts can enhance success rates and cost-effectiveness. Successful programs exhibit a commitment to monitoring participant progress, making real-time adjustments, and refining program design as needed. Many large-scale programs have demonstrated agility by adding or removing components, adjusting component sequencing, or making other significant modifications to enhance quality.

FIGURE ES.6   **Percentage of Programs in Which External Organizations Are Involved in Program Service Delivery**

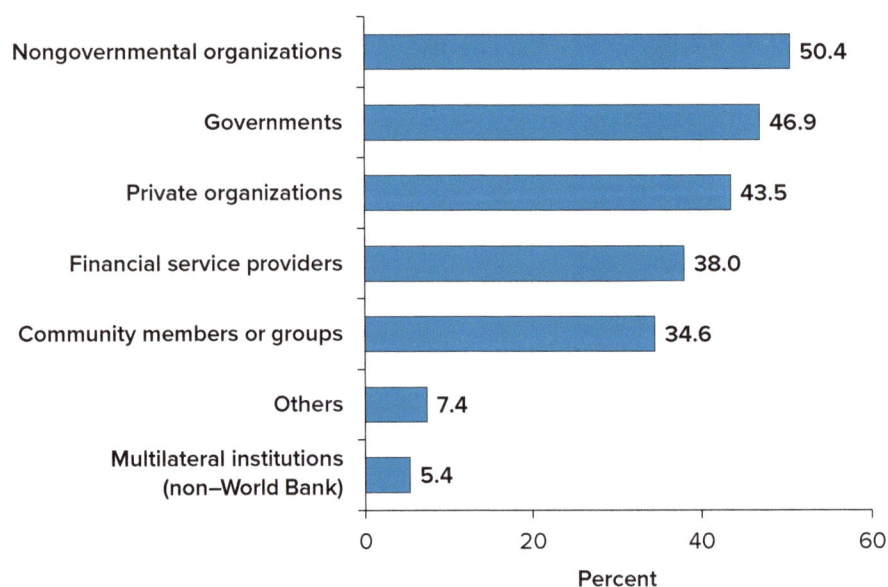

Source: Partnership for Economic Inclusion, World Bank.
Note: Figure shows the percentage of all programs ($N = 405$).

Message 6: Utilizing Community Structures in Program Delivery Can Facilitate Local Buy-In

Economic inclusion programs use community structures and groups across the delivery chain, including for targeting and enrollment, component provision, monitoring, and grievance and case management. Engaging community groups bolsters the social inclusion of participants, encourages active participation in developing and implementing programs, and fosters acceptance and ownership within the community, improving program uptake and sustainability.

Some programs formally engage community members in implementation by introducing selection criteria for their participation as facilitators. These community facilitators are assigned well-defined roles and responsibilities in program activities at both the individual or household and group levels. Notably, a deliberate emphasis on prioritizing women encourages gender inclusion and augments female participation in program delivery. Scaling up programs using local individuals for service delivery can also enhance cost-effectiveness.

Community-led producer groups can support the creation of rural enterprise ecosystems. Programs in both the agricultural and nonagricultural sectors collaborate with producer groups within community structures. These programs encourage smallholder farmers to form groups, thereby improving their market access and economic well-being. By acting collectively, groups can pool their resources, share knowledge, and negotiate together with buyers, boosting their bargaining power. Community savings groups promote financial inclusion and empower individuals, particularly those in economically vulnerable situations, to save money, access financial services, and benefit from financial inclusion. Program facilitators work with community members to form small savings groups based on common interests, geographical proximity, or other relevant criteria.

Message 7: Digital Tools and Technologies Are Playing an Increasing Role in Program Delivery

Digital tools and technologies are contributing to enhanced efficiency, accessibility, and effectiveness of program delivery. Ninety-three percent of programs use digital technologies across the delivery chain, particularly for targeting and enrollment and for monitoring and evaluation (refer to figure ES.7). Governments are using digital tools to deliver business capital. Digital financial services and electronic payment systems, including mobile money and direct bank transfers, are commonly used to disburse cash and grants. These methods enhance transparency, reduce leakage, and give beneficiaries convenient and secure access to funds. Expansion of the digital government-to-person payments model underscores the potential to scale up the cash-based components of economic inclusion interventions.

The use of digital technologies holds great promise, especially for reaching remote communities and tailoring interventions for targeted groups. However, design and delivery must account for the digital literacy levels of both program implementers and participants and ensure appropriate training for effective implementation, especially in rural contexts.

FIGURE ES.7   **Percentage of Programs Using Digital Technology for Program Management and Delivery**

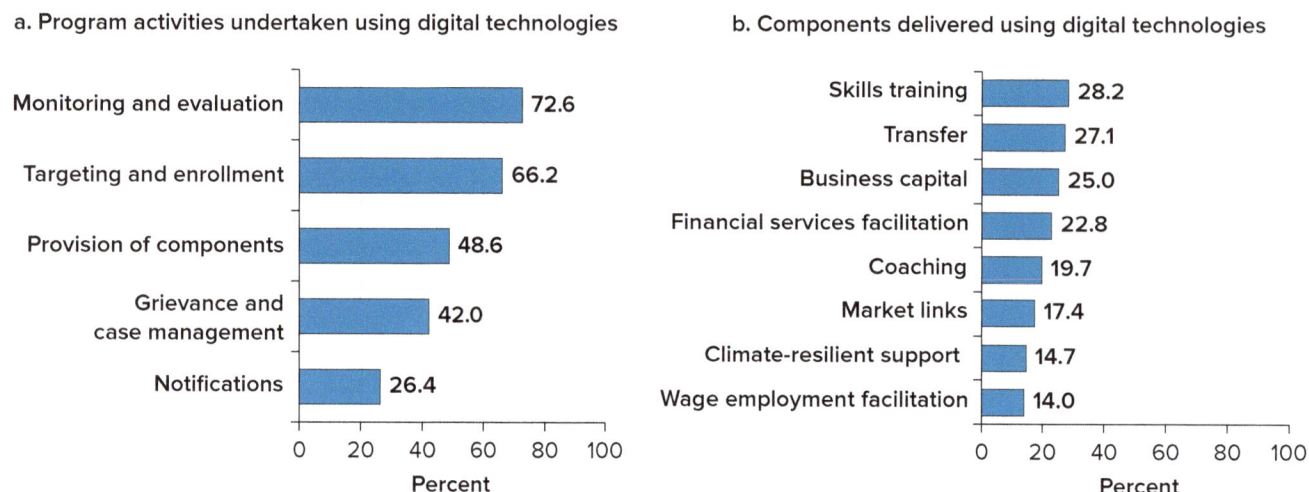

a. Program activities undertaken using digital technologies

Activity	Percent
Monitoring and evaluation	72.6
Targeting and enrollment	66.2
Provision of components	48.6
Grievance and case management	42.0
Notifications	26.4

b. Components delivered using digital technologies

Component	Percent
Skills training	28.2
Transfer	27.1
Business capital	25.0
Financial services facilitation	22.8
Coaching	19.7
Market links	17.4
Climate-resilient support	14.7
Wage employment facilitation	14.0

Source: Partnership for Economic Inclusion, World Bank.

Note: Panel a shows the percentage of all programs ($N = 405$). Panel b shows the percentage of programs providing components digitally out of those providing a given component (skills training, $N = 387$; transfer, $N = 218$; business capital, $N = 312$; financial services facilitation, $N = 298$; coaching, $N = 361$; market links, $N = 299$; climate-resilient support, $N = 266$; and wage employment facilitation, $N = 136$). Multiple responses were possible.

Message 8: Expanding Coverage While Addressing the Jobs Challenge, Especially Among Youth, and Enhancing Women's Economic Empowerment Are Needed

While the number of individuals participating in economic inclusion programs has increased by 50 percent since 2021, this figure still constitutes a small fraction of the global population living in poverty, especially considering the projected increase in poverty due to crises and climate change. In addition, not all programs target the extreme-poor population. Therefore, prioritizing the inclusion of the most-poor and most-vulnerable individuals should be a key focus of scale-up efforts.

At a time of overlapping crises and job displacement due to climate change, addressing the jobs challenge for poor and vulnerable individuals will be an overriding policy challenge. Currently, few programs (34 percent) facilitate wage jobs for participants. However, programs in upper-middle-income countries focus more on wage job opportunities (44 percent of all programs) than in low-income countries (31 percent), particularly in urban areas. Given the characteristics of the local economy and target populations, the majority of programs develop self-employment opportunities through livelihood support and, increasingly, linking participants to markets. A comprehensive set of policies will be necessary to address the job challenges for poor and vulnerable individuals to facilitate their economic and social inclusion.

Programs that integrate young people into the economy are critical given widespread youth unemployment, especially in countries facing a "youth bulge." At present, 65 percent of programs target youth, with 40 percent of these programs facilitating wage employment. Understanding the market failures that prevents youth from accessing job opportunities in urban areas, bridging the socioemotional skills gap, and providing access to apprenticeships in collaboration with the private sector are all important agendas for youth's economic inclusion.

Similarly, although most economic inclusion programs target women and include some measures to support women, more programs could take a gender-intentional approach to design and delivery. About one-third of programs cite women's economic empowerment as a core objective and indicate that they use deliberate strategies to strengthen women's economic inclusion. However, more programs can benefit from taking a more-systematic approach to addressing women's constraints, which could involve addressing social norms, tailoring the timing and nature of program activities, and including components such as childcare to ensure that women can and do succeed. Lessons learned from these innovations must be further mainstreamed.

Message 9: Building Climate Resilience Is Emerging as the Next Frontier for Programming

Economic inclusion programs strive to build resilience by helping participants become better able to adapt to and recover from multiple and recurrent shocks. However, there is growing recognition that programs must be designed so that they also address the medium- to long-term threats to economic inclusion posed by climate change. People living in extreme poverty, especially women, face many environmental and natural resources management challenges, with climate change being an accelerating factor.

A new generation of climate-resilient economic inclusion (CREI) programs is needed to build adaptive capacity to respond to climatic threats, to directly contribute to climate mitigation, and to reduce the negative impacts of climate mitigation policies. At present, 66 percent of programs, benefiting more than 58 million individuals, are adapting existing components by introducing climate-smart practices or developing new components to help participants build climate resilience. Some innovations include climate risk insurance, payment for ecosystems, and low-cost green technology. Geographically, 65 percent of CREI programs are in Sub-Saharan Africa, 14 percent in South Asia, and 8 percent in Latin America and the Caribbean (refer to map ES.1).

Despite these seemingly large numbers, this is a nascent agenda, and programs vary considerably in the degree to which they align climate and poverty objectives and how effectively they incorporate climate-resilient activities and outcomes in program design. Three overlapping program areas show high potential for positive climate-resilience outcomes: (1) adaptive safety nets and adaptive social protection that build resilience to climate events and incentivize sustainable livelihoods, (2) sustainable food and ecosystems that enhance natural assets and restore ecosystems, and (3) green livelihoods and jobs that facilitate a transition from extractive and resource-dependent livelihoods (Costella et al. 2023). However, the results of these programs on climate-resilient outcomes remain to be fully assessed.

Going forward, it is critical to build deeper links among adaptive social protection, agrifood programs, and natural resources management programs to enhance climate resilience in economic inclusion efforts. This work will require sustained collaboration at the design, implementation, and evaluation stages for the evidence-informed design of future CREI programs.

MAP ES.1   CREI Programs and Climate Vulnerability

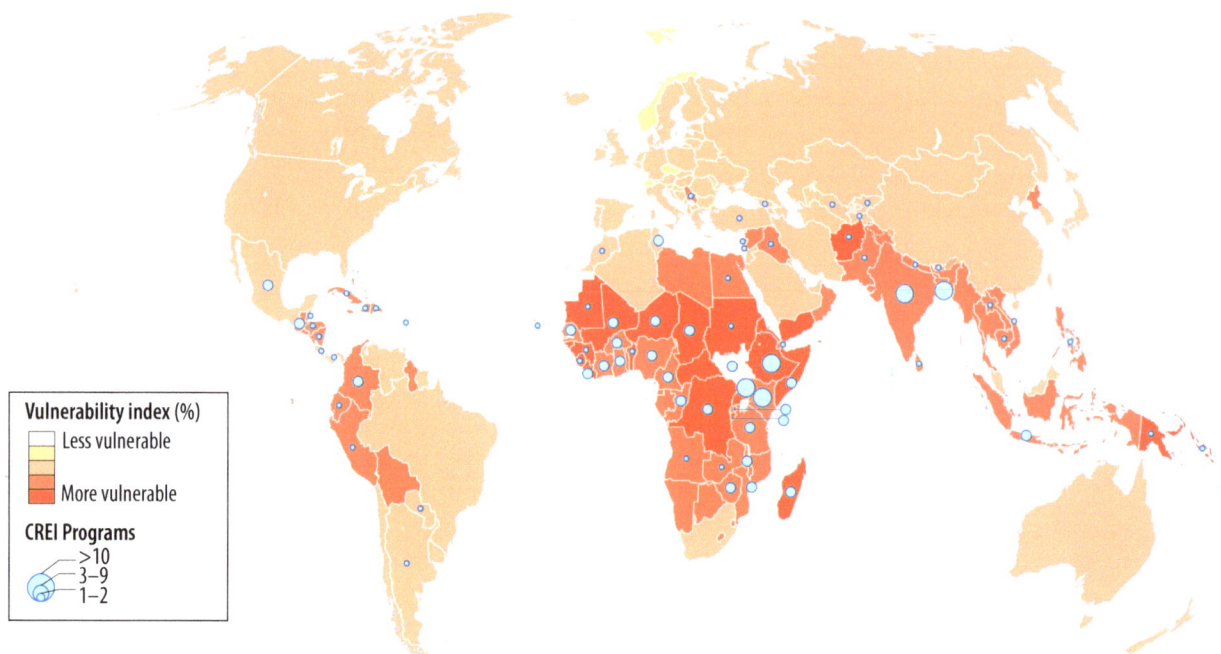

Vulnerability index (%)
- Less vulnerable
- More vulnerable

CREI Programs
- >10
- 3–9
- 1–2

IBRD 48228 | June 2024

Sources: University of Notre Dame 2023; Partnership for Economic Inclusion, World Bank.

Note: Climate data measure a country's level of vulnerability and readiness to adapt. On the map, the darker the color, the more vulnerable a country is to climate impacts and the less prepared it is. Blue dots indicate the locations of all programs. CREI = climate-resilient economic inclusion.

Message 10: Sustainable Financing Remains Critical for Piloting and Scaling Up Programs

Finally, although examples of successful policy integration are emerging, sustainable financing remains critical for piloting and scale-up. In many countries, economic inclusion programs are a key feature in social protection and jobs policies. Even though most governments are funding economic inclusion programs to some extent, most programs still rely primarily on donors for funding and sustainability (refer to figure ES.8).[3] However, information on the share of government financing of programs is limited. Country-specific reviews of government expenditures are needed for a deeper understanding of government versus external funding. For nongovernment-led programs, bilateral agencies, the private sector, and regional multilateral institutions remain the key donors.

Given that economic inclusion programs are designed to tackle enduring challenges such as poverty, inequality, and vulnerability, securing adequate and consistent funding is pivotal for attaining lasting impact. In this context, evolving collaboration among philanthropic donors, NGOs, and government-led initiatives offers a promising avenue for donor funding to play a catalytic role in advancing economic inclusion while simultaneously leveraging existing government investments.

FIGURE ES.8 **Percentage of Government- and Nongovernment-Led Programs Financed by External Institutions**

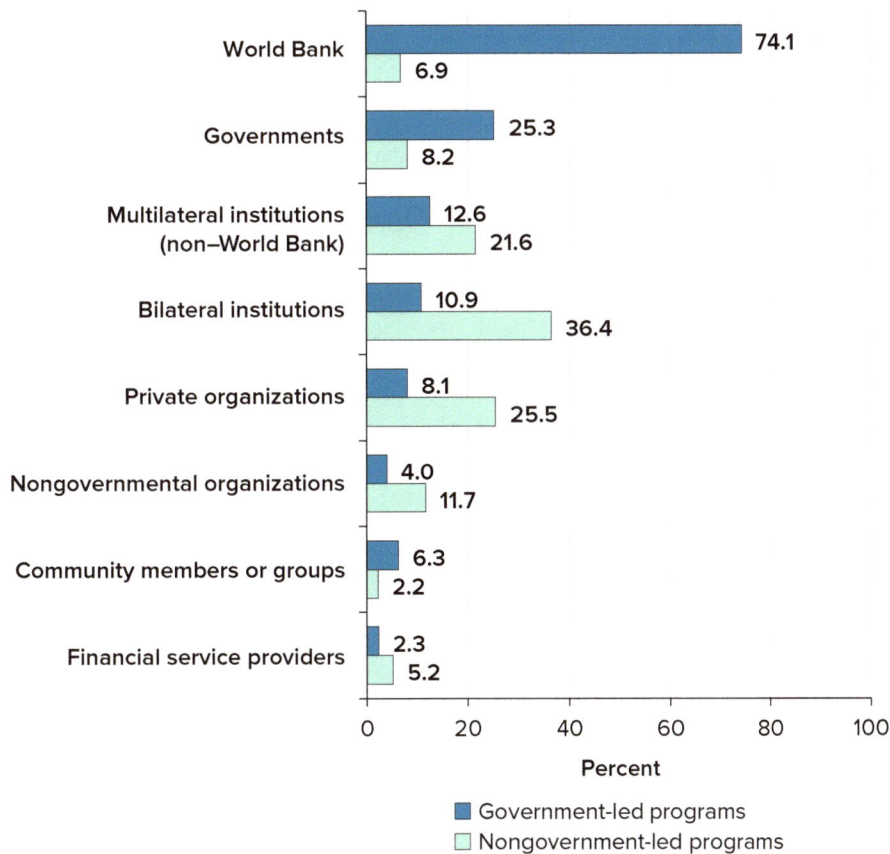

Source: Partnership for Economic Inclusion, World Bank.

Note: Figure shows the percentage of government- and nongovernment-led programs (N_1 = 174 and N_2 = 231).

Notes

1. The Partnership for Economic Inclusion (PEI) is a global platform that unites nongovernmental organizations, UN agencies, research institutions, funding partners, and the World Bank to support government adoption and scale-up of economic inclusion programs, empowering extreme-poor and vulnerable people to lift themselves out of poverty.
2. The report draws on the Landscape Survey of Economic Inclusion Programs 2023 (Landscape Survey 2023), as well as operational insights garnered through PEI's collaboration with its partners. All the data points in the executive summary and the report are from the 405 surveyed programs.
3. According to the Landscape Survey 2023, 74 percent of the surveyed government-led programs are funded by the World Bank and 20 percent by other multilateral or bilateral donors. However, the coverage of the survey is biased toward the World Bank, because most of its programs responded to the survey, and programs funded by bilateral or other multilateral institutions are not fully represented.

References

Andrews, Colin, Aude de Montesquiou, Inés Arévalo-Sánchez, Puja Vasudeva Dutta, Boban
Varghese Paul, Sadna Samaranayake, Janet Heisey, Timothy Clay, and Sarang Chaudhary.
2021. *The State of Economic Inclusion Report 2021: The Potential to Scale*. Washington, DC:
World Bank. http://hdl.handle.net/10986/34917.

Bossuroy, Thomas, Markus Goldstein, Bassirou Karimou, Dean Karlan, Harounan Kazianga,
William Parienté, Patrick Premand, Catherine C. Thomas, Christopher Udry, Julia Vaillant,
and Kelsey A. Wright. 2022. "Tackling Psychosocial and Capital Constraints to Alleviate
Poverty." *Nature* 605 (7909): 291–97. https://doi.org/10.1038/s41586-022-04647-8.

Bossuroy, Thomas, Dean Karlan, William Parienté, Patrick Premand, Christopher Udry, Julia
Vaillant, and Kelsey Wright. 2024. "Impact des mesures d'inclusion productive du programme
Yom Kom Kom au Sénégal." Banque Mondiale, Washington, DC.

Botea, Ioana, Andrew Brudevold-Newman, Markus Goldstein, Corrine Low, and Gareth Roberts.
2023. "Supporting Women's Livelihoods at Scale: Evidence from a Nationwide Multi-
Faceted Program." NBER Working Paper No. w31625. Cambridge, MA: National Bureau of
Economic Research. http://www.nber.org/papers/w31625.

Costella, Cecilia, Timothy Clay, Manann Donoghoe, and Liz Giron. 2023. "Pathways to Climate-
Resilient Economic Inclusion: A Framework for Integrating Climate Action in Economic
Inclusion Programs." *PEI in Practice, Volume 9*. World Bank, Washington, DC. http://hdl
.handle.net/10986/40542.

IPCC (Intergovernmental Panel on Climate Change). 2022. *Climate Change 2022: Impacts,
Adaptation, and Vulnerability. Contribution of Working Group II to the Sixth Assessment
Report of the Intergovernmental Panel on Climate Change*. H.-O. Pörtner, D. C. Roberts,
M. Tignor, E. S. Poloczanska, K. Mintenbeck, A. Alegría, M. Craig, S. Langsdorf, S. Löschke,
V. Möller, A. Okem, and B. Rama, eds. Cambridge, UK: Cambridge University Press.
https://doi.org/10.1017/9781009325844.

J-PAL (Abdul Latif Jameel Poverty Action Lab). 2023. "Building Stable Livelihoods for
Low-Income Households." *J-PAL Policy Insights*. https://www.povertyactionlab.org/policy
-insight/building-stable-livelihoods-low-income-households.

Sachs, Jeffrey D., Guillaume Lafortune, Grayson Fuller, and Eamon Drumm. 2023. *Sustainable
Development Report 2023: Implementing the SDG Stimulus*. Dublin: Dublin University Press.
https://doi.org/10.25546/102924.

World Bank. 2022. "Poverty and Shared Prosperity: Correcting Course." World Bank,
Washington, DC. https://doi.org/10.1596/978-1-4648-1893-6.

Abbreviations

AI	artificial intelligence
ASP	adaptive social protection
BRLP	Bihar Rural Livelihoods Project (JEEViKA, local acronym, India)
BRLPS	Bihar Rural Livelihoods Promotion Society (India)
COMSIP	Community Savings and Investment Promotion Cooperative Union Limited (Malawi)
CREI	climate-resilient economic inclusion
DIB	development impact bond
DREAMS	Delivering Resilient Enterprises and Market Systems (Ethiopia and Uganda)
ECLAC	Economic Commission for Latin America and the Caribbean
EPA	Environmental Protection Agency (Ghana)
ESSRP	Emergency Social Stabilization and Resilience Project (Iraq)
FAO	Food and Agriculture Organization of the United Nations
FCV	fragility, conflict, and violence
FOMENTAR	Promoting Better Jobs through Integrated Labor and Skills Programs Program (Argentina)
G2P	government-to-person
ICM	International Care Ministries
ILO	International Labour Organization
INADEH	National Professional Training Institute (Panama)
IPCC	Intergovernmental Panel on Climate Change
J-PAL	Abdul Latif Jameel Poverty Action Lab
JEEViKA	local acronym for Bihar Rural Livelihoods Project (BRLP, India)
LLA	locally led adaptation
MPG	Minimum Package for Graduation (Rwanda)
MITRADEL	Ministry of Education and Ministry of Labor (Panama)
MLNR	Ministry of Lands and Natural Resources (Ghana)
MoDEE	Ministry of Digital Economy and Entrepreneurship (Jordan)
MOLSA	Ministry of Labor and Social Affairs (Iraq)
MoU	memorandum of understanding
NASSP	National Social Safety Nets Project (Nigeria)
NBS	nature-based solution
NGO	nongovernmental organization
NG-CARES	Nigeria COVID-19 Action Recovery and Economic Stimulus
NPL	national poverty line
ORKOY	Forest and Village Relations Program (Türkiye)

OGM	General Directorate of Forestry (Türkiye)
PAD	project appraisal document
PEI	Partnership for Economic Inclusion
PES	payments for ecosystem services
PP	project paper
PPP	purchasing power parity
REAP	Rural Entrepreneur Access Project (Kenya)
SDG	Sustainable Development Goal (United Nations)
SEI	State of Economic Inclusion (World Bank)
SHG	self-help group
SJY	Satat Jeevikoparjan Yojana (Bihar, India)
SLWMP	Sustainable Land and Water Management Project (Ghana)
SMS	short message service
TDA	Text and Data Analytics team (World Bank)
UNDESA	United Nations Department of Economic and Social Affairs
UNDP	United Nations Development Programme
UNHCR	United Nations High Commissioner for Refugees
UPSNJP	Urban Productive Safety Net and Jobs Project (Ethiopia)
YESSO	Youth Employment and Social Support Operation (Nigeria)
YKK	Yook Koom Koom (Senegal)
YTJ	Youth, Technology and Jobs (Jordan)

Note: All dollar amounts in this publication are U.S. dollars unless otherwise indicated.

Introduction

Partnership for Economic Inclusion and *The State of Economic Inclusion Report*

The State of Economic Inclusion Report (SEI) is a flagship initiative of the Partnership for Economic Inclusion (PEI), a global platform that supports the adoption and scale-up of government-led economic inclusion programs that increase the earnings and assets of extreme-poor and vulnerable households. Hosted by the World Bank's Social Protection Global Practice, PEI brings together diverse networks of governments, the United Nations, nongovernmental organizations (NGOs), researchers, and other organizations and institutions.

The first report in this series, *The State of Economic Inclusion Report 2021: The Potential to Scale* (SEI 2021; Andrews et al. 2021) established a baseline of the global landscape and introduced a common framework for understanding these programs as they move to scale. A central focus of SEI 2021 was the integration of new data and evidence regarding program design and implementation, impacts, and costs. Through the Landscape Survey 2020, the report consolidated formerly disconnected strands of experiences in government and nongovernment programs across various sectors. The impact review documented experiences from quantitative evaluations of 80 programs in 37 countries. In addition, the report introduced the Quick Costing Tool 2020 as a starting point to inform discussions on cost optimization and efficiency. Key data collected throughout the report was published on the PEI Open Access Data Portal at http://peiglobal.org.

The current report—*The State of Economic Inclusion Report 2024: Pathways to Scale* (SEI 2024)—complements SEI 2021 by exploring efforts to scale up policy and programming, including progress and challenges around government-led programs, and the interplay with nongovernment actors and the private sector. This report analyzes shifts in the global landscape over the past three years, including the degree to which economic inclusion programs are being customized in vastly different contexts and the growing role of economic inclusion in building resilience and providing job opportunities to the poor population in the context of overlapping crises. Box I.1 defines the terms used in this report.

BOX I.1   Key Terms Used in SEI 2024

- **Economic inclusion.** The gradual integration of individuals and households into broader economic and community development processes. Integration is achieved by addressing the multiple constraints or structural barriers faced by poor people at different levels: the household (for example, human and physical capacity), the community (social norms), the local economy (access to markets and services), and formal institutions (access to political and administrative structures).
- **Economic inclusion program.** Bundle of coordinated, multidimensional interventions that support individuals, households, and communities to sustainably increase their incomes and assets. Economic inclusion program are also known as *productive inclusion programs.*
- **Opportunity.** Increasing the probability of individuals, households, and communities to capture and capitalize on chances to improve incomes and assets that they would otherwise miss (Hernandez 2020; Ralston, Andrews, and Hsiao 2017). This helps propel individuals and households out of poverty through improved productivity and access to jobs but requires both access to such chances and the capacity to take advantage of them (World Bank 2012).
- **Resilience at the household level.** The strengthened ability of households to manage risk and respond to and cope with sudden shocks that are likely to overwhelm them. Resilience depends on a set of interconnected capacities that span across the before, during, and post-shock continuum: *anticipatory,* the ability to anticipate shocks through preparedness and planning; *absorptive,* the ability to absorb the impacts during and after shocks have occurred; and *adaptive,* the ability to adapt, learn, and adjust after a disaster occurs (Bahadur et al. 2015).
- **Resilience at the system level.** The ability of a system—social, economic, or environmental—to continue to function over time in the wake of a shock. *Climate resilience* refers to the capacity of social and economic systems and ecosystems to cope with hazardous events, trends, or disturbances by responding or reorganizing in ways that maintain their essential function, identity, and structure, as well as biodiversity in the case of ecosystems, while also maintaining the capacity for adaptation, learning, and transformation (Costella et al. 2023).

Landscape Survey 2023

The report draws on the Landscape Survey of Economic Inclusion Programs 2023 (Landscape Survey 2023),[1] as well as on the operational insights garnered through PEI's collaboration with its partners. In 2023, PEI identified 570 ongoing economic inclusion programs in 105 countries (refer to box I.2), or more than double the number of programs identified in 2020. Of the programs identified, 405 programs in 88 countries completed PEI's Landscape Survey 2023.[2] Sixty-three percent of surveyed programs have emerged since the Landscape Survey 2020. In addition to the 570 ongoing programs, more than 70 programs, mostly government led, are expected to be operational in the near future.

BOX I.2　Landscape Survey of Economic Inclusion Programs 2023

The following is general information about the Landscape Survey of Economic Inclusion Programs 2023. Appendix A in this report includes a full description of the survey methodology.

Sampling frame

The Partnership for Economic Inclusion (PEI) team built a sampling frame based on the 2020 sample, partner outreach, and a scan of the World Bank's portfolio and pipeline of projects to identify those with an economic inclusion focus. The team also scanned existing databases and sources of information, including the database of the Economic Commission for Latin America and the Caribbean on productive inclusion programs and the Atlas of Social Protection Indicators of Resilience and Equity. From this process, the PEI team identified 645 economic inclusion programs globally in 2023. Of these, 570 programs were under way, and 75 were in the pipeline.

Questionnaire

The Landscape Survey 2023 captured data on program objectives, coverage, profiles of targeted participants, component design and delivery, institutional arrangements, and research and evaluation plans using an online tool that built on the survey questionnaire used in the 2020 round. The 2020 questionnaire was revised to add clarity and granularity to some of the questions and was expanded slightly to capture information on design and implementation features relevant to PEI's priority topics: women's economic empowerment and climate resilience. The 2023 questionnaire was designed to be completed by staff from the lead implementing agency or from partner organizations using an online survey tool that is publicly available (the survey tool is available on the SEI 2024 publication landing at peiglobal.org/state-of-economic-inclusion-report).

Response rate

All 570 identified ongoing programs were invited to complete the online survey tool. Of these, 405 completed the survey, for a 71 percent response rate. The distribution of responses, by type of lead agency and income, aligns with the distribution of all identified programs. Of those who completed the survey, 92 programs (23 percent) were also included in PEI's Landscape Survey 2020. Of the 313 programs in the Landscape Survey 2023 but not in the 2020 round, 247 programs (79 percent) started after the 2020 survey had closed, 55 programs (18 percent) had not been identified, 9 programs (3 percent) did not meet the criteria for inclusion, and 2 programs (less than 1 percent) did not respond to the survey in 2020.

How to Navigate SEI 2024

This report consists of four chapters, policy recommendations, three spotlights, and a special focus on climate resilience.

- **Chapter 1** discusses the role of economic inclusion programs in building resilience and creating jobs, especially in the context of overlapping crises. It draws on key data points from the Landscape Survey 2023.

- **Chapter 2** reviews the evolving landscape, global footprint, and key objectives and design features of economic inclusion programs based on the Landscape Survey 2023. It also includes comparisons with the Landscape Survey 2020, which underpinned SEI 2021, where relevant.

- **Chapter 3** builds on the scale framework introduced in SEI 2021, using survey data and country cases to review the programmatic dimensions of scaling up economic inclusion, focusing on increased coverage and functional expansion.

- **Chapter 4** addresses the institutional aspects of scaling up economic inclusion programs, examining diverse arrangements for achieving scale in light of operational and organizational challenges.

- **Spotlight 1** summarizes the emerging evidence from government-led economic inclusion programs and highlights key knowledge gaps.

- **Spotlight 2** places economic inclusion programs in the context of the challenges faced by youth in the labor market and offers youth-focused design considerations.

- **Spotlight 3** demonstrates the significant potential digital technologies hold for economic inclusion programming, providing an overview of emerging innovations for digital delivery.

- The **Special Focus** section explores the emerging agenda of designing economic inclusion programs to enhance the climate resilience of poor and vulnerable individuals and communities. It presents current experiences from programs intentionally designed to support climate-resilient development.

- **Policy Recommendations** include five recommendations based on the in-depth review of the current landscape of economic inclusion programs.

- **Appendix A** provides an overview of the methodology used in executing the Landscape Survey 2023 and the analysis underpinning this report.

- **Appendix B** compares the landscape data findings included in *The State of Economic Inclusion Report 2021* and *The State of Economic Inclusion Report 2024.*

- **Appendix C** provides a list and key data points for the economic inclusion programs surveyed globally for this report.

Notes

1. The survey captures data on the programs' objectives, coverage and profile of targeted participants, component design and delivery, institutional arrangements, and research and evaluation plans. Refer to box I.2 for details. The data collected for the 2023 survey are publicly available through PEI's Open Access Data Portal at https://www.peiglobal.org/pei-data-portal. For information on PEI's Landscape Survey 2020, refer to Andrews et al. (2021).
2. PEI identified 645 economic inclusion programs globally in 2023, of which 570 programs were ongoing (that is, already serving participants or about to do so) and 75 were in the pipeline.

References

Andrews, Colin, Aude de Montesquiou, Inés Arévalo-Sánchez, Puja Vasudeva Dutta, Boban Varghese Paul, Sadna Samaranayake, Janet Heisey, Timothy Clay, and Sarang Chaudhary. 2021. *The State of Economic Inclusion Report 2021: The Potential to Scale.* Washington, DC: World Bank. http://hdl.handle.net/10986/34917.

Bahadur, Aditya, Emma Lovell, Emily Wilkinson, and Thomas Tanner. 2015. *Resilience in the SDGs: Developing an Indicator for Target 1.5 That Is Fit for Purpose.* London: Overseas Development Institute.

Costella, Cecilia, Timothy Clay, Manann Donoghoe, and Liz Giron. 2023. *Pathways to Climate-Resilient Economic Inclusion: A Framework for Integrating Climate Action in Economic Inclusion Programs. PEI in Practice, Volume 9.* Washington, DC: World Bank. http://hdl.handle.net/10986/40542.

Hernandez, Emilio. 2020. "Financial Inclusion for What?" *CGAP Blog,* February 5. https://www.cgap.org/blog/financial-inclusion-what.

Ralston, Laura, Colin Andrews, and Allan Jer-Yu Hsiao. 2017. "The Impacts of Safety Nets in Africa: What Are We Learning?" Policy Research Working Paper No. 8255, World Bank, Washington, DC. https://ssrn.com/abstract=3076234.

World Bank. 2012. *Resilience, Equity, and Opportunity: The World Bank's Social Protection and Labor Strategy 2012–2022.* Washington, DC: World Bank. http://documents.worldbank.org/curated/en/443791468157506768/Resilience-equity-and-opportunity-the-World-Banks-social-protection-and-labor-strategy-2012-2022.

CHAPTER 1
Economic Inclusion in Overlapping Crises

KEY MESSAGES

- Economic inclusion programs are expanding in number and reach, shaped by the growing evidence of their effectiveness at building resilience and facilitating job opportunities for poor and vulnerable people in the face of overlapping global crises.

- Improving food security and short- and long-term resilience to various shocks are hallmarks of well-designed economic inclusion programs. Climate resilience can be enhanced by addressing challenges at the intersection of climate change and poverty.

- Economic inclusion programs can play a role in improving job opportunities for poor people by facilitating self-employment opportunities, establishing market links, and providing access to value chains. They can also facilitate access to wage employment opportunities, particularly in urban areas.

Introduction

There has been a sustained surge in the number of economic inclusion programs in recent years. A significant number of ongoing programs have expanded despite, or in some cases in response to, the current context of overlapping crises. In 2023, the Landscape Survey identified 570 ongoing economic inclusion programs in 105 countries, with many more programs expected to be operational in the future. This figure is more than double the number of programs identified in 2020, reflecting a steady expansion of economic inclusion programming.

This surge comes at a time when the world has been grappling with repeated shocks and crises, from the COVID-19 pandemic to disruptions in global trade and markets to inflation and a global economic slowdown. The effects of these overlapping crises have been felt globally, but they have affected poor and vulnerable populations disproportionately, derailing progress toward achieving the Sustainable Development Goals (SDGs) (Sachs et al. 2023).

This chapter illustrates the role of economic inclusion programs in building resilience and promoting job opportunities specifically in the context of overlapping crises. Drawing on key data points extracted from the Landscape Survey 2023,[1] the chapter focuses on the following topical concerns about how economic inclusion programs are improving job outcomes for poor and vulnerable populations against a background of overlapping crises and building long-term resilience to shocks, especially threats to food security and climate risks.

Safeguarding Poor and Vulnerable Populations Amid Overlapping Crises

Global trends in poverty reduction have reversed for the first time in decades as a result of COVID-19 (World Bank 2022a). Recent estimates suggest that, although poverty rates are falling again (World Bank 2023d), it is at a slower rate than before the pandemic; factors include uneven recoveries and the effects of overlapping crises, including steep increases in the cost of living and economic losses arising from conflicts and climate shocks (Yonzan, Gerszon Mahler, and Lakner 2023). All of these issues are taking place against a backdrop of climate change and other global megatrends, such as fragility, conflict, and demographic change, that have implications for poverty reduction and are hampering efforts to achieve the SDGs (refer to box 1.1). Meanwhile, debt distress in many countries and worsening financial conditions are limiting the efforts to promote an inclusive and resilient recovery. However, efforts to specifically target those disproportionately affected by the overlapping crises are now more important than ever.

BOX 1.1   **Global Megatrends with Implications for Poverty Reduction**

The following global megatrends have implications for poverty reduction:

- **Fragility, conflict, and violence (FCV).** Countries classified as FCV face "extremely low levels of institutional and governance capacity" or "acute insecurity" (World Bank 2024a). These challenging conditions impede poverty reduction because poverty and conflict can mutually reinforce each other, raising the risk of turning extreme poverty into a chronic problem, particularly in Sub-Saharan Africa where FCV conditions are concentrated (Tetteh and Lakner 2023). By 2030, up to two-thirds of the world's extreme-poor individuals could live in these settings, even though the affected countries account for only 10 percent of the world's population (Corral et al. 2020).

- **Climate change.** The Earth's climate is changing rapidly due to human activity (Hallegatte et al. 2017; IPCC 2022). Climate change is leading to losses of biodiversity, soil erosion, sea-level rise, and less clean water. In addition, it is having other significant effects on the natural environment by increasing the frequency and intensity of climate-induced natural disasters, such as droughts, cyclones, and floods (IPCC 2022). Poor people are most vulnerable to the effects of climate change because of their reliance on agriculture and natural resources and because they lack the resources to recover from losses after experiencing an extreme climate event or to adapt to and recover from climate-induced shocks and stressors. By 2030, climate change could increase the number of people living in extreme poverty by 122 million (IPCC 2022), reversing some of the progress in poverty reduction in recent decades.

- **Demographic change.** Current estimates suggest the world's population will grow at a slower rate than in recent decades, reaching 9.7 billion by 2050 (UNDESA 2019). Worldwide, the population is aging due to rising longevity and lower fertility levels, thereby putting pressure on contributory social protection systems that require a sufficient proportion of working-age adults to pay into and sustain the system (UNDESA 2019). However, these growth trends will be uneven across regions. Sub-Saharan Africa will likely experience a "youth bulge" and so could achieve development gains if it creates job opportunities and integrates youth into the workforce. In contrast, East and Southeast Asia, Europe, and North America, with their aging populations, must develop systems that can affordably provide for the health care and financial support that older people need. Such regional demographic imbalances, paired with uneven economic performance and increasing fragility, conflict, and violence in some parts of the world, will likely lead to growing migration, which, if managed well, could benefit both origin and destination countries (World Bank 2023e).

- **Urbanization.** The percentage of people living in urban areas rose from 25 percent of the world's population in 1950 to 56 percent in 2022 and is expected to continue growing in the coming years (UN Habitat 2022; World Bank 2023f). As urbanization continues and urban poverty rises, urban development strategists must find ways to address the needs of poor and vulnerable populations and to prevent the exclusion of these groups from local economic processes and prevent the emergence of poverty traps in urban areas (Baker et al. 2023).

With the overarching goal of building resilience and creating jobs for poor and vulnerable people, economic inclusion programs can be used to address different needs in different contexts. Investing in economic inclusion programs pays off in the long run, with the benefits significantly outweighing the initial costs. The original graduation pilots in six countries showed positive returns ranging from 133 percent to 433 percent (Banerjee et al. 2015). A recent meta-analysis highlights evidence from studies conducted in Afghanistan, Bangladesh, the Democratic Republic of Congo, Ghana, Nepal, and Niger revealing cost-benefit ratios between 121 percent and 379 percent and internal rates of return[2] ranging from 16 percent to 66 percent (J-PAL 2023). For policy makers, this robust evidence from diverse settings demonstrates that economic inclusion programs consistently deliver economic benefits that surpass the initial investment, can be considered effective tools for poverty alleviation, and are wise investments with considerable returns, leading to broader social and economic development (refer to spotlight 1 for emerging evidence from government-led programs).[3]

Building Long-Term Resilience to Shocks

Economic inclusion programs help build households' resilience to intermittent shocks and stressors by, for example, providing access to regular and predictable cash transfers; facilitating asset accumulation, income diversification, and access to financial services; and strengthening social networks (Andrews et al. 2021). Several studies show that households participating in economic inclusion programs were better able to cope with shocks than were nonparticipants. Nonparticipants resorted to negative coping strategies, such as selling assets or reducing food consumption, and so they experienced reductions in well-being more than participant households (Bedoya Argüelles et al. 2023; Hernandez et al. 2016; HTSPE 2011; Siddiki et al. 2014; Smith et al. 2019).

In overlapping crises, however, the ability of poor and vulnerable households to withstand and recover from shocks is seriously undermined, reducing their resilience to future shocks (D'Errico et al. 2021). This finding highlights the importance of explicitly incorporating program elements specifically intended to build participants' long-term resilience. Such elements should help participants not only cope with the immediate effects of a crisis but also develop their capacity to adapt to and recover from shocks. Box 1.2 illustrates how economic inclusion programs built resilience in this way in response to the COVID-19 pandemic.

Food security and climate resilience are deeply interconnected. Achieving food security requires a transformation of food systems to ensure they are both nutritionally robust and adaptable to changing climate conditions. The World Bank's Global Challenge Programs on Food and Nutrition Security underscores the importance of building resilience to climate impacts, recognizing that without it, food systems remain vulnerable to disruptions (World Bank 2023b). This vulnerability has both immediate and longer-term consequences: climate-induced degradation of soil, water, and biodiversity not only undermines the current capacity to produce sufficient and nutritious food but also jeopardizes the future sustainability of food systems.

BOX 1.2   Building Resilience After the COVID-19 Pandemic

The COVID-19 pandemic undermined the ability of millions of people to sustain themselves and their families, especially those in poor and vulnerable households. In response, many economic inclusion programs adapted ongoing interventions to better support participants. Early responses focused on providing the immediate support households needed, and many programs provided emergency support through cash transfers or transfer top-ups to alleviate income losses as economic activity came to a halt. Some economic inclusion programs that built on existing cash transfers used existing delivery systems, such as social registries, to provide a timely response.

Although the initial effects of COVID-19 on economic activity were temporary during lockdowns (such as movement restrictions and market closures), its effects on people's livelihoods and overall well-being outlasted the lockdown period and were further exacerbated by the trickle-down effects of the pandemic, including the effects of supply chain disruptions on inflation and access to markets. Poor and vulnerable people were particularly affected because of their weaker access to resources and fewer positive or neutral coping mechanisms.

Some longer-lasting effects of COVID-19 were compounded by subsequent crises, and many economic inclusion programs were designed to respond to these events. For example, the Nigeria COVID-19 Action Recovery and Economic Stimulus Program, led by the Federal Ministry of Budget and Economic Planning, was designed to mitigate the impacts of COVID-19 on the livelihoods of poor and vulnerable households, communities, and micro and small enterprises. It expands their access to livelihood support and food security services by providing cash transfers, livelihood grants, agricultural inputs, and basic community infrastructure, as well as skills training and coaching. The program also strengthens the institutions for delivery of adaptive and shock-responsive social protection services.

Enhancing Long-Term Food Security and Reducing Reliance on Negative Coping Strategies

Food insecurity can be detrimental to people's ability to engage in productive work and function effectively in daily life, and it can have long-lasting impacts on the physical, cognitive, and psychosocial development of young children (Gallegos et al. 2021). In the event of a shock, poor and vulnerable households use coping mechanisms differently from those of other groups, and reducing the amount and quality of consumed food is among the main strategies used (D'Errico et al. 2021).

In recent years, food insecurity has dramatically increased globally as a result of overlapping crises. Since 2019, an additional 150 million people have become food insecure because of COVID-19 (FAO et al. 2023), and between 2019 and 2022, the number of people facing severe food insecurity more than doubled (UNDESA 2023). Despite some recent improvements, food security and nutrition are worse today than before the pandemic (FAO et al. 2023) due to inflation, food supply disruptions, and the economic effects of recent crises. Increasing exposure to the effects of climate change poses additional risks (FAO 2023) and will likely make food security a pervasive issue (World Bank 2022b).

Food security is a core objective in 24 percent of all programs. A higher proportion of programs in Sub-Saharan Africa than in other regions have food security as a core objective (30 percent in East Africa versus 26 percent in West Africa and 19 percent in the rest of the world), a reflection of the higher food insecurity in these regions (FAO et al. 2023). Economic inclusion programs have been found to increase food security in general, but programs that deliberately include food security and nutrition elements can help their participants overcome constraints in accessing a healthy diet (Bouguen and Dillon 2021; Kang et al. 2023; Technical and Operational Performance Support Uganda Graduation Randomized Control Trial Associate Award 2022).[4] Economic inclusion programs support food security and nutrition in ways that are consistent with strengthening households' long-term resilience. This finding is particularly important because evidence suggests that improvements in food security through social assistance or livelihood support do not necessarily translate into improvements in anthropometric indicators such as stunting and child height and weight (Technical and Operational Performance Support Uganda Graduation Randomized Control Trial Associate Award 2022; World Bank 2022b).

Beyond addressing shorter-term needs, programs build longer-term resilience and food security by supporting efforts to increase productivity, especially that of farmers and food producers through access to improved inputs (such as seeds and fertilizers) and technologies, as well as markets. Economic inclusion packages that support the development of agrifood systems show great potential for enhancing food security and nutrition and reducing poverty. Developing community groups, building local infrastructure, and strengthening local institutions are critical to building resilient and inclusive value chains and food systems (IFPRI 2023). For instance, Yemen's Food Security Response and Resilience Project combines short-term immediate support interventions to mitigate the humanitarian crisis's impact with medium- to long-term strategies aimed at enhancing resilience. The interventions encompass community-based agricultural production infrastructure, including small-scale irrigation, water harvesting and storage, land protection, terrace rehabilitation, and farm-to-field roads. In addition, the project support to resilience building includes agricultural services such as animal health and seed production and multiplication (using certified seeds on a farm to produce clean seeds that can be used by other farmers as alternatives to the often-unaffordable and -unavailable certified seeds), as well as assistance to agrifood service providers.

Building Climate Resilience in the Long Term

The lives and livelihoods of billions of people worldwide are significantly affected by climate change, which intensifies levels of extreme poverty and vulnerability. Each year, climate-magnified natural disasters such as droughts, floods, and windstorms cause more than US$300 billion in damages and more than US$500 billion in welfare and consumption losses worldwide (Hallegatte et al. 2017). Addressing climate change is a monumental challenge that cannot be separated from efforts to alleviate poverty. Moreover, climate change is also expected to lead to widespread hunger as a result of crop failures and higher mortality due to changing temperatures and greater exposure to diseases, such as malaria and diarrhea (WHO 2023). Poor people often must cope with these shocks in ways that further deteriorate their surrounding natural environment, reinforcing a vicious cycle of poverty and environmental degradation. Thus, global efforts to reduce poverty must be paired with efforts to combat the effects of climate change, and vice versa.

Economic inclusion programs are well placed to enable climate-resilient development by supporting climate adaptation and mitigation, going beyond short-term shock-responsiveness. These programs are designed to improve resilience, and many of their features are particularly well suited for addressing the challenges to economic inclusion posed by climate change. The Landscape Survey 2023 finds that 66 percent of economic inclusion programs include interventions designed to build resilience to climate change.[5] However, these numbers are misleading, and programs vary considerably in the degree to which they align climate and poverty objectives and how effectively they incorporate climate-resilient activities and outcomes in program design (Costella et al. 2023a).

Despite the growing importance of the climate-resilience agenda, cumulative experience is still limited within economic inclusion programs. Three program areas show high potential for positive climate-resilience outcomes: (1) adaptive safety nets and adaptive social protection (refer to box 1.3) that build resilience to climate events and incentivize sustainable livelihoods; (2) sustainable food and ecosystems that enhance natural assets and restore ecosystems; and (3) green livelihoods and jobs that facilitate a transition from extractive and resource-dependent livelihoods (Costella et al. 2023a). This report's section with the special focus on climate resilience delves deeper into these areas and presents emerging evidence and experiences from economic inclusion programs intentionally supporting climate-resilience development.

BOX 1.3   **Adaptive Social Protection and Climate Resilience**

Adaptive social protection (ASP) is a dynamic strategy for addressing poverty and food insecurity in the context of climate-resilient economic inclusion. Unlike traditional social protection, ASP integrates disaster risk management and climate change adaptation to enhance the capacity of vulnerable households and communities to prepare for, cope with, and adapt to various shocks, including natural disasters, economic crises, and climate change (Bowen et al. 2020). Against the backdrop of COVID-19 and the ensuing overlapping crises, diverse audiences related to climate, financing, and food security now recognize the potential of an adaptive approach (Costella et al. 2023b; World Bank 2023c).

A notable example of effective ASP is the Sahel Adaptive Social Protection Program, which supports six countries (Burkina Faso, Chad, Mali, Mauritania, Niger, and Senegal) in building adaptive systems to help vulnerable households adapt to the impacts of climate change and other shocks. This comprehensive initiative includes a spectrum of policies, instruments, and initiatives designed to enhance the human capital, productivity, and resilience of the most vulnerable populations in the region. By enabling these communities to effectively confront and adapt to shocks, the program's economic inclusion measures strive to have large positive impacts such as reducing poverty levels, addressing food insecurity, boosting productivity, and enhancing resilience among program participants. Furthermore, the program is anticipated to have broader effects on local economies, societies, and future generations.

Creating Jobs for the Poorest People

Economic growth is not always inclusive, and access to jobs is particularly challenging for poor and vulnerable individuals, especially women (refer to box 1.4). With an insufficient demand for paid labor, the wage sector remains thin in most developing countries, where levels of informality in labor markets are high—reaching 70 percent of employment in emerging markets and developing economies (Ohnsorge and Yu 2022). Creating better jobs is more difficult in informal settings due to capital constraints, low productivity, and fewer available resources to support investments (World Bank 2023a). Addressing the job challenges for poor and vulnerable individuals cannot be left solely to overall economic growth and instead requires a comprehensive set of policies.

BOX 1.4   The Jobs Challenge and Women

Women tend to be disadvantaged across the board in comparison with men, particularly in accessing earning opportunities (Fields 2011). A key barrier is that women are often expected to carry the burden of unpaid care work for children or elderly individuals, which limits the time they can engage in paid work. Other external factors hindering women's ability to work are lack of safe transport options, long working hours, customary practices or laws that restrict their rights to property or work, discrimination in hiring and retention, and limited access to education and training, among other things. Social norms, such as the widespread expectation that women will raise children and manage their households, also undermine their ability to find jobs. Married women, particularly those with young children, face the greatest number of barriers to entering or remaining in the labor market (UN Women and ILO 2020).

As a result, from 2011 to 2022, an average of 50 percent of women globally participated in the labor force, compared with 70 percent of men (World Bank 2024b). Moreover, jobs are often subject to gender bias, with women's jobs overwhelmingly in the informal economy where jobs pay less and are less secure. In 2022, for example, four-fifths of the jobs created for women were in the informal economy compared with two-thirds of jobs for men (ILO 2023). Women are also more likely than men to change their status in the labor market; they face greater difficulties moving to formal jobs and are more likely than men to lose their jobs (OECD 2024).

These factors are heightened when a woman takes on the role of mother. Research suggests that, even in high-income countries, female labor force participation and earnings drop after a woman has her first child. In low- and middle-income countries, there is more variation in the duration of the impacts, resulting in a higher overall cost to women's earnings (Bandiera et al. 2022).

As a result, women are more vulnerable to poverty than men. According to Bandiera et al. (2022, 236–237), "gender is a stronger predictor of the levels of work than wealth: women are less likely to work than men in every wealth class." Given this context, economic inclusion actors must design programs that consider the specific limitations women face and help them overcome structural and social barriers to successfully engage in economic activities.

The upcoming Jobs Flagship Report from the World Bank recommends an ambitious policy agenda to address market and policy failures that is centered on three broad pillars:

- *Production policies* can help by removing barriers that hold back private businesses;

- *Policies for people* should address inefficiencies in education and training to ensure a steady supply of a qualified workforce; and

- *Policies for places* will improve productivity through agglomeration economies, better market access, lower trade costs, and reduced barriers to migration.

Policies in each of these areas have impacts that cut across the four dimensions of jobs, as outlined in the report: sectoral, spatial, occupational, and organizational (World Bank, forthcoming).

Economic inclusion programs play a pivotal role in unlocking the productive potential of the poorest and most vulnerable individuals, gradually integrating them into broader economic development processes. Through a multidimensional approach these programs address multiple constraints faced by poor and vulnerable people. The programs can boost the productivity of people across the four dimensions of jobs. In terms of sectoral, labor productivity is improved as programs promote income diversification from subsistence farming to nonfarm enterprises. Spatially, programs support the creation of businesses in less developed areas and the poorest regions. Foundational technical and business skills are improved, enhancing the occupational choices for poor individuals. Finally, household enterprises are linked to markets, expanding value chains, and improving the productivity of producer organizations.

Overcoming the Constraints to Jobs

It is crucial to acknowledge the existence of "poverty traps" and understand that unlocking the productive potential of people living in poverty requires addressing various constraints. These constraints, stemming from households, communities, local economies, and institutions, can disproportionately affect the poorest and most vulnerable populations (Andrews et al. 2021). Economic inclusion programs address multiple constraints that prevent poor and vulnerable people from tapping into economic activities and participating in structural transformation processes.

Yet, how these programs enhance access to job opportunities for poor and vulnerable populations largely depends on the local economy and the characteristics of targeted households. Most economic inclusion programs are aimed at enhancing self-employment opportunities (84 percent of surveyed programs).[6] In low-income countries, programs targeting extreme-poor and ultra-poor people exclusively, mostly in rural contexts, more often focus on supporting income diversification, increasing resilience, and moving participants from unpaid or casual work to self-employment, as well as increasing income through improved self-employment activities. These goals are mostly carried out by providing business capital and by facilitating access to financial services (81 percent and 75 percent of programs that seek to enhance self-employment opportunities, respectively).

A much smaller share of programs facilitates access to wage employment opportunities (34 percent of surveyed programs). In lower- and upper-middle-income countries, the focus is much more on wage employment opportunities than in low-income countries, particularly in urban areas where the context for the poor population changes significantly, influencing the design of programs (refer to chapter 3). A large proportion of programs that facilitate access to wage employment do so by linking participants to apprenticeships, which is always combined with training for better positive employment and income outcomes (Bertrand and Crepon 2023). Ethiopia's Urban Productive Safety Net and Jobs Project offers six-month apprenticeships to unemployed youth with high school diplomas or less. These apprenticeships, hosted by private and public firms, provide a stipend during the program and for three months after, helping support the transition into work. In addition, the project offers life skills, digital training, and job search support to further boost employment prospects.

Creating Market Access and Boosting Local Economies

Combining livelihood support with activities aimed at increasing the market access of poor and vulnerable households can effectively increase productivity and incomes (World Bank 2022c). Economic inclusion programs are increasingly linking these households to market systems and local economic processes. In fact, 23 percent of programs have "increased market access" as their core objective. This approach emphasizes the need to address constraints beyond the household and the community levels and pave the way for greater integration into the local economy to support more and better income-generating opportunities for poor and vulnerable populations. This issue is particularly true in agrifood economies and low-income countries, where fragmentation of production and weak market links lead to low productivity and low incomes (World Bank 2022c).

However, poor infrastructure and producer capacity in these contexts make it more challenging to improve market access (World Bank 2022c). Forty percent of economic inclusion programs support the organization of farmers through cooperatives and other types of producer organizations. These organizations can facilitate market integration, enhance coordination, and improve production capacity for smallholder farmers (Sparkman et al. 2022; World Bank 2022c). Programs can also use producer organizations as a platform to provide additional support such as skills training, capacity development, and access to finance and technology (refer to chapter 4 for more on the role of producer organizations and other community structures). Programs can be designed to assist in the organization and specialization of these producer groups and tailor support for them, depending on the initial level of specialization and formalization (refer to box 1.5 for an example).

BOX 1.5   Facilitating Access to Markets and Better Job Opportunities in Ethiopia

The Livestock and Fisheries Sector Development Project in Ethiopia is a good example of how economic inclusion programs can help link poor farmers to higher-value markets. The program targets government-defined cluster areas with select value chains (poultry, dairy, red meat, and fish) and supports smallholder farmers, unemployed youth, and female-headed households. The program seeks to increase the productivity and commercialization of farmers through a bundle of interventions customized as these farmers increase their productivity and become part of more-specialized producer organizations (refer to figure B1.5.1).

(Box continues next page)

BOX 1.5   **Facilitating Access to Markets and Better Job Opportunities in Ethiopia** *(continued)*

FIGURE B1.5.1   **Components and Objectives of the Livestock and Fisheries Sector Development Project in Ethiopia**

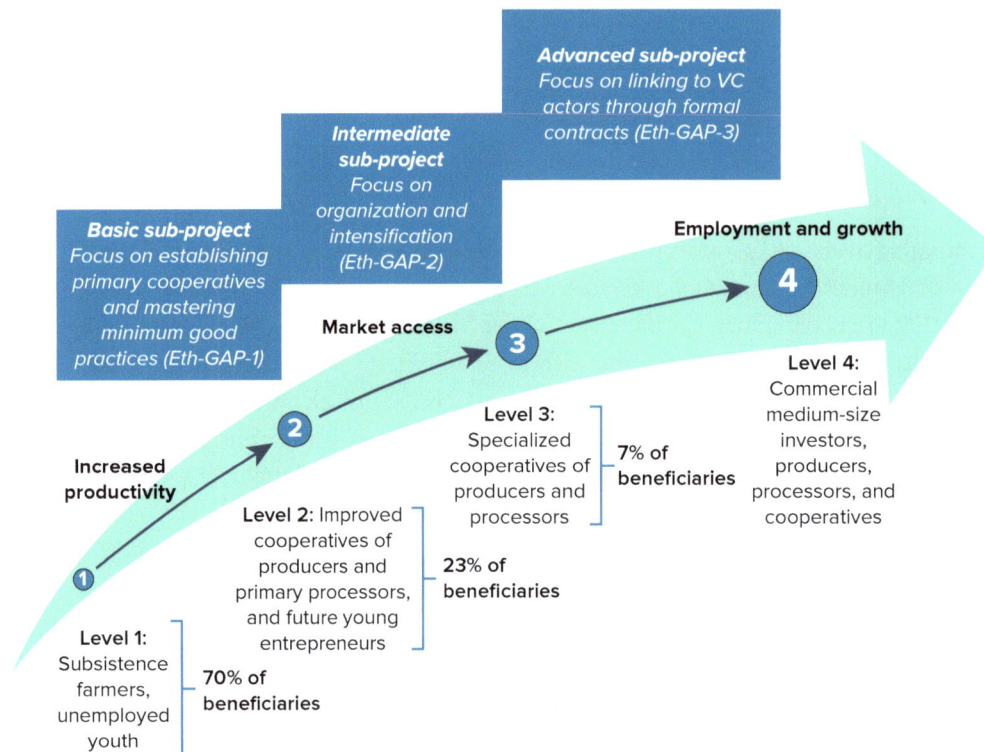

Source: World Bank 2017.

Note: Eth-GAP-1: extension and advisory services (health, feed, breed); Eth-GAP-2: intensive and specialized adult training (FFS); Eth-GAP-3: specialized support, coaching on marketing, quality and food safety, organizational management. FFS = Farmer Field Schools; VC = value chain.

The support package consists of business capital, financial and business management skills training, coaching, facilitation of access to credit and savings, and links to markets. At level 1, the program supports farmers in establishing primary cooperatives and improving their business management skills. Once participants become part of cooperatives, productive partnerships are established at level 2 between the cooperatives and market actors. At this level, participants are further supported through additional training (following the Food and Agriculture Organization's Farmer Field Schools approach) and access to inputs. As cooperatives strengthen further, the program continues to support them through more specialized partnership contracts, training, coaching, and inputs (level 3). The program also supports access to equipment and improved productive and processing infrastructure. At level 4, producers and processors are expected to be able to access private financing and are no longer supported by the program.

Many economic inclusion programs are embedded in broader multisectoral interventions that address constraints beyond the household level, including barriers at the community, local economy, and institutional levels. The interventions may include developing local infrastructure (such as irrigation), building the capacity of government and nongovernment actors (through training and service integration), and initiating changes in policies such as land reform that govern access to and ownership of resources for target populations. Such steps can increase program effectiveness by better connecting poor and vulnerable populations to markets, ultimately contributing to more inclusive local economic development. For example, investments in rural roads, marketing, storage, and collection were important for productivity and inclusion enhancement at the farm and cooperative levels in the Agricultural Growth Project in Ethiopia and the Rural Alliances Project in Bolivia (World Bank 2022c).

Notes

1. Refer to box 1.2 for details.
2. The *internal rate of return* is the annual rate of growth that an investment is expected to generate.
3. Refer also to SEI 2021 for a review of impact evidence from both government and nongovernment programs (Andrews et al. 2021).
4. For instance, cash transfers can also help households be better prepared for future shocks by building assets and undertaking productive investments and income diversification (IFPRI 2023). Some programs help households increase the availability of food through business grants and training, and even the production of high-nutrient foods (for example, Graduating to Resilience program in Uganda). The coaching component of this project included topics on food and nutrition, particularly for pregnant and lactating women and children, and provided guidance on meal planning and cooking demonstrations.
5. Meanwhile, there is large overlap with programs operating in FCV settings: 76 percent of programs in these settings support program participants to build climate resilience versus 61 percent in non-FCV settings.
6. This includes programs that seek to enhance self-employment opportunities, support income diversification, and increase productivity.

References

Andrews, Colin, Aude de Montesquiou, Inés Arévalo-Sánchez, Puja Vasudeva Dutta, Boban Varghese Paul, Sadna Samaranayake, Janet Heisey, Timothy Clay, and Sarang Chaudhary. 2021. *The State of Economic Inclusion Report 2021: The Potential to Scale.* Washington, DC: World Bank. http://hdl.handle.net/10986/34917.

Baker, Judy, Narae Choi, Manuel Gonzalez-Schuler, and Dmitry Sivaev. 2023. "Cities, Jobs, and Local Economic Development: A Guidance Note for Task Teams." World Bank, Washington, DC. http://documents.worldbank.org/curated/en/099050124115510113/P17499 110dc93c05e1a12c18622fa73b0a9.

Bandiera, Oriana, Ahmed Elsayed, Anton Heil, Andrea Smurra. 2022. "Presidential Address 2022: Economic Development and the Organisation of Labour: Evidence from the Jobs of the World Project." *Journal of the European Economic Association* 20 (6): 2226–2270. https://doi.org/10.1093/jeea/jvac056.

Banerjee, Abhijit, Esther Duflo, Nathanael Goldberg, Dean Karlan, Robert Osei, William Parienté, Jeremy Shapiro, Bram Thuysbaert, and Christopher Udry. 2015. "A Multifaceted Program Causes Lasting Progress for the Very Poor: Evidence from Six Countries." *Science* 348 (6236): 1260799. https://www.science.org/doi/10.1126/science.1260799.

Bedoya Argüelles, Guadalupe, Yulia Belyakova, Aidan Coville, Thomas Escande, Mohammad Isaqzadeh, and Aminata Ndiaye. 2023. "The Enduring Impacts of a Big Push during Multiple Crises: Experimental Evidence from Afghanistan (English)." Policy Research Working Paper No. WPS 10596; Impact Evaluation Series, Knowledge for Change Program World Bank, Washington, DC. http://documents.worldbank.org/curated/en/099837211062311087/IDU1 e486b8ed1e7a114d231a60d1848c87baeeb1.

Bertrand, Marianne, and Bruno Crepon. 2023. "Vocational and Skills Training Programs to Improve Labor Market Outcomes," Abdul Latif Jameel Poverty Action Lab. https://www .povertyactionlab.org/policy-insight/vocational-and-skills-training-programs-improve-labor -market-outcomes.

Bouguen, Adrien, and Andrew Dillon. 2021. "The Impact of a Nutrition-Focused Livelihoods Program on Child Nutrition in Burkina Faso." https://poverty-action.org/sites/default/files /publications/Child-Health-Nutrition-Burkina-Faso_Endline_3.4.22.pdf.

Bowen, Thomas Vaughan, Carlo Del Ninno, Colin Andrews, Sarah Coll-Black, Ugo Gentilini, Kelly Johnson, Yasuhiro Kawasoe, Adea Kryeziu, Barry Patrick Maher, and Asha M. Williams. 2020. *Adaptive Social Protection: Building Resilience to Shocks* (English). International Development in Focus Series. Washington, DC: World Bank. http://documents.worldbank.org/curated/en/579641590038388922 /Adaptive-Social-Protection-Building-Resilience-to-Shocks.

Corral, Paul, Alexander Irwin, Nandini Krishnan, Daniel Gerszon Mahler, and Tara Vishwanath. 2020. *Fragility and Conflict: On the Front Lines of the Fight against Poverty.* Washington, DC: World Bank. http://hdl.handle.net/10986/33324.

Costella, Cecilia, Timothy Clay, Manann Donoghoe, and Liz Giron. 2023a. *Pathways to Climate-Resilient Economic Inclusion: A Framework for Integrating Climate Action in Economic Inclusion Programs. PEI in Practice, Volume 9.* Washington, DC: World Bank. http://hdl.handle.net/10986/40542.

Costella, Cecilia, Maarten van Aalst, Yola Georgiadou, Rachel Slater, Rachel Reilly, Anna McCord, Rebecca Holmes, Johnathan Ammoun, and Valentina Barca. 2023b. "Can Social Protection Tackle Emerging Risks from Climate Change, and How? A Framework and a Critical Review." *Climate Risk Management*, Article 100501. https://www.sciencedirect.com/science /article/pii/S221209632300027X?via%3Dihub.

D'Errico, Marco, Jeanne Pinay, Anh Luu, and Ellestina Jumbe. 2021. "Drivers and Stressors of Resilience to Food Insecurity—Evidence from 35 Countries." FAO Agricultural Development Economics Working Paper 21-09. FAO, Rome. https://doi.org/10.4060/cb7411en.

FAO (Food and Agriculture Organization). 2023. "Global Food Security Challenges and Its Drivers: Conflicts and Wars in Ukraine and Other Countries, Slowdowns and Downturns, and Climate Change." FAO Council, Hundred and Seventy-Second Session, CL 172/5. FAO, Rome. https://www.fao.org/3/nl652en/nl652en.pdf.

FAO (Food and Agriculture Organization), IFAD (International Fund for Agricultural Development), UNICEF (United Nations Children's Fund), WFP (UN World Food Programme), and WHO (World Health Organization). 2023. *The State of Food Security and Nutrition in the World 2023. Urbanization, Agrifood Systems Transformation and Healthy Diets across the Rural–Urban Continuum.* Rome: FAO. https://doi.org/10.4060 /cc3017en.

Fields, Gary S. 2011. "Labor Market Analysis for Developing Countries." *Labour Economics* 18 (Suppl. 1): S16–S22. https://doi.org/10.1016/j.labeco.2011.09.005.

Gallegos, Danielle, Areana Eivers, Peter Sondergeld, and Cassandra Pattinson. 2021. "Food Insecurity and Child Development: A State-of-the-Art Review." *International Journal of Environmental Research and Public Health* 18 (17): 8990. https://www.mdpi.com/1660-4601/18/17/8990.

Hallegatte, Stephane, Adrien Vogt-Schilb, Mook Bangalore, and Julie Rozenberg. 2017. *Unbreakable: Building the Resilience of the Poor in the Face of Natural Disasters.* Climate Change and Development. Washington, DC: World Bank. http://documents.worldbank.org /curated/en/512241480487839624/Unbreakable-building-the-resilience-of-the-poor-in-the-face -of-natural-disasters.

Hernandez, Ricardo, Akhter U. Ahmed, Arifeen Akter, Nusrat Zaitun Hossain, Samira Choudhury, and Mehrab Malek. 2016. *An Evaluation of the Program on Enhancing Resilience to Natural Disasters and the Effects of Climate Change in Bangladesh.* Dakar, Senegal: International Food Policy Research Institute. https://ebrary.ifpri.org/digital/api/collection/p15738coll2/id /130841/download.

HTSPE. 2011. *Bangladesh: Independent Impact Assessment of the Chars Livelihoods Programme: Phase 1 Final Report.* Hemel Hempstead, UK: HTSPE. https://assets.publishing.service.gov.uk /media/5a7b9d8c40f0b62826a04b62/Evaluation-chars-livelihoods-prog-bangladesh.pdf.

IFPRI (International Food Policy Research Institute). 2023. *2023 Global Food Policy Report: Rethinking Food Crisis Responses.* Washington, DC: IFPRI. https://doi.org/10.2499/9780 896294417.

ILO (International Labour Organization). 2023. "World Employment and Social Outlook: Trends 2023." ILO Flagship Report, Geneva, Switzerland. https://www.ilo.org/wcmsp5/groups/public /---dgreports/---inst/documents/publication/wcms_865332.pdf.

IPCC (Intergovernmental Panel on Climate Change). 2022. "Climate Change 2022: Impacts, Adaptation, and Vulnerability. Contribution of Working Group II to the Sixth Assessment Report of the Intergovernmental Panel on Climate Change." H.-O. Pörtner, D. C. Roberts, M. Tignor, E. S. Poloczanska, K. Mintenbeck, A. Alegría, M. Craig, S. Langsdorf, S. Löschke, V. Möller, A. Okem, and B. Rama, eds. Cambridge University Press. Cambridge, UK, https:// doi.org/10.1017/9781009325844.

J-PAL (Abdul Latif Jameel Poverty Action Lab). 2023. "Building Stable Livelihoods for Low-Income Households." *J-PAL Policy Insights.* https://www.povertyactionlab.org/policy -insight/building-stable-livelihoods-low-income-households.

Kang, Yunhee, Indira Prihartono, Md. Iqbal Hossain, Shinhye Min, Heeyeon Kim, Yoonho Cho, Seungheon Han, Hee Sun Kim, and Jaganmay P. Biswas. 2023. "Impact Evaluation of a Community Nutrition and Livelihood Program on Child Nutrition in Rural Bangladesh." *Maternal & Child Nutrition* 19 (2): e13461. https://doi.org/10.1111/mcn.13461.

OECD (Organisation for Economic Co-operation and Development). 2024. *Breaking the Vicious Circles of Informal Employment and Low-Paying Work.* Paris: OECD Publishing. https://doi .org/10.1787/f95c5a74-en.

Ohnsorge, Franziska, and Shu Yu, eds. 2022. *The Long Shadow of Informality: Challenges and Policies.* Washington, DC: World Bank. https://openknowledge.worldbank.org /bitstream/handle/10986/35782/The-Long-Shadow-of-Informality-Challenges-and-Policies .pdf?sequence=5&isAllowed=y.

Sachs, Jeffrey D., Guillaume Lafortune, Grayson Fuller, and Eamon Drumm. 2023. *Sustainable Development Report 2023: Implementing the SDG Stimulus.* Dublin: Dublin University Press. https://sdgtransformationcenter.org/reports/sustainable-development-report-2023.

Siddiki, Omar Faruque, Rebecca Holmes, Ferdous Jahan, Fahim Subhan Chowdhury, and Jessica Hagen-Zanker. 2014. *How Do Social Safety Nets Contribute to Social Inclusion in Bangladesh? Evidence from the Chars Livelihoods Programme and the Vulnerable Group Development Programme.* London: Overseas Development Institute.

Smith, Lisa, Tim Frankenberger, Karyn Fox, S. Nelson, and Tiffany Griffin. 2019. "Ethiopia Pastoralist Areas Resilience Improvement and Market Expansion (PRIME) Project Impact Evaluation: Endline Survey Report." US Agency for International Development, Washington, DC. https://pdf.usaid.gov/pdf_docs/PA00WCWT.pdf.

Sparkman, Tim, Jill Sackett, Jorge Avalos, and Boban Varghese Paul. 2022. *Enhancing Links of Poor Farmers to Markets: A Practice Review for Economic Inclusion in Zambia. PEI in Practice, Volume 5.* Washington, DC: World Bank. http://hdl.handle.net/10986/38035.

Technical and Operational Performance Support (TOPS) Uganda Graduation Randomized Control Trial Associate Award. 2022. *Endline Report of the Resilience Food Security Activity Graduating to Resilience in Uganda, Cohort 1.* Washington, DC: The TOPS Program. https://pdf.usaid.gov/pdf_docs/PA00ZNCJ.pdf.

Tetteh Baah, Samuel Kofi, and Christoph Lakner. 2023. "Fragility and Poverty in Sub-Saharan Africa: Two Sides of the Same Coin." *World Bank Blogs.* https://blogs.worldbank.org/opendata/fragility-and-poverty-sub-saharan-africa-two-sides-same-coin.

UNDESA (United Nations, Department of Economic and Social Affairs). 2023. *World Economic Situation and Prospects 2023.* New York: UNDESA Publications. https://desapublications. un.org/publications/world-economic-situation-and-prospects-2023#:~:text=The%20 World%20Economic%20Situation%20and,headwinds%20will%20begin%20to%20 subside.

UNDESA (United Nations, Department of Economic and Social Affairs, Population Division). 2019. "World Population Prospects 2019: Highlights" (ST/ESA/SER.A/423). https://www .un.org/es/desa/world-population-prospects-2019-highlights#:~:text=The%20world's%20 population%20is%20expected,United%20Nations%20report%20launched%20today.

UN Habitat. 2022. *World Cities Report.* Nairobi, Kenya: UN Habitat. https://doi.org/10.18356 /9789210028592.

UN Women and ILO (International Labour Organization). 2020. *Spotlight on Goal 8: The Impact of Marriage and Children on Labour Market Participation.* New York: UN Women. https:// data.unwomen.org/sites/default/files/inline-files/Spotlight-goal8-spread.pdf.

WHO (World Health Organization). 2023. "Climate Change." World Health Organization, Geneva. https://www.who.int/news-room/fact-sheets/detail/climate-change-and -health#:~:text=Research%20shows%20that%203.6%20billion,diarrhoea%20and%20 heat%20stress%20alone.

World Bank. 2017. "International Development Association Project Appraisal Document on a Proposed Credit in the Amount of SDR 121.1 Million (US$170 Million Equivalent) to the Federal Democratic Republic of Ethiopia for a Livestock and Fisheries Sector Development Project." World Bank, Washington, DC. https://documents1.worldbank.org/curated/en /982381513306833652/pdf/ETHIOPIA-PAD-with-Map-11212017.pdf.

World Bank. 2022a. *Poverty and Shared Prosperity: Correcting Course.* Washington, DC: World Bank. https://doi.org/10.1596/978-1-4648-1893-6.

World Bank. 2022b. *Social Protection, Food Security and Nutrition—An Update of Concepts, Evidence and Select Practices in South Asia and Beyond.* Washington, DC: World Bank. http:// documents.worldbank.org/curated/en/099210010212228485/P1758650cf037303809a2104 ce42f5d81cc.

World Bank. 2022c. "Toward Productive, Inclusive, and Sustainable Farms and Agribusiness Firms: An Evaluation of the World Bank Group's Support for the Development of Agrifood Economies (2010–20)." Independent Evaluation Group, World Bank, Washington, DC. http:// documents.worldbank.org/curated/en/099603508292232536/SECBOS0a0aea3e0d70bd 9006aa69c788243.

World Bank. 2023a. *An Evaluation of World Bank Group Support to Jobs and Labor Market Reform through International Development Association Financing.* Independent Evaluation Group (IEG) Approach Paper. Washington, DC: World Bank. http://documents.worldbank .org/curated/en/099714203202319117/SECBOS0bebfd900e80a69a061a2e3fc2881.

World Bank. 2023b. *Second Update on Food and Nutrition Security (FNS).* Washington, DC: World Bank. https://documents1.worldbank.org/curated/en/099041823184562589/pdf/BOSI B03f1e3a4d067093680ee9c8ff5f269.pdf.

World Bank. 2023c. *Ending Poverty on a Livable Planet: Report to Governors on World Bank Evolution.* Development Committee. Washington, DC: World Bank. http://documents .worldbank.org/curated/en/099092823122522428/BOSIB0c8b6a4f20d90b86e035c5e46c8414.

World Bank. 2023d. "2023 in Nine Charts: A Growing Inequality." https://www.worldbank.org /en/news/feature/2023/12/18/2023-in-nine-charts-a-growing-inequality?cid=ECR_E_News letterWeekly_EN_EXT&deliveryName=DM205045.

World Bank. 2023e. *World Development Report 2023. Migrants, Refugees, and Societies.* Washington, DC: World Bank. https://www.worldbank.org/en/publication/wdr2023.

World Bank. 2023f. "Urban Development Overview." World Bank, Washington, DC. https://www .worldbank.org/en/topic/urbandevelopment/overview.

World Bank. 2024a. "Classification of Fragility and Conflict Situations (FCS) for World Bank Group Engagement." World Bank, Washington, DC. https://thedocs.worldbank.org/en/doc /fb0f93e8e3375803bce211ab1218ef2a-0090082023/original/Classification-of-Fragility-and -Conflict-Situations-FY24.pdf.

World Bank. 2024b. "Global Economic Prospects." World Bank, Washington, DC. https:// openknowledge.worldbank.org/server/api/core/bitstreams/08b387d9-cc44-496e-8e78-e311 c88185d7/content.

World Bank. Forthcoming. "Jobs for Development: Facts and a Framework for Policy." World Bank, Washington, DC.

Yonzan, Nishant, Daniel Gerszon Mahler, and Christoph Lakner. 2023. "Poverty Is Back to Pre-COVID Levels Globally, but Not for Low-Income Countries." *World Bank Blogs.* World Bank, Washington, DC. https://blogs.worldbank.org/opendata/poverty-back-pre-covid -levels-globally-not-low-income-countries.

A Look at the Evidence Emerging from Government-Led Programs

Introduction

The *State of Economic Inclusion Report 2021* (SEI 2021; Andrews et al. 2021) presented a comprehensive review of impact evaluations of 80 economic inclusion programs in 37 countries. The findings revealed that a diverse array of economic inclusion initiatives exhibit promising and potentially sustained impacts for outcomes including income, assets, consumption, and savings, among others. Notably, most of the compelling evidence emerged from nongovernmental organization pilots (Banerjee et al. 2015; Bandiera et al. 2017). SEI 2021 conscientiously acknowledged the existing knowledge gaps and underscored the need to recalibrate the discourse surrounding program impacts. Because a growing number of governments were scaling up these programs, the report emphasized the need to establish the impact of government-led programs and to systematize evidence by using comparable outcomes and indicators.

SEI 2024 summarizes the evidence emerging from government-led economic inclusion programs. This discussion is limited to the evaluations of government-led economic inclusion programs, as defined in box I.1, that were not covered in SEI 2021[1] and whose results were published or presented in the public domain after publication of SEI 2021 (refer to table S1.1 for the list of studies and programs included in this review).

Program Examples

Government-led, multifaceted economic inclusion programs are demonstrating robust impacts on key economic outcomes among poor and vulnerable populations. Emerging evidence underscores substantial improvements in key indicators, including food security, consumption, income, business revenues, and asset accumulation. For example, the economic inclusion interventions in a national safety net program in Niger increased consumption by 15 percent and food security by 19 percent after 18 months of intervention. Remarkable increases in business revenue were also observed, with households experiencing a 102 percent rise in monthly revenues, primarily attributed to new income streams from off-farm business activities (Bossuroy et al. 2022).

Similarly, Zambia's Supporting Women's Livelihood intervention exhibited a 28 percent aggregate increase in household income, driven by a substantial 45 percent boost in household business profits arising from income-generating activities led by women. Household consumption also increased by 19 percent 12 months after the intervention (Botea et al. 2023). In Nigeria, a livelihood package provided as part of its National Social Safety Nets Program increased the total household earnings of program participants by 24 percent and profits from household enterprises by 45 percent (Ajayi et al., forthcoming). In Mauritania, a significant 137 percent increase was observed in monthly business revenues for economic inclusion program participants (Bossuroy et al. 2024a). Senegal's Yook Koom Koom program implemented in urban settings produced a 22-percent increase in business revenues for participants (Bossuroy et al. 2024b).

TABLE S1.1   Studies Noted in This Spotlight

Program	Country	Components	Study	Program cost per household (US$)
Targeting Ultra-poor	Afghanistan	Cash grant, life skills training, business training, coaching, access to markets, community savings and loan groups, community sensitization on aspirations and norms	Bedoya Argüelles et al. 2023	$1,675
Social Safety Net Project	Burkina Faso	Cash grant, life skills training, business training, coaching, access to markets, community savings and loan groups, community sensitization on aspirations and norms	Bossuroy et al. 2024c	$430
Youth Employment Program	Côte d'Ivoire	Cash grant, life skills training, business training, coaching, access to markets, community savings and loan groups	Marguerie and Premand 2023	—
Social Safety Net Project	Mauritania	Cash grant, life skills training, business training, coaching, access to markets, community savings and loan groups, community sensitization on aspirations and norms	Bossuroy et al. 2024a	$446
National Safety Net Project	Niger	Cash grant, life skills training, business training, coaching, access to markets, community savings and loan groups, community sensitization on aspirations and norms	Bossuroy et al. 2022	$584
Refugees and Host Communities Support Project	Niger	Cash grant, life skills training, business training, coaching, access to markets, community savings and loan groups	Fernandez et al. 2024	—
National Social Safety Net Project	Nigeria	Cash grant, co-responsibility training, life skills training, business training, coaching, access to markets, community savings and loan groups	Ajayi et al., forthcoming	—
Yook Koom Koom	Senegal	Cash grant, life skills training, business training, coaching, access to markets, community savings and loan groups, community sensitization on aspirations and norms	Bossuroy et al. 2024b	$442

(Table continues next page)

TABLE S1.1   Studies Noted in This Spotlight *(continued)*

Program	Country	Components	Study	Program cost per household (US$)
Tanzania Social Action Fund Program	Tanzania	Cash grant, business training	Baird et al. 2024	—
Supporting Women's Livelihood	Zambia	Cash grant, life skills training, business training, coaching, community savings and loan groups	Botea et al. 2023	$384

Source: Original table for this publication.

Note: — = not available.

Economic inclusion programs also help rural households become more resilient to shocks over the long run. Evidence suggests diversification of women's economic activities, which is a key pathway to resilience. For example, in Afghanistan, participant households had 32 percent higher income and business revenue five years after an intervention than control households. The economic inclusion program helped households endure a series of droughts and conflict shocks (Bedoya Argüelles et al. 2023). Strong impacts on savings and financial inclusion, which contribute to resilience, were also observed.

Government programs also have positive impacts on the psychosocial well-being of women participants and on women's empowerment (refer to box 3.2). Early evidence from programs operating in a forced displacement context is also revealing positive impacts on population subgroups. One example is Niger's Refugees and Host Communities Support and Youth Employment and Productive Inclusion projects. Significant effects have been observed on household income, employment, and economic activities (World Bank, forthcoming).

The results emerging from broader fragile, conflict, and violent contexts are, however, mixed. Although the long-term results of the program in Afghanistan have had sustained impacts on income, the impact of a government-led program in post-conflict Côte d'Ivoire has had a higher impact on savings. Instead of investing the start-up capital in businesses, participants saved a substantial share (30 percent) of the grant, pointing to high precautionary savings motives. Indeed, results from participants who received only a savings-focused intervention without a capital grant were encouraging, with participants shifting the saving toward investments over time (Marguerie and Premand 2023). Similarly in Burkina Faso over 90 percent of former participants remained active members of savings groups two years after the end of the program, increasing the contributed amounts by two-and-a-half times. However, the impacts on business revenues were muted (Bossuroy et al. 2024c).

Although the evidence is limited to a few studies, multifaceted programs, when implemented through government systems, have been shown to be cost-effective, high-return investments. For example, in Niger, 18 months after the intervention the overall cost-effectiveness was high, with a cost-benefit ratio of 127 percent.

In Zambia, the cost-effectiveness was lower, but the program broke even within 12 months. Assuming persistent impacts, both Niger and Zambia were yielding positive returns on investment at 73 percent and 36 percent, respectively (Bossuroy et al. 2022; Botea et al. 2023).

Even though some multifaceted programs led by governments have remarkable impacts, certain variations in economic inclusion programming yield cautionary results. In Tanzania, a study of a former economic inclusion program assessed the impact of business grants given to groups combined with consumption support and training delivered by Tanzania's Social Action Fund program. Surprisingly, the program had no impact, and businesses operated by the groups were unprofitable. The study underscores that for a group-based model to succeed, members must overcome the *tragedy of the commons*,[2] invest assets for collective endeavors, and remain committed to the initiative for an extended period (Baird et al. 2024). The program has incorporated lessons learned and is now scaling up a redesigned multifaceted program with individual business grants and coaching layered on consumption support and life and business skills training.

Knowledge Gaps and Learning Priorities as Economic Inclusion Programs Move to Scale

Notably, the emerging evidence from government-led programs is predominantly from Sub-Saharan Africa and does not adequately represent the diversity of economic inclusion programs implemented in various contexts and regions. Evidence and a research agenda are needed to assess the impact and cost-effectiveness of large-scale government-led programs across different contexts. Specifically, there are critical learning gaps where additional impact evidence is needed on how to optimally design economic inclusion programs to achieve impacts and cost-effectiveness at scale.

The scale-up of programs should be aided by exploring several research priorities, including determining how alternative delivery modalities that enhance scalability, such as group coaching and digitally delivered training, influence program impact and cost-effectiveness. It is also important to identify the appropriate package that can achieve maximum impact in a specific context and for specific target groups. Even within successful programs, not all participants benefit equally. Understanding the factors contributing to this heterogeneity is crucial for creating equitable program designs. This work involves examining participant trajectories to identify those who benefit significantly less and then tailoring interventions to better support these individuals.

To understand the sustainability of these programs, conducting long-term evaluations (seven years or more following program completion) is necessary. A detailed list of knowledge gaps and research questions is provided in table S1.2. By addressing these research questions, policy makers and practitioners can enhance the design and implementation of economic inclusion programs to better serve poor and vulnerable populations and achieve sustainable impacts at scale.

A new wave of evaluations of government-led economic inclusion programs is also in the pipeline to assess the opportunities and challenges in moving these interventions to scale. With more than 25 evaluations currently ongoing, the next wave of evaluations will bridge critical learning gaps on how to optimally design economic inclusion programs to achieve impact and cost-effectiveness at scale.

TABLE S1.2   Key Policy-Relevant Knowledge Gaps in the Economic Inclusion Literature

Thematic priorities	Impact evidence and cost-effectiveness research questions
Effectiveness at scale	• What is the cost-effectiveness of large-scale government-led programs? • What is the nature and extent of spillovers on the local economy and general equilibrium effects?
"Scalable" delivery modalities	• How do alternative delivery modalities that enhance scalability affect program impact and cost-effectiveness (for example, low-cost versus high-cost; low-intensity versus high-intensity; digital versus face-to-face; individual versus group-based; nongovernment organization versus government)?
Dynamics over time	• How do impacts vary over time? Are they sustained in the short term to long term? • How does impact over time affect cost-benefit analysis?
Bundling of interventions	• What is the marginal contribution of constituent interventions (including cash) to overall impact and overall cost? What is the appropriate bundle to achieve maximum impact in a given context? • Does the timing, sequencing, and intensity of interventions matter? • What is the role of psychosocial interventions or behavioral nudges to bring about sustained economic inclusion? • What is the impact of low-intensity "refresher" interventions? • What is the effect of add-on interventions to promote women's economic empowerment? • Are interventions facilitating referrals with service providers effective, or linkages with value chains effective?
Targeting and heterogeneity	• What is the cost-effectiveness of economic inclusion programs across population groups? • What modifications in bundle design and delivery are necessary to increase cost-effectiveness for different subgroups?
External validity across settings	• How to adapt economic inclusion programs in urban; fragility, conflict, and violence; and displacement-affected contexts?
Resilience and shock-responsiveness	• Do economic inclusion programs improve households' resilience to shocks (for example, climate, conflict, or economic)? How? • What elements in the bundle can help beneficiaries build resilience? • How can economic inclusion programs be tailored to improve resilience? • Are economic inclusion programs also effective to build resilience in conflict-affected and shock-prone areas?

Source: Original table for this publication.

Notes

1. Refer to appendix B, table B.1 for the list of evaluations covered in SEI 2021 at https://www.peiglobal.org/sites/pei/files/2021-01/Appendixes.pdf.
2. The *tragedy of the commons* is an economic and environmental theory that describes a situation in which individuals act in their own self-interest and deplete a shared resource, which can lead to negative consequences for everyone.

References

Ajayi, Kehinde, Robin Audy, Thomas Bossuroy, Ayodele Fashogbon, and Oyebola Okunogbe. Forthcoming. "National Social Safety Net Project." Working Paper. World Bank, Washington, DC.

Baird, Sarah, Craig McIntosh, Pape Utz, and Özler Berk. 2024. "Asset Transfers and Anti-Poverty Programs: Experimental Evidence from Tanzania." *Journal of Development Economics* 166: 103182. https://doi.org/10.1016/j.jdeveco.2023.103182.

Bandiera, Oriana, Robin Burgess, Narayan Das, Selim Gulesci, Imran Rasul, and Munshi Sulaiman. 2017. "Labor Markets and Poverty in Village Economies." *Quarterly Journal of Economics* 132 (2): 811–70. https://doi.org/10.1093/qje/qjx003.

Banerjee, Abhijit, Esther Duflo, Nathanael Goldberg, Dean Karlan, Robert Osei, William Parienté, Jeremy Shapiro, Bram Thuysbaert, and Christopher Udry. 2015. "A Multifaceted Program Causes Lasting Progress for the Very Poor: Evidence from Six Countries." *Science* 348 (6236): 1260799. https://www.science.org/doi/10.1126/science.1260799.

Bedoya Argüelles, Guadalupe, Yulia Belyakova, Aidan Coville, Thomas Escande, Mohammad Isaqzadeh, and Aminata Ndiaye. 2023. "The Enduring Impacts of a Big Push during Multiple Crises: Experimental Evidence from Afghanistan (English)." Policy Research Working Paper No. WPS 10596, Impact Evaluation Series. World Bank, Washington, DC. http://documents.worldbank.org/curated/en/099837211062311087/IDU1e486b8ed1e7a 114d231a60d1848c87baeeb1.

Bossuroy, Thomas, Markus Goldstein, Bassirou Karimou, Dean Karlan, Harounan Kazianga, William Parienté, Patrick Premand, Catherine C. Thomas, Christopher Udry, Julia Vaillant, and Kelsey A. Wright. 2022. "Tackling Psychosocial and Capital Constraints to Alleviate Poverty." *Nature* 605 (7909): 291–97. https://doi.org/10.1038/s41586-022-04647-8.

Bossuroy, Thomas, Dean Karlan, William Parienté, Patrick Premand, Christopher Udry, Julia Vaillant, and Kelsey Wright. 2024a. "Impact des mesures d'inclusion productive du programme Tekavoul en Mauritanie." Banque Mondiale, Washington, DC.

Bossuroy, Thomas, Dean Karlan, William Parienté, Patrick Premand, Christopher Udry, Julia Vaillant, and Kelsey Wright. 2024b. "Impact des mesures d'inclusion productive du programme Yom Kom Kom au Sénégal." Banque Mondiale, Washington, DC.

Bossuroy, Thomas, Dean Karlan, William Parienté, Patrick Premand, Christopher Udry, Julia Vaillant, and Kelsey Wright. 2024c. "Impact des mesures d'inclusion productive du programme Burkin Naong Sa Ya au Burkina Faso." Banque Mondiale, Washington, DC. https://documents.banquemondiale.org/fr/publication/documents-reports/documentdetail/099 836302282427372/idu115bad4921bdf414c131a54a1683d2d194245.

Botea, Ioana, Andrew Brudevold-Newman, Markus Goldstein, Corrine Low, and Gareth Roberts. 2023. "Supporting Women's Livelihoods at Scale: Evidence from a Nationwide Multi-Faceted Program." NBER Working Paper No. w31625. Cambridge, MA: National Bureau of Economic Research. http://www.nber.org/papers/w31625.

Fernandez, Chloë, Samih Ferrah, Andrea Guariso, Marcus Holmlund, Tara Mitchell, and Carol Newman. 2024. "Entrepreneurship Support for Host and Displaced Communities in Niger." World Bank, Washington, DC.

Marguerie, Alicia Charlene, and Patrick Premand. 2023. "Savings Facilitation or Capital Injection? Impacts and Spillovers of Livelihood Interventions in Post-Conflict Côte d'Ivoire." Policy Research Working Paper No. WPS 10563. World Bank, Washington, DC. http://documents.worldbank.org/curated/en/099439409082319139 /IDU016356e4e01f4704759089a00b05060f249c1.

World Bank. Forthcoming. "Niger Refugees and Host Communities Support." Impact Evaluation Indicative Results. World Bank, Washington, DC.

CHAPTER 2
A Growing Global Footprint—Economic Inclusion Is Expanding

KEY MESSAGES

- More than 70 million people in 88 countries benefited either directly or indirectly from economic inclusion programs in 2023—over 50 percent more than in 2020. Those numbers are likely to increase exponentially as government-led programs mature and programs now in the pipeline begin serving participants. However, millions more poor and vulnerable people remain economically and socially excluded.

- The landscape reveals a greater diversity of programs, with programs in more countries and in more-diverse contexts, serving more population groups and implemented by a wider range of institutions. Meanwhile, programs strive to maximize the quality of impact while optimizing costs.

- This report identifies two complementary programs reflected in the landscape: (1) *household-focused programs,* which are targeted to offer comprehensive support to households in extreme poverty to build assets and market links while preparing participants to access broader systems and services, and (2) *area-focused programs,* which are targeted to offer support to a broader community in a geographic area or a system to improve access to markets or services, while also providing extensive assistance to households in extreme poverty.

The Global Footprint of Economic Inclusion Programs Is Growing

Despite the global economic slowdown that began in 2020, a renewed surge in the number of economic inclusion programs is under way globally. The Landscape Survey 2023 covers 405 programs in 88 countries, whereas the 2020 survey covered 219 programs in 75 countries. Many ongoing programs have expanded despite, or in some cases in response to, the current overlapping crises. Programs currently operating support more than 15 million households and benefit more than 70 million individuals, directly or indirectly,[1] for an increase of more than 50 percent in the reach of economic inclusion programs. *The State of Economic Inclusion Report 2021* (SEI 2021; Andrews et al., 2021) reported that programs surveyed by the Partnership for Economic Inclusion were supporting 9.8 million households and benefiting more than 45.8 million individuals, directly or indirectly.[2]

Current estimates of the number of people engaged in and benefiting from these programs are probably conservative because of the robust pipeline of economic inclusion programs. These estimates also mask the impressive outreach of these programs over time. Since starting operations, 338 programs report having served nearly 25 million households, thereby benefiting more than 111 million people worldwide cumulatively and over time.[3] They include not only programs squarely targeting extreme-poor and ultra-poor individuals but also many programs supporting economic inclusion for people from a wider range of economic groups.

The 96 ongoing programs that target only extreme-poor and ultra-poor individuals and that reported beneficiary data support more than 2.3 million households and benefit more than 11 million people. Over time, these programs have supported more than 6.6 million households and benefited more than 29 million extreme-poor and ultra-poor individuals. However, this number represents a fraction of the total coverage of these poverty groups because these numbers do not include the coverage of extreme-poor and ultra-poor households by programs that are targeted more widely.[4]

Governments Lead the Effort to Scale Up

The 43 percent of all surveyed programs (and 35 percent of surveyed programs with participant data) that are government-led account for approximately 74 percent of all participants (refer to figure 2.1). These government-led programs often build on existing programs in social assistance, agriculture, environment, and other sectors that provide an entry point for organizations to build a multifaceted economic inclusion intervention. Many government-led programs build their economic inclusion efforts on an existing safety net, such as a cash transfer or a public works program (refer to box 2.1).

FIGURE 2.1   **Percentage of Economic Inclusion Programs and Participants, by Lead Institution**

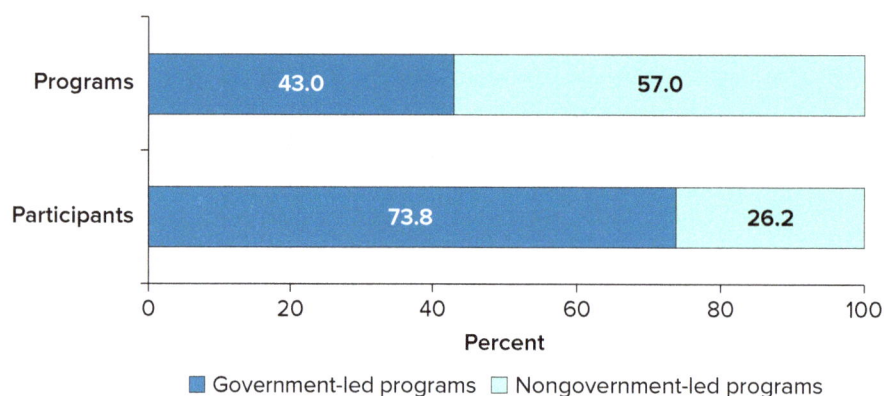

Source: Partnership for Economic Inclusion, World Bank.

Note: Data on the number of participants are missing for 72 programs (16 nongovernment-led and 56 government-led programs), most of which were in the last phases of preparation before actual delivery of support for participants began. Overall, 405 programs were surveyed (231 nongovernment-led and 174 government-led programs). The total number of participants is 15,323,059, and the total number of beneficiaries, which includes direct participants and indirect beneficiaries, is 70,043,913.

BOX 2.1   Social Assistance Programs Provide a Solid Foundation for Scaling Up

Many government-led programs build their economic inclusion efforts on existing social assistance programs. *The State of Economic Inclusion Report 2024* reports data from 91 government-led programs in 54 countries that layer additional economic inclusion measures on existing social protection programs, including social assistance and labor market programs. These programs currently serve more than 5 million households directly and 24.3 million individuals directly or indirectly. Most of these programs layer on safety nets supporting self-employment opportunities, diversifying income sources, and boosting productivity. Most programs layer four or more components on top of cash transfers or in-kind support to address the multiple constraints faced by poor and vulnerable groups.

Some economic inclusion programs layered on social assistance programs are already operating at scale. These existing programs offer a robust institutional framework and delivery mechanism to effectively integrate and scale-up economic inclusion interventions. The Productive Social Safety Net Project in Tanzania reaches about 100,000 households, providing economic inclusion measures in addition to public works and cash transfers. Similarly, the Social Support for Resilient Livelihoods Project in Malawi enhances the productive capacity of 357,359 households in the Social Cash Transfer and Climate Smart Public Works Programs. This capacity building focuses on savings and income-generating skills, enabling these households to sustainably improve their livelihoods, become resilient to shocks, and transition out of poverty through a graduation pathway.

Nongovernment organizations, mostly nongovernmental organizations (NGOs), lead 57 percent of economic inclusion programs and serve 26 percent of participants. New programs have emerged, but some nongovernment-led programs have also been sustained and scaled up since 2021, which explains why in 2023 these programs represent a higher proportion of total participants than in SEI 2021. NGOs play a critical role by piloting economic inclusion approaches in new geographic areas or with different population groups or by testing new methods or approaches. These organizations also play a key role in government-led programs as service providers and technical assistance providers, helping to increase the capacity of government agencies to implement and scale-up economic inclusion programs (refer to chapter 4).

Both government-led and nongovernment-led programs will likely continue to scale up—a necessity in view of the overlapping crises and the growing number of people living in extreme poverty. The strongest potential for scaling up economic inclusion programs continues to rest with governments because of the many government-led programs in the pipeline and the potential to build on existing and strengthened government systems. Some nongovernment-led programs will also continue to scale up with significant capital investments from a range of donors. Others may continue to operate on a smaller scale but play a critical role in reaching vulnerable populations not served by other means and by innovating in new contexts and with new approaches. Whatever lies ahead, all varieties of economic inclusion programs must ensure they are delivering quality programs using evidence-backed strategies or those tested over multiple rounds of economic inclusion implementation.

Scale-Up Is Under Way but Falling Significantly Short of Needs

The scale of a program is most often defined by the number of participants.[5] Fifty-eight percent of government-led programs serve at least 10,000 households, compared with 17 percent of nongovernment-led programs. Also, as shown in figure 2.2, older programs are larger than newer ones. The fact that economic inclusion programs are reaching ever more people is important, but the quality of impact and sustainability of coverage, as well as the processes of change and adaptation, are equally important (chapters 3 and 4 explore some of the challenges associated with scaling up).

Despite a notable increase in coverage, the current scale does not meet the need. Although the number of individuals participating in these programs has increased by more than 50 percent, this number remains small when compared with the overall population living in poverty. Today, about 700 million people live in extreme poverty, a figure that could rise due to ongoing economic shocks, conflicts, and the effects of climate change (World Bank 2023c). While economic growth is essential for poverty reduction and addressing structural challenges, economic inclusion programs focus specifically on reaching and empowering those who may be left behind or excluded from the benefits of growth.

Another way of looking at the scale of economic inclusion programs is by analyzing the number of participants relative to the population. Figure 2.3 shows the distribution of programs by their coverage of participants as a share of the population living below the national poverty line. Because of the emergence of new programs, a larger proportion of programs than in 2020 are reaching less than 1 percent of poor people. Although the absolute number of people engaged in these programs has increased by more than 50 percent, it continues to be small relative to the number of people living in poverty.

FIGURE 2.2   **Percentage of Economic Inclusion Programs, by Number of Current Direct Participants**

Percent

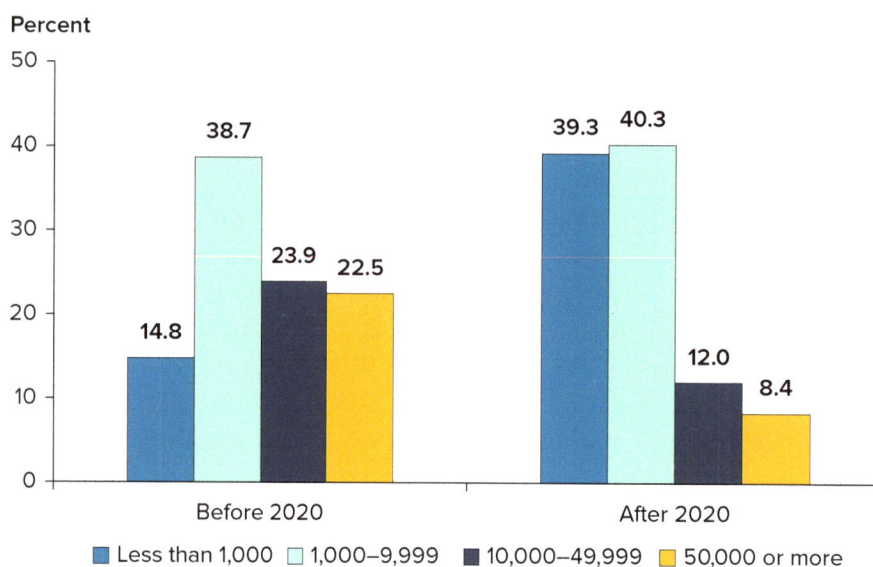

Legend: ■ Less than 1,000   □ 1,000–9,999   ■ 10,000–49,999   □ 50,000 or more

Source: Partnership for Economic Inclusion, World Bank.

Note: Figure shows the percentage of programs with participant data that were under way before the Landscape Survey 2020 underpinning SEI 2021 was completed in January 2020 (142 programs) and those that began after the 2020 survey was completed (191 programs). SEI 2021 = *The State of Economic Inclusion Report 2021.*

FIGURE 2.3   **Distribution of Program Coverage Rates, by Share of Population Living in Poverty**

Percent

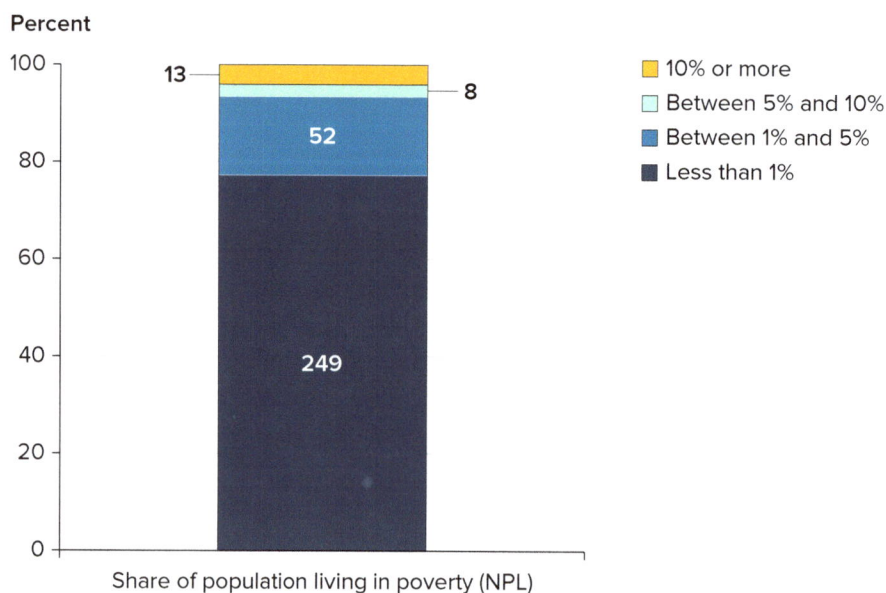

Legend: □ 10% or more   □ Between 5% and 10%   ■ Between 1% and 5%   ■ Less than 1%

Share of population living in poverty (NPL)

Source: Partnership for Economic Inclusion, World Bank.

Note: The analysis is based on 322 programs (those providing data on the number of beneficiaries in countries where data on poverty headcount is available), representing 69 countries. Data are presented by program. The poverty headcount is missing for nine countries. This figure assumes perfect targeting. NPL = national poverty line.

The Greater Diversity of Programs Is Evident

With a range of objectives, economic inclusion programs are widely implemented globally serving poor and vulnerable populations. These programs, traditionally rural focused, are increasingly expanding to urban and peri-urban areas. They target various vulnerable groups, including the ultra-poor, extreme-poor, and poor populations, with some programs also addressing the needs of the "missing middle" affected by economic shocks like COVID-19. In addition, there is a growing emphasis on supporting groups such as women, youth, forcibly displaced populations, and people with disabilities, reflecting responses to global demographic shifts and the unique barriers these groups face in achieving economic inclusion.

Programs Operate in Diverse Contexts in 88 Countries

Economic inclusion programs are used in many regions and contexts to build resilience and create jobs for poor and vulnerable people, but most programs are in low-income and lower-middle-income countries (79 percent of surveyed programs), in line with what was reported in SEI 2021. As in SEI 2021, most programs (and participants) are in Sub-Saharan Africa (refer to figure 2.4), although in 2023 a higher proportion of participants are in that region. The increase in the proportion of beneficiaries in Sub-Saharan Africa is driven by a relative (as well as an absolute) increase in the number of programs in the region, as well as by the expansion of existing programs.

Most programs continue to operate in rural areas (84 percent of surveyed programs and 43 percent are exclusively rural), where most of the world's extreme-poor population live (World Bank 2022). However, economic inclusion programs, particularly more recent ones, are increasingly operating in urban areas, and 38 percent of surveyed programs serve urban

FIGURE 2.4 **Percentage of Economic Inclusion Programs and Participants, by Region**

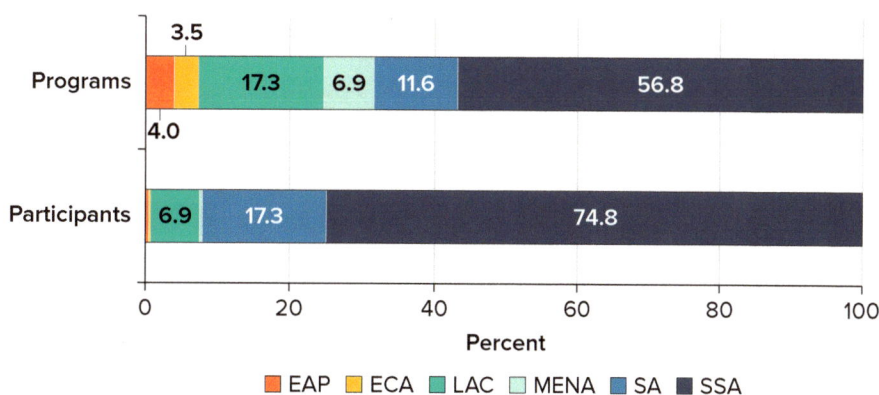

Source: Partnership for Economic Inclusion, World Bank.

Note: The figure is based on survey data for 405 programs: 16, EAP; 14, ECA; 70, LAC; 28, MENA; 47, SA; and 230, SSA. The total number of participants is 15,323,059 and beneficiaries is 70,043,913, which includes direct participants and indirect beneficiaries. Data on number of participants are missing for 72 programs, most of which were in the last phases of preparation before actual delivery of support for participants began. EAP = East Asia and Pacific; ECA = Europe and Central Asia; LAC = Latin America and the Caribbean; MENA = Middle East and North Africa; SA = South Asia; SSA = Sub-Saharan Africa.

or peri-urban populations. This figure includes programs that have national coverage or were designed to serve both urban and rural areas of the country, as well as programs that started in rural areas and have expanded to serve urban and peri-urban populations. It also includes several government-led economic inclusion programs that build on social safety nets, such as Ethiopia's Productive Safety Net Program, which began by serving exclusively rural areas of the country and is now covering urban settings as well.

Targeted Groups Include a Range of Vulnerable Populations

Economic inclusion programs typically target vulnerable populations at the lower end of the income distribution, including the ultra-poor (40 percent of surveyed programs), extreme-poor (53 percent), and poor (55 percent) populations (refer to figure 2.5, panel a, as well as box 2.2 for key definitions).[6] Some programs have a strong mandate to focus on the extreme-poor and ultra-poor populations, and 26 percent of programs target extreme-poor and ultra-poor people exclusively, particularly nongovernment-led programs (34 percent versus 14 percent of government-led programs). In some contexts, policy makers and organizations with other institutional mandates may face demands for targeting poor people more broadly. Some programs are also expanding across the income distribution to achieve greater scale and support segments of the population that may have been previously excluded from government support. This population includes the so-called "missing middle"—that is, workers in the informal economy who were particularly vulnerable to the economic impacts of COVID-19 due to a lack of social protection coverage.

FIGURE 2.5   **Poverty Segments and Population Groups Targeted: Percentage of Programs**

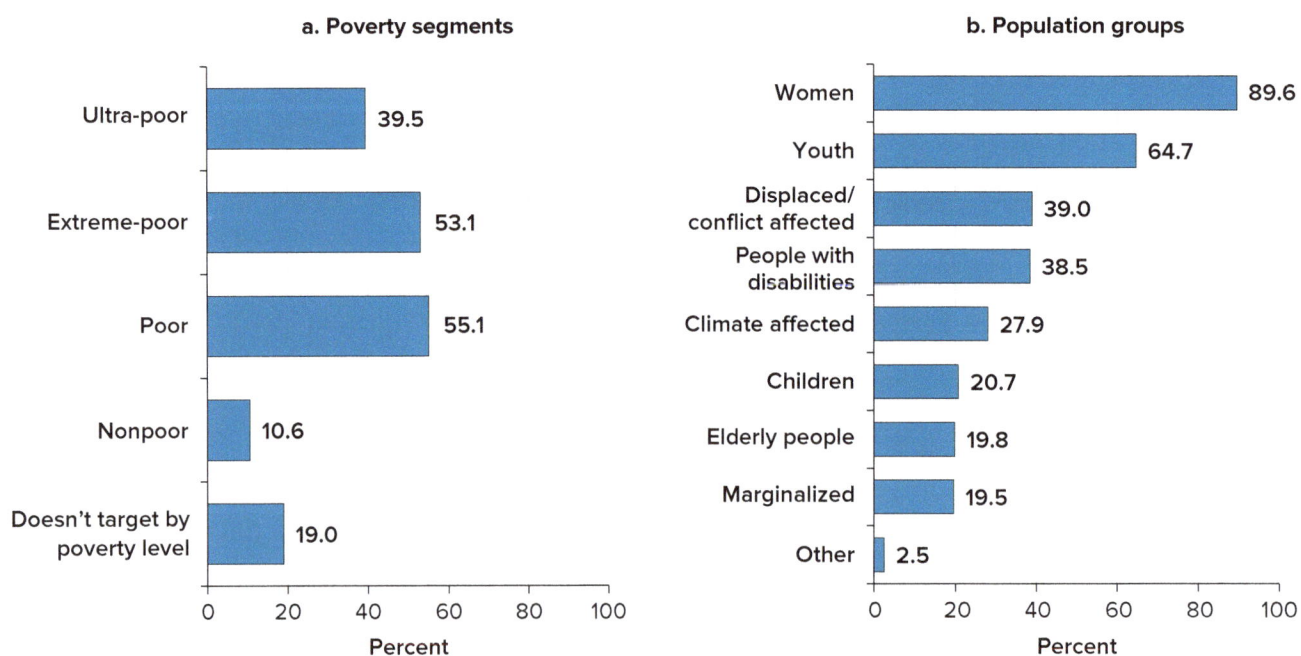

Source: Partnership for Economic Inclusion, World Bank.

Note: Both panels provide the percentage of all programs *(N = 405)*. Programs may target more than one poverty segment or population group.

BOX 2.2   **Definitions of Poverty and Vulnerability Segments from the Landscape Survey 2023**

The following are definitions of poverty and vulnerability segments from the Landscape Survey 2023:

- **Poor population.** People whose consumption is below the national poverty line, as defined by the government.

- **Extreme-poor population.** People whose consumption is below US$2.15 per day (at 2017 US$ purchasing power parity [PPP]) and who can work on a sustained basis. Also defined as the bottom 50 percent of the poor population in a country or those unable to meet basic needs.

- **Ultra-poor population.** People whose consumption is below $1.08 per day (at 2017 US$, PPP). Also defined as those experiencing the severest forms of deprivation, such as being persistently hungry or lacking sources of income.

- **Vulnerable populations.** People who, because of their personal or community characteristics, face barriers in accessing opportunities to earn sustainable livelihoods and have elevated risks of being or staying in poverty or being socially marginalized.

Source: PEI Landscape Survey 2023.

Almost 11 percent of programs target nonpoor households, whereas 19 percent of programs do not target by poverty level (refer to figure 2.5, panel a), which may reflect a program's focus on supporting the development of a given geographical area or work at the community or system level, especially programs that build on agricultural and environmental interventions.[7]

Many programs have an additional focus on specific population groups such as women (90 percent of programs), youth (65 percent), displaced and conflict-affected populations (39 percent), and people with disabilities (39 percent) (refer to figure 2.5, panel b). At the regional level, programs in the Middle East and North Africa (MENA) and the Sub-Saharan Africa (SSA) regions, which are experiencing a youth bulge, have a stronger focus on supporting the access of youth to better economic opportunities than those in other regions (86 percent of MENA programs and 70 percent of SSA programs, compared with 51 percent of Latin America and the Caribbean programs and 55 percent of South Asia programs).

Overall, more programs target youth and older populations today than in SEI 2021, which is likely a response to global demographic shifts (refer to box 1.1). Meanwhile, a higher proportion of programs than in SEI 2021 target people with disabilities (39 percent versus 26 percent) and those affected by forced displacement (38 percent versus 32 percent). Although these vulnerable groups share some of the same constraints to economic inclusion, understanding specific barriers to engaging in income-generating activities is key to supporting them effectively (refer to chapter 3).

Program Objectives Vary Across Context and Target Groups

With the overall goal of transforming the lives of poor and vulnerable people—by building resilience and creating job opportunities—economic inclusion programs are driven by a range of objectives (refer to figure 2.6, panel a). Programs continue to focus on supporting self-employment opportunities, including through enhancing self-employment opportunities (47 percent of all programs), diversifying income sources (36 percent), and increasing productivity (31 percent). Increasing financial inclusion and food security also continue to be features, and about one-fourth of all economic inclusion programs have these as core objectives, similar to what was observed in SEI 2021. In response to increased recognition of the need to deliberately address specific barriers to women's economic empowerment, there is a substantial increase in the percentage of programs that seek to empower women (33 percent in 2023 versus 17 percent in SEI 2021). Similarly, a higher percentage of programs seek to enhance market access (24 percent in 2023 versus 10 percent in SEI 2021; refer to appendix B in this report).

FIGURE 2.6   **Main Program Objectives Overall and by Poverty Focus**

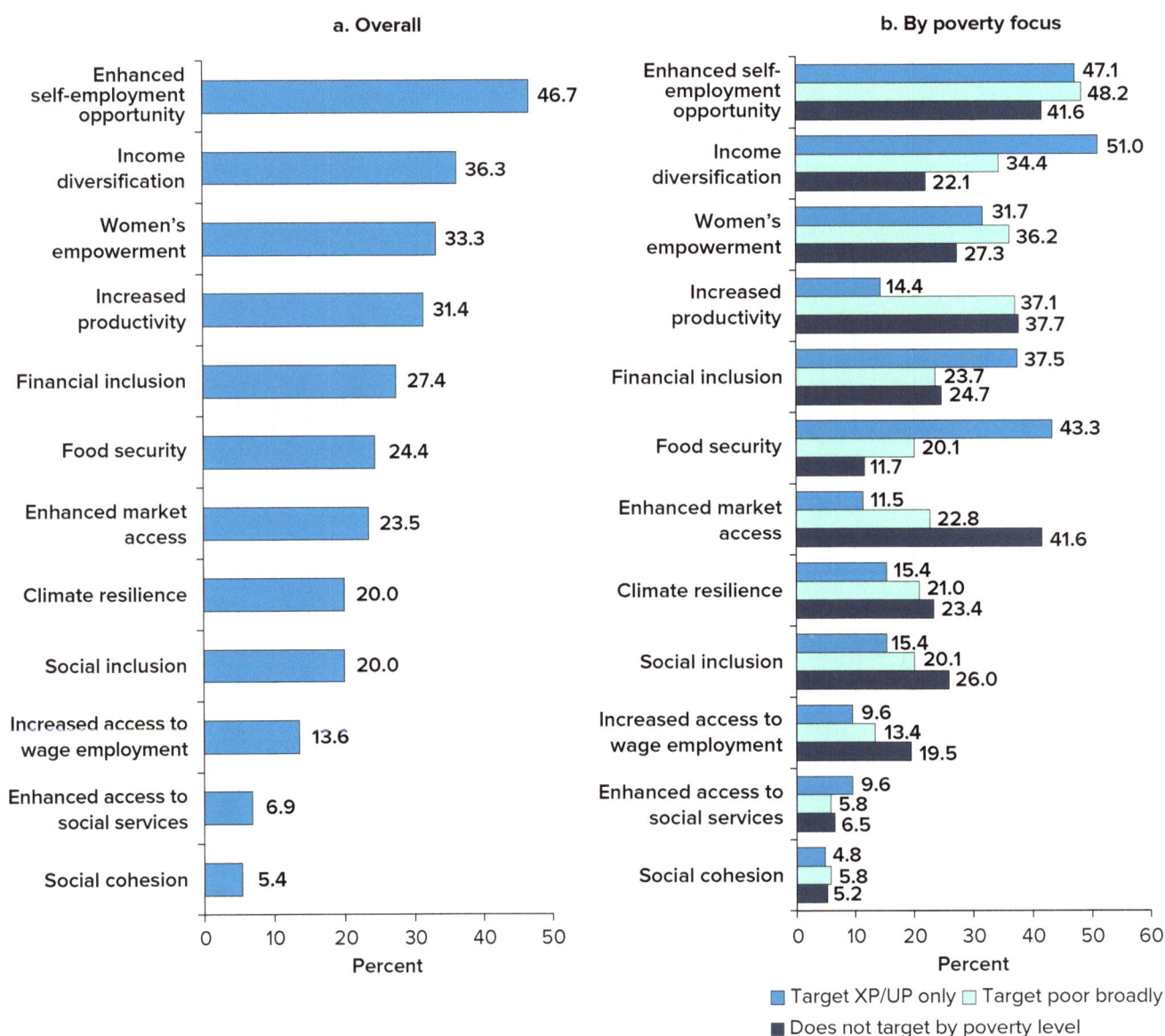

Source: Partnership for Economic Inclusion, World Bank.

Note: Panel a provides the percentage of all programs (*N* = 405) and panel b the percentage of programs targeting only extreme-poor and ultra-poor groups (*N* = 104), targeting the poor population broadly (*N* = 224), and not targeting by poverty level (*N* = 77). Respondents were asked to report a maximum of three main objectives. XP/UP = extreme-poor/ultra-poor.

The Landscape Survey 2023 reveals heterogeneity in program design, driven partly by the objectives, targeted groups, or the context in which they operate. Interesting differences emerge, for example, when analyzing target groups and core objectives together. Programs focusing exclusively on the extreme-poor and ultra-poor populations focus more strongly on income diversification, food security, and financial inclusion, suggesting that building resilience is a core driver. However, increasing productivity and enhancing market access are often the core objectives of programs that do not target by poverty level or that target the poor population more broadly (refer to figure 2.6, panel b).

Similarly, program objectives vary across countries in different income categories: programs in low-income countries focus more on food security and income diversification than those in middle-income countries as a response to greater food insecurity and more unstable income streams for poor people in low-income settings. To illustrate this finding, table 2.1 shows some notable differences in the core objectives and target groups of four countries in four income settings.

TABLE 2.1   Examples of Economic Inclusion in Four Country Income Groups

Key indicators	Bangladesh	Colombia	Ethiopia	Panama
Income category	Lower middle income	Upper middle income	Low income	High income
Fragile and conflict-affected situation	No	No	Yes (conflict)	No
Poverty rate at US$2.15 (2017 PPP)	13.5%	9.4%	27.0%	1.1%
Poverty rate at US$3.65 (2017 PPP)	42.3%	16.0%	65.0%	4.3%
Poverty rate at US$6.85 (2017 PPP)	83.1%	39.2%	90.9%	12.9%
Population size	169.4 million	51.5 million	120.3 million	4.4 million
Number of programs (number of government-led)	15 (6)	12 (2)	21 (7)	6 (3)
Number of participants (direct and indirect)[a]	4,872,657	249,402	21,168,051	12,977
Top objectives	Women's empowerment Self-employment Increased productivity Food security	Self-employment Wage employment Food security Women's empowerment Social inclusion	Income diversification Increased productivity Food security Self-employment Climate resilience	Self-employment Wage employment Increased productivity Social cohesion
Rural (number of programs of total)	11/15	6/12	17/21	3/6
Urban/peri-urban (number of programs of total)	8/15	9/12	11/21	4/6
Top three targeted vulnerable groups	1. Women 2. People with disabilities 3. Climate affected	1. Women 2. Displacement affected 3. Children	1. Women 2. Youth 3. Displacement affected	1. Women 2. Displacement affected 3. Youth

Sources: World Bank 2023a, 2023b; World Bank Development Indicators; and Partnership for Economic Inclusion.

Note: Data on participants and programs summarize results for all programs in a country based on individual program responses to the Landscape Survey 2023. Top core objectives and targeted vulnerable groups are ranked based on the total number of programs.

Most Programs Have at Least Five Components, Delivering Them In Sequence for Up to 3 Years

Economic inclusion programs often consist of five or six components (refer to figure 2.7, panel a),[8] including training (96 percent), coaching (89 percent), business capital (77 percent), and market links (74 percent) (refer to figure 2.7, panel b). There is little change from SEI 2021, except that a lower percentage of programs provide a transfer to smooth consumption (54 percent versus 68 percent), and a higher percentage of programs help participants build their climate resilience (66 versus 57 percent).[9]

The components of economic inclusion programs are most frequently provided in sequence to ensure that participants receive support when they can benefit most from it. For example, programs often provide skills training before transferring business capital so that participants can apply recently acquired skills when they invest in their productive activities through the capital delivered by the program. Avoiding delays in the delivery of components, while ensuring other aspects of quality, is critical if participants are to make the most of program interventions (chapter 3). In 63 percent of programs, economic inclusion interventions are provided over a period of between 12 and 36 months. A higher proportion of programs than in SEI 2021 support participants for more than three years, perhaps a reflection that a larger number of programs build on agricultural and environmental interventions, which tend to be of longer duration than other programs.

FIGURE 2.7 **Distribution of Programs, by Number and Type of Components, Sequencing, and Duration**

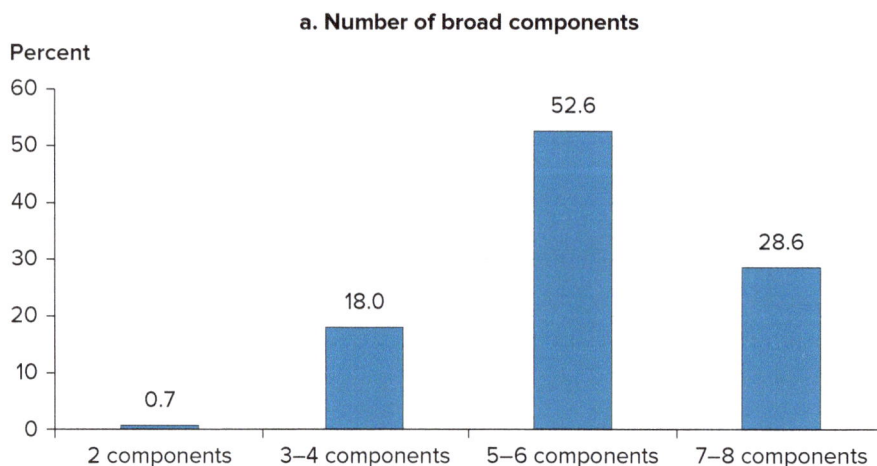

a. Number of broad components

(Figure continues next page)

FIGURE 2.7   Distribution of Programs, by Number and Type of Components, Sequencing, and Duration *(continued)*

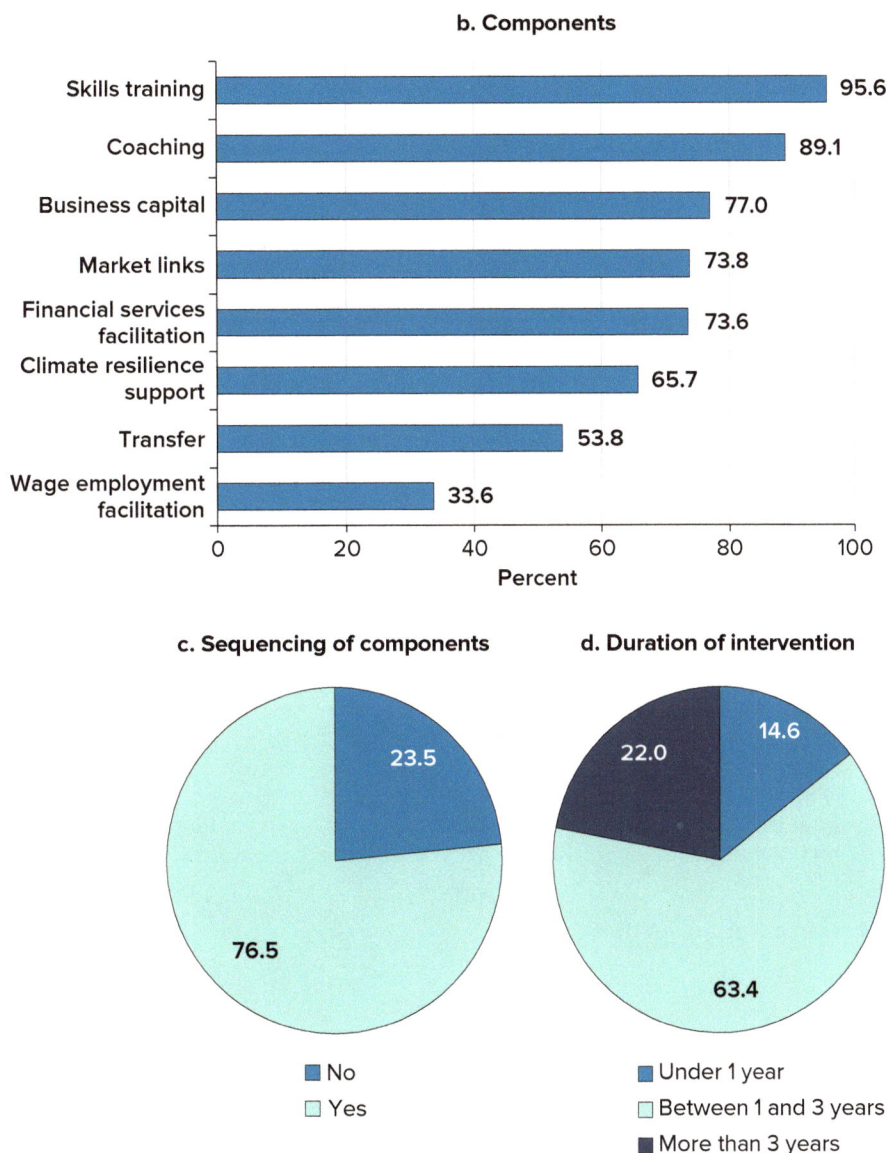

b. Components

Component	Percent
Skills training	95.6
Coaching	89.1
Business capital	77.0
Market links	73.8
Financial services facilitation	73.6
Climate resilience support	65.7
Transfer	53.8
Wage employment facilitation	33.6

c. Sequencing of components

- No: 23.5
- Yes: 76.5

d. Duration of intervention

- Under 1 year: 14.6
- Between 1 and 3 years: 63.4
- More than 3 years: 22.0

Source: Partnership for Economic Inclusion, World Bank.

Note: Figure shows the percentage of all programs (*N* = 405).

The Surge in Programs Has Prompted an Update of the Economic Inclusion Framework

As reflected in the surge and scale-up of programs, economic inclusion has become a popular strategy for engaging people living in extreme poverty. Therefore, this report reintroduces the Pathways to Economic Inclusion at Scale framework (refer to figure 2.8) from SEI 2021, which has been revised slightly to acknowledge the changing landscape. The framework outlines the pathways to scale for economic inclusion programs (refer to box I.1 for key definitions).

Economic inclusion programs are designed to respond to national or regional contexts and the populations served, and each develops in its own institutional structures.

FIGURE 2.8   Pathways to Economic Inclusion at Scale: A Framework

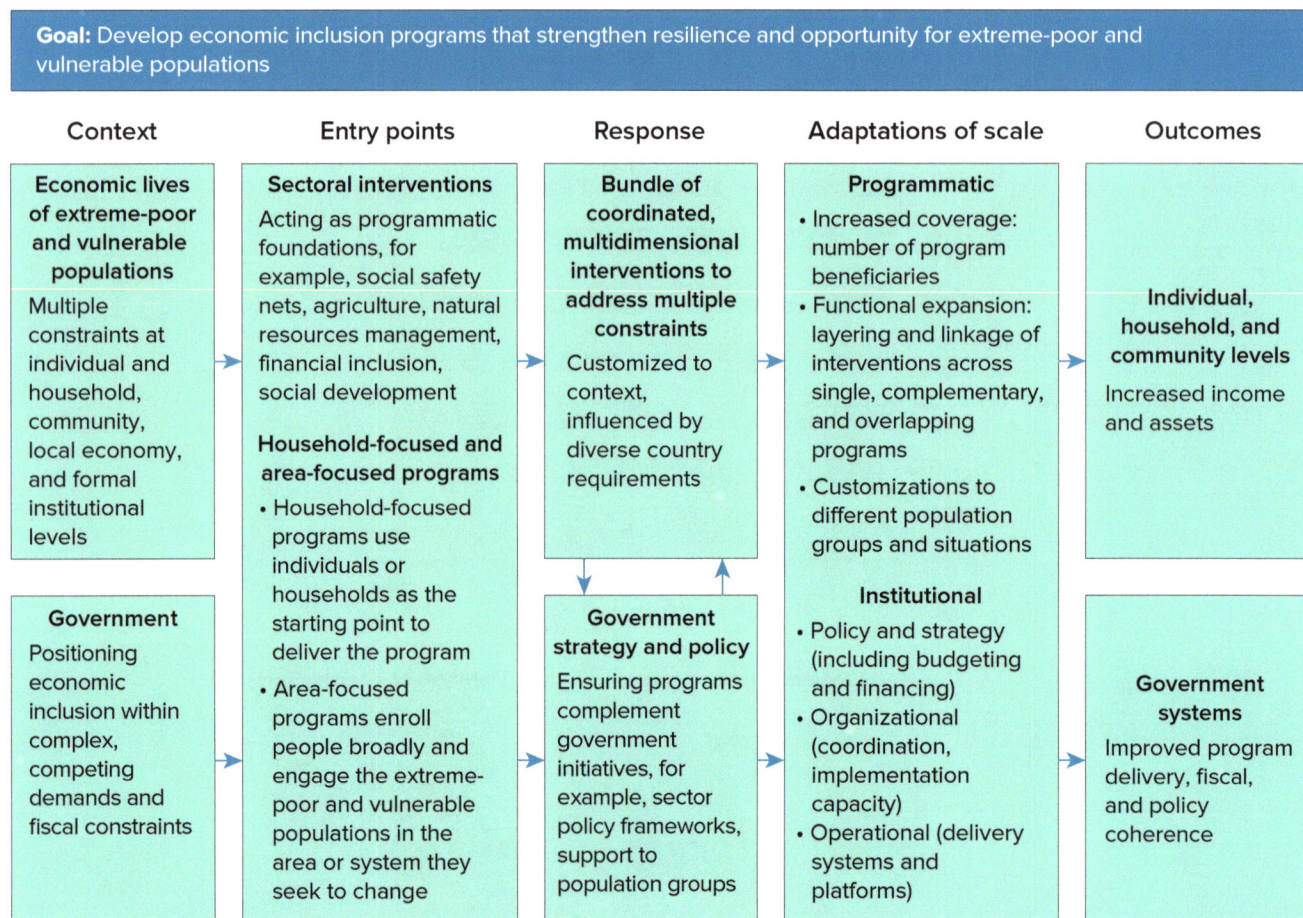

Goal: Develop economic inclusion programs that strengthen resilience and opportunity for extreme-poor and vulnerable populations

Context	Entry points	Response	Adaptations of scale	Outcomes
Economic lives of extreme-poor and vulnerable populations Multiple constraints at individual and household, community, local economy, and formal institutional levels	**Sectoral interventions** Acting as programmatic foundations, for example, social safety nets, agriculture, natural resources management, financial inclusion, social development **Household-focused and area-focused programs** • Household-focused programs use individuals or households as the starting point to deliver the program • Area-focused programs enroll people broadly and engage the extreme-poor and vulnerable populations in the area or system they seek to change	**Bundle of coordinated, multidimensional interventions to address multiple constraints** Customized to context, influenced by diverse country requirements **Government strategy and policy** Ensuring programs complement government initiatives, for example, sector policy frameworks, support to population groups	**Programmatic** • Increased coverage: number of program beneficiaries • Functional expansion: layering and linkage of interventions across single, complementary, and overlapping programs • Customizations to different population groups and situations **Institutional** • Policy and strategy (including budgeting and financing) • Organizational (coordination, implementation capacity) • Operational (delivery systems and platforms)	**Individual, household, and community levels** Increased income and assets **Government systems** Improved program delivery, fiscal, and policy coherence
Government Positioning economic inclusion within complex, competing demands and fiscal constraints				

Source: Partnership for Economic Inclusion, World Bank.

They are also shaped by policy, political economy, institutional arrangements, and other factors. Program designers and policy makers often face trade-offs between program quality—what level of services is optimal to enable people living in extreme poverty to seize opportunities and become resilient—versus what is financially feasible given the many competing priorities. Programs must also balance the desire to maximize the number of people served with capacity constraints and the limitations of operating systems and financing. This framework underpins the detailed analysis in chapters 3 and 4 on the design and delivery of programs as they move to scale.

Household- and Area-Focused Programs Provide Insight into the Diverse Approaches to Economic Inclusion

The design of an economic inclusion program is shaped by the goal of the institution launching the program. For example, a social safety net program will design an economic inclusion component with different features than, say, a watershed development program or a community-driven development program. Each economic inclusion program generally includes a core intervention, such as cash transfers in a social safety net or agriculture extension services in an agricultural development intervention (refer to figure 2.9). Layers of economic inclusion components or services are then added and refined to address the constraints faced by the extreme-poor and vulnerable populations.

The core interventions are more wide-ranging than in the past.[10] For example, more agrifood systems development and the sustainable management of ecosystems and landscapes programs are integrating economic inclusion interventions. This surge reflects, in part, the growing emphasis on building climate resilience.[11]

The most common type of program targets the households. A "push" strategy enables a household, by the time it completes the program, to build the assets, income, knowledge, and confidence it needs to access services and engage in broader systems, including market systems, not accessible to them before. Many household-focused programs include graduation features that combine sequenced inputs to give a household a "big push," thereby improving its overall economic and social well-being. Research suggests that providing an initial amount of capital above a critical threshold ultimately determines whether households can capture higher productivity opportunities and move out of poverty (Parry, Burgess, and Bandiera 2020).

Area-focused programs have broader objectives associated with community-, region-, market-, or system-level interventions. These programs, typically including people living in one or more of the poverty categories and delivering two or more components, use a "pull" strategy. They enroll people broadly and, for those living in extreme poverty, try to engage them in the community, region, market, or other systems that the program seeks to change (refer to figure 2.9).

FIGURE 2.9   **Complementary Approaches to Economic Inclusion at the Household and Area (System) Levels**

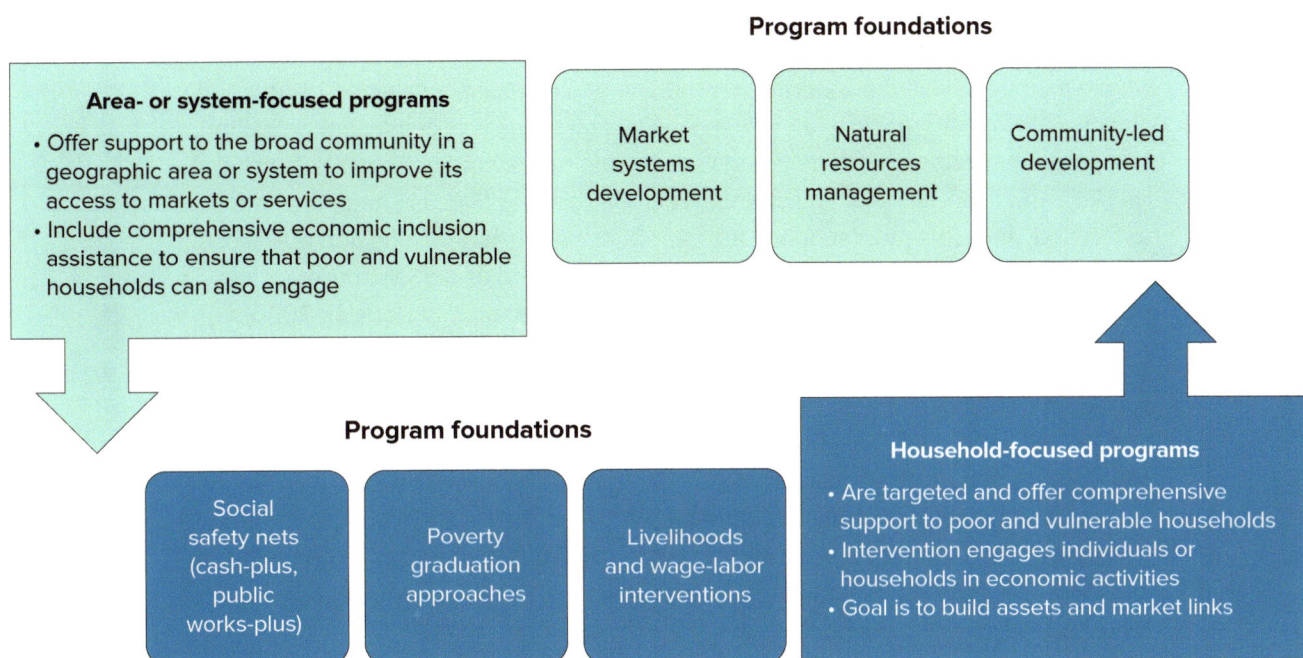

Program foundations

Area- or system-focused programs
- Offer support to the broad community in a geographic area or system to improve its access to markets or services
- Include comprehensive economic inclusion assistance to ensure that poor and vulnerable households can also engage

Market systems development

Natural resources management

Community-led development

Program foundations

Social safety nets (cash-plus, public works-plus)

Poverty graduation approaches

Livelihoods and wage-labor interventions

Household-focused programs
- Are targeted and offer comprehensive support to poor and vulnerable households
- Intervention engages individuals or households in economic activities
- Goal is to build assets and market links

Source: Partnership for Economic Inclusion, World Bank.

Household-focused programs are more likely to target people living in ultra-poverty or extreme poverty and help them increase their income and assets, but they may serve people at other poverty levels as well. Area-focused programs typically target a larger population group and use economic inclusion strategies to reach people living in extreme poverty (refer to table 2.2 for a comparison of the two types of programs and boxes 2.3 and 2.4 for examples of each program). Both types of interventions are affected by and work to transform macro-level policies to improve outcomes for people in extreme poverty.

TABLE 2.2   Household- and Area-Focused Programs: A Comparison

Type	Household-focused program	Area-focused program
Focus	Household	Geography or systems
Goal	Build the assets, income, knowledge, and confidence to access services and engage in broader systems, including market systems. Objectives may also be associated with poverty alleviation such as food security or resilience.	Pursue community-, region-, market-, or system-level interventions to create sustainable economic opportunities; build resilience; and foster long-term poverty reduction.
Target	Often a specific poverty group, such as the ultra-poor or extreme-poor populations. Target may also be specific populations such as youth, displaced people, or people with disabilities.	Poorest geographic areas; a particular system such as markets; or traditionally vulnerable populations such as women, refugees, people with disabilities, or others, across wealth categories.
Example	Programs building on social safety nets (cash plus, public works plus) and graduation programs.	Community-led development projects, watershed development projects, market systems development projects, and agrifood system development projects.

Source: Original table for this publication.

BOX 2.3   Examples of Household-Focused Economic Inclusion Programs

Ethiopia's Urban Productive Safety Net and Jobs Project features a public works and livelihood program targeting the ultra-poor, extreme-poor, and poor urban households whose members have the capacity to work. The households are selected using a combination of geographic and proxy means test targeting and community validation. The program unfolds over three years: year 1—employment in public works, training in life skills and financial skills, and savings; year 2—business planning, technical training as needed, and job search support; and year 3—based on the training and business plan, a livelihood grant and coaching to ease the transition as participants work less time in public works (Ethiopia Ministry of Urban Development and Housing 2020).

BRAC's Ultra-Poor Graduation program targets the ultra-poor population using poverty maps, a climate vulnerability index, participatory rural appraisals, focus group discussions, and verification processes. It offers a transfer to smooth consumption, life and skills training, business capital, market and government service links, coaching, and savings, together with other components. The program is a combination of holistic, climate-sensitive, context-specific, time-bound, and sequenced sets of interventions that provide a "big push" to overcome poverty traps and establish sustainable economic inclusion and social empowerment.

Source: PEI's Landscape Survey 2023.

BOX 2.4   Examples of Area-Focused Economic Inclusion Programs

The Kenya Development Response to Displacement Impacts Project, which supports more than 230,000 participants, seeks to improve access to basic social services, expand economic opportunities, and enhance environmental management for communities hosting refugees for a protracted period of time. The project targets the poor population broadly and focuses on women, female-headed households, and youth who are disproportionately affected by displacement. The objectives are to improve social cohesion, to restore environmental and natural resources that suffered from the inflow of refugees, to offer economic support to host communities, and to balance the support provided to refugees by the United Nations High Commissioner for Refugees with comparable support to host communities—all of this while building a collective understanding that both hosts and refugees have ownership over, and the right to access, natural resources (Partnership for Economic Inclusion 2021). This desire to foster cohesion results in a focus on whole communities. All participants receive coaching, while a subset of participants receive cash transfers, training, access to financial services, business transfers, integration into markets, and support for building climate resilience.

The Lao Landscape and Livelihoods Project promotes sustainable forest management and seeks to improve protected area management and enhance livelihood opportunities in eight provinces in the Lao People's Democratic Republic. It works with partners and villagers living in and around forests to invest in the natural wealth and resilience of landscapes while creating jobs that benefit both village communities and protect forests.

Among other project activities, livelihood development grants are provided to more than 500 villages (about 72,000 households) that receive grants of US$10,000. Vulnerable households, including the elderly population, widows, people with disabilities, single mothers, and disaster-affected households, are prioritized with 20 percent of the grant allocated to these approximately 5,000 households. The remaining 80 percent of the grants operate as a revolving fund in the village using the existing government Village Development Fund architecture. This fund supports farm and nonfarm forest-smart livelihood activities, including agroforestry and small-scale tree plantations.

The grants to villages act as incentives for diversifying away from activities that negatively affect forests. The project also offers agricultural and forest extension support and vocational training to help villagers take advantage of new job opportunities.

Source: PEI's Landscape Survey 2023.

As governments, in particular, consider scaling up, a strategic approach will involve understanding the interplay between household- and area-focused interventions to catalyze sector-wide transformation. This approach could result in the inclusion of the poorest and most vulnerable individuals in national jobs policies and interventions that foster informal micro and small enterprises. Using both household- and area-focused interventions could drive comprehensive transformation in sectors and enhance economic inclusion for poor and vulnerable people.

Large-Scale Programs Bring to Light Diverse Approaches

A review of the top 20 economic inclusion programs serving the most participants cumulatively demonstrates the growing diversity in programs since 2021 (refer to table 2.3). Eleven programs are in Africa, four in Asia, four in Latin America, and one in Europe. In this mixture of household- and area-focused programs, the newest were launched in 2021 and the oldest in 2002. The smallest program has served 320,000 people and the largest 2.5 million people directly. Together, these 20 programs have served 15.8 million people with economic inclusion services since they began operations.

A closer look at the programs reveals important differences. Fifteen are government-led and five are nongovernment-led. Some government-led programs appear to be achieving scale by establishing large programs serving participants from several poverty segments.

Only four programs have reached more than 1 million participants, and each of these programs must be considered in relation to the size of their country's poor or ultra-poor populations. The government-led initiative that tops the list (Ethiopia's Second Agricultural Growth Program) is led by the Ministry of Agriculture. This area-focused program seeks to increase the agricultural productivity of smallholder farmers by providing household- and small-scale irrigation, training, coaching, and links to value chains. It does not target by poverty level and includes multiple wealth categories in its program, from subsistence smallholder farmers with a half to a 1.5-hectare landholding to people living in extreme poverty, including subsistence farmers.

By contrast, Haku Wiñay is a household-focused program embedded in the government's social protection system. It provides a specific segment of the population with multidimensional services, complementing the work of other programs serving other poverty segments in communities across Peru.

Among the nongovernment-led programs, four of five target only the extreme-poor or ultra-poor populations, whereas one program does not target by poverty. Two programs that target the extreme-poor and ultra-poor groups take distinct approaches. International Care Ministries (ICM) in the Philippines has served 320,000 participants cumulatively, while BRAC in Bangladesh has served more than 2.2 million people cumulatively. Both have achieved these numbers by gradually increasing the number of participants over time, with ICM currently serving more than 41,000 participants and BRAC serving 70,000 with its context-specific and targeted population-centric interventions. While BRAC uses the graduation approach, ICM uses a more streamlined approach to reducing poverty. Key to its model is the use of savings groups to reach more people, with a cascade training approach in which the program trains a savings group leader who then trains other members.

Notably, only a few programs among these top 20 have a strong evidence base with BRAC's Ultra-Poor Graduation program in Bangladesh standing out with the most robust evidence. This underscores the need to develop a strong research and learning agenda to gain a deeper understanding of the impact at scale on the economic lives of poor and vulnerable people. Programs on this list and those at earlier stages of implementation must also balance the desire for quality of impact with the need to optimize costs. As more programs progress in scale-up and as the evidence base continues to evolve, much can be learned from operational experience, in particular from more mature programs that have improved over time. What follows in chapters 3 and 4 is a summary of the Landscape Survey 2023 data, available evidence, and program learning for each dimension of scale.[12]

TABLE 2.3   Top 20 Programs, by Cumulative Participants

No.	Program name	Country	Lead implementer	Lead type	Start year	Cumulative participants	Current participants	Targeting strategy	Area / HH
1	Second Agricultural Growth Project	Ethiopia	Ministry of Agriculture	Government	2015	2,500,000	2,348,576	Does not target by poverty level	Area
2	Ultra Poor Graduation Program	Bangladesh	BRAC	Nongovernment	2002	2,312,477	70,000	Targets XP/UP only	HH
3	Urban Productive Safety Net and Jobs Project	Ethiopia	The Ministry of Urban Development and Infrastructure	Government	2020	1,440,472	1,440,472	Targets poor broadly	HH
4	AgriFin Digital Farmer 2	Kenya	Mercy Corps Kenya	Nongovernment	2021	1,356,089	1,356,089	Does not target by poverty level	Area
5	Resilience, Entrepreneurship, and Livelihood Improvement Project	Bangladesh	Social Development Foundation	Government	2021	804,000	804,000	Targets poor broadly	HH
6	Nigeria COVID-19 Action Recovery and Economic Stimulus Program	Nigeria	Federal CARES Support Unit, created under the Federal Ministry of Finance, Budget and National Planning	Government	2021	739,461	173,415	Targets poor broadly	Area
7	Productive Social Safety Net Program	Tanzania	Tanzania Social Action Fund	Government	2012	716,327	313,411	Targets XP/UP only	HH
8	Human Development Credit	Ecuador	Ministry of Economic and Social Inclusion	Government	2007	681,722	36,015	Targets poor broadly	HH
9	National Agricultural and Rural Inclusive Growth Project	Kenya	Ministry of Agriculture and Livestock Development	Government	2017	528,000	528,000	Targets poor broadly	Area
10	Forest and Village Relations (ORKOY) Program	Türkiye	General Directorate of Forest	Government	1974	526,797	11,127	Does not target by poverty level	Area
11	Youth Employment and Social Support Operations Project	Nigeria	Ministry of Humanitarian Affairs, Disaster Management and Social Development	Government	2013	486,904	486,904	Targets XP/UP only	HH

(Table continues next page)

TABLE 2.3   Top 20 Programs, by Cumulative Participants (*continued*)

No.	Program name	Country	Lead implementer	Lead type	Start year	Cumulative participants	Current participants	Targeting strategy	Area / HH
12	VenEsperanza	Colombia	Mercy Corps	Nongovernment	2019	477,425	60,798	Targets XP/UP only	HH
13	Climate Resilient Agriculture and Productivity Enhancement Project	Chad	Ministry of Agriculture, Irrigation and Agricultural Equipment	Government	2018	476,000	476,000	Targets poor broadly	HH
14	Sowing Life Program	Mexicc	Secretary of Welfare	Government	2019	450,038	450,038	Targets poor broadly	HH
15	The Sustainable Livelihoods Enhancement Scheme	Rwanda	Local Administrative Entities Development Agency	Government	2017	447,247	141,539	Targets poor broadly	HH
16	Tamil Nadu Rural Transformation Project	India	Tamil Nadu Rural Transformation Society	Government	2017	432,191	432,191	Targets poor broadly	Area
17	Nigeria for Women Project	Nigeria	Federal and State Ministries of Women Affairs	Government	2018	406,805	406,805	Targets poor broadly	HH
18	Haku Wiñay Program	Peru	Ministry of Development and Social Inclusion	Government	2014	353,566	148,800	Targets poor broadly	HH
19	Social Support for Resilient Livelihoods Project	Malawi	Community Savings and Investment Promotion Cooperative Union Limited	Nongovernment	2020	345,742	345,742	Targets XP/UP only	HH
20	Transform	Philippines	International Care Ministries	Nongovernment	2009	320,000	41,456	Targets XP/UP only	HH

Source: Partnership for Economic Inclusion, World Bank.

Note: Cumulative participants refer to the cumulative number of direct participant households that have received the economic inclusion package to date. Current participants refer to the number of direct participant households currently participating in the program and that are receiving the economic inclusion package. Area = area-focused programs; HH = household-focused programs; XP/UP = extreme-poor/ultra-poor.

Notes

1. Data on program participants are available for 333 programs (215 nongovernment- and 118 government-led programs) and are missing for 72 programs (16 nongovernment- and 56 government-led programs). The current number of participants in the missing programs is unavailable because they were in the process of finalizing preparatory work.

2. SEI 2021 reports a significantly higher number of economic inclusion participants (nearly 92 million people, including indirect beneficiaries) than what is reported here (nearly 46 million people, including indirect beneficiaries). Data checks performed as part of the Landscape Survey 2023 revealed that the data reported in 2020 on the Satat Jeevikoparjan Yojana program, led by India's Bihar Rural Livelihoods Promotion Society (BRLPS), included beneficiaries of various programs implemented by BRLPS.

3. Fifty-two percent of these programs were launched in 2020 or earlier, and some have been under way for more than 20 years, mostly nongovernment-led programs, including BRAC's Ultra-Poor Graduation program and several of Women for Women International's Stronger Women, Stronger Nations programs: https://www.womenforwomen.org/stronger-women -stronger-nations-program. Some recent programs build on previous programs or earlier phases of the same program. For example, Argentina's Promoting Better Jobs through Integrated Labor and Skills Program (FOMENTAR Program) started in 2022, but it builds on the implementation of the More and Better Work for Young People, which launched in 2008. It is likely, then, that the cumulative number of participant households reported in the Landscape Survey 2023 does not fully capture participants in previous programs or earlier phases of the same program.

4. The 128 ongoing programs that support the poor population more broadly do include extreme-poor or ultra-poor households. Their coverage of these households could not be disentangled from the total coverage figures because the survey was designed to capture the total number of direct participants and indirect beneficiaries of each program and did not ask for the breakdown of coverage figures by target group.

5. Establishing an absolute threshold of participants above which a program is considered to be operating at scale is somewhat arbitrary. Such a threshold is unlikely to reflect program priorities or the needs in its context. Instead, the PEI team looked at size ranges of economic inclusion programs to provide an overview of their scale of current participants.

6. While poverty definitions provide a broad understanding of economic deprivation, they may not always align with the targeting criteria used in economic inclusion programs. Eighty-one percent of programs targeting poor people combine more than one targeting methodology, which may include geographical, categorical, community bases, and proxy means-tests for effectively identifying and reaching the most poor and vulnerable populations.

7. PEI's Landscape Survey 2023 was designed to capture more granularity on the profile of target participants, based on their poverty level, than the Landscape Survey 2020. The question on poverty groups targeted by programs was changed slightly from how it was posed in the Landscape Survey 2020 (where the question did not ask programs whether they target nonpoor and do not by poverty level), and thus comparisons across the two survey rounds are not possible for this question.

8. This is in line with what was reported in the SEI 2021, where 56 percent of programs included five or six components, 27 percent included seven or eight, and the rest four or fewer components.

9. This comparison should be regarded with caution, as the question varied slightly in the two survey rounds: "Does the program support beneficiaries to build climate resilience?" (2023 survey) versus "Does the program seek to support sustainable natural resources management and/or climate change adaptation?" (2020 survey).

10. The three entry points in the SEI 2021 framework are (1) social safety net interventions such as cash transfer and public works programs, (2) single (or limited) intervention livelihoods

and job programs such as training or labor intermediation services, and (3) financial inclusion programs such as micro saving schemes or financial literacy programs. The past 3 years have seen a renewed surge in economic inclusion programs that build on additional sectoral interventions. Thus, a slightly revised version of the framework accounts for the wider range of sectoral interventions that act as an entry point to multifaceted economic inclusion programs.

11. SEI 2021 identified 17 World Bank–supported environmental projects, while this report mapped 41.

12. Since the SEI 2021 report, there has been an effort to collect policy and program documents, share emerging good practices, and assess what works in different contexts. The sheer number of economic inclusion programs has made tracking and analyzing this documentation and learning a challenge. Inevitably, programmatic lessons are better documented than policy or institutional lessons, and both country and political context are important to understand to interpret these lessons and consider their applicability elsewhere.

References

Andrews, Colin, Aude de Montesquiou, Inés Arévalo-Sánchez, Puja Vasudeva Dutta, Boban Varghese Paul, Sadna Samaranayake, Janet Heisey, Timothy Clay, and Sarang Chaudhary. 2021. *The State of Economic Inclusion Report 2021: The Potential to Scale.* Washington, DC: World Bank. http://hdl.handle.net/10986/34917.

Ethiopia Ministry of Urban Development and Housing. 2020. *Urban Productive Safety Net and Jobs Project Operations Manual 2020.* Addis Ababa: Ministry of Urban Development and Housing.

Parry, Katie, Robin Burgess, and Oriana Bandiera. 2020. "Is It Time to Rethink Poverty Policy?" *VoxDev*, February 14. https://voxdev.org/topic/it-time-rethink-poverty-policy.

Partnership for Economic Inclusion. 2021. "Country Innovation Exchange on Economic Inclusion and Forced Displacement." Webinar. December 2. Notes not public. World Bank, Washington, DC.

World Bank. 2022. "Poverty and Shared Prosperity: Correcting Course." World Bank, Washington, DC. https://doi.org/10.1596/978-1-4648-1893-6.

World Bank. 2023a. "FY24 List of Fragile and Conflict-affected Situations: Brief." World Bank, Washington, DC. https://www.worldbank.org/en/topic/fragilityconflictviolence/brief/harmonized-list-of-fragile-situations.

World Bank. 2023b. "Macro Poverty Outlook: Country-by-Country Analysis and Projections for the Developing World 2023." World Bank, Washington, DC. https://thedocs.worldbank.org/en/doc/77351105a334213c64122e44c2efe523-0500072021/related/mpo-am23.pdf.

World Bank. 2023c. "2023 in Nine Charts: A Growing Inequality." World Bank, Washington, DC. https://www.worldbank.org/en/news/feature/2023/12/18/2023-in-nine-charts-a-growing-inequality?cid=ECR_E_NewsletterWeekly_EN_EXT&deliveryName=DM205045.

CHAPTER 3
Program Design for Scale

KEY MESSAGES

- Programs are scaling up along five dimensions, including by increasing coverage, adding components, institutionalizing through policy or strategy, increasing organizational capacity, and leveraging delivery systems. Expanding to new populations or geographies while ensuring strong program quality requires adopting good diagnostics, tailoring program components, and sequencing components.

- The economic empowerment of women is a core objective of a larger proportion of programs than reported in SEI 2021. More programs could take a gender-intentional approach to design and delivery by addressing social norms, tailoring the timing and nature of program activities, and including components such as childcare to ensure that women can succeed.

- Monitoring participant progress, making real-time adjustments, and refining program design are hallmarks of success, but programs should balance participant need, cost, and complexity plus feedback from monitoring data to inform good design.

Introduction

All economic inclusion programs take a different pathway to scaling up because each one is customized for geography, population, institutional arrangements, and funding. As a result, program designs and scale trajectories are diverse, making it difficult to consolidate lessons on good practice when scaling up. However, good information on design and trends has emerged from the 405 programs currently supporting over 15 million households and benefiting more than 70 million people, directly or indirectly; 50 percent more than the number reported in *The State of Economic Inclusion Report 2021* (SEI 2021; Andrews et al. 2021).

The Partnership for Economic Inclusion's (PEI) Pathways to Economic Inclusion at Scale framework identifies two programmatic and three institutional dimensions of scale and their expected results in greater detail (refer to table 3.1). The first programmatic dimension of scale results in an increase in coverage (the number of participants served) by including more people or communities in existing program areas or expanding to different locations. The second programmatic dimension includes functional expansion that increases the scope of activities (or program components) with the goal of improving, widening, or deepening outcomes. This chapter more closely examines these aspects of scaling up economic inclusion.

For the institutional dimensions, sustainable scale-up of government-led programs entails several adaptations of the institutions that implement them. The institutional aspects of scale include the efforts to align economic inclusion programs with national institutions, strategies, financing, and policies to improve efficiency, fiscal coherence, policy coherence, or all of these. Program delivery, policy, and strategy are explored in chapter 4.

Programs may use more than one of these programmatic and institutional dimensions as they move to scale. However, technical decisions on program design and implementation must be balanced with political economy considerations that can limit options, such as fiscal constraints, major shocks, or population trends. Political opportunities—for example, at the start of a new administration or with new funding opportunities—should be considered as well.

TABLE 3.1 Dimensions of Scale: Programmatic and Institutional

Focus and dimension of scale	Description	Expected results
Programmatic aspects		
Increased coverage	Expansion of programmatic coverage by including more people and/or communities in a given location or replication in different locations	
Functional expansion	Expansion by increasing the scope of activity, in which a program starts with a single focus but then layers in or links additional multisectoral interventions	Improve, widen, and/or deepen program outcomes
Institutional aspects		
Policy and strategy	Institutionalization through policy, strategy, and programming decisions—reinforced by legal, budgetary, and financing decisions to allow effective performance at scale	
Organizational	Expansion of organizational coordination and capacity at different levels (central, local, community level); identification of overall governance mechanisms (including cross-ministerial); and engagement of partnerships (including with groups at the community level, nongovernmental organizations, and private sector)	Improve efficiency; improve fiscal and policy coherence
Operational	Operationalization through building or leveraging delivery systems, especially with respect to digital and community platforms	

Source: World Bank, with adaptations from Carter, Joshi, and Remme 2018; Cooley and Linn 2014.

Five Dimensions of Scale Reflect Program Growth Beyond Coverage

Seventy-four percent of economic inclusion programs have scaled up along at least one dimension. Many of these programs are well integrated with related programs and are well targeted. One means of scaling up is by increasing program coverage (the number of participants served) by adding new populations within the same geographic area, expanding to new geographic areas, or both. Fifty-four percent of programs report scale-up through increased coverage. Scaling up can also be achieved by adding functions or strengthening program components to increase participant outcomes—so-called "functional expansion." Twenty-nine percent of programs have scaled up in this fashion.

More than half (57 percent) of programs have reported institutional scale-up over the past 2 years. This scale-up has taken various forms, including expanding capacity within implementing organizations or establishing new partnerships or institutions (26 percent) and integrating economic inclusion programs into government structures through policy, programming, and political, legal, budgetary, or other systemic changes (16 percent). Forty-five percent of programs have begun to use digital tools or introduced other changes to program delivery, which is reflected in the operational aspects of scaling up (refer to figure 3.1).

FIGURE 3.1   Programs Have Scaled Up Along Core Dimensions

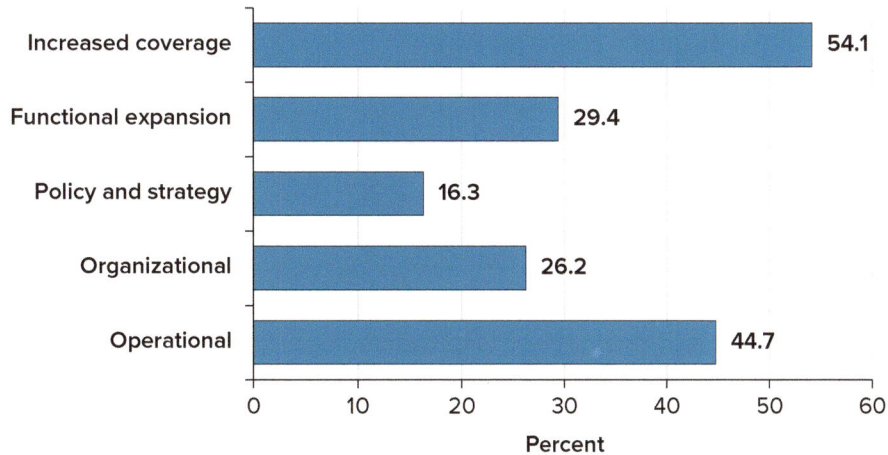

Source: Partnership for Economic Inclusion, World Bank.
Note: Figure shows the percentage of all programs (*N* = 405).

Deciding how to scale depends on the nature of the program, its needs, and the rationale for including more people. Some programs start relatively small to test the program design and scale by including more geographic areas and people. Other programs (including some area-focused) seek to achieve a specific time-bound outcome and may not have an objective to scale. Examples include a market development program focusing on specific value chains or a watershed development program focusing on managing and protecting resources in a specific geographic area. They may not seek to scale up to the national level but rather to integrate good practices into future project design.

Programs Can Scale Up by Adding New Population Groups

Programs successfully implemented with one population group can also expand by including either a different demographic group or a different poverty segment. For example, a program targeting the poorest people in a village may decide to include a nearby group of refugees, or a program may decide to include people with disabilities. An example of targeting an additional poverty segment is a program aiming to mitigate the impacts of climate change that decides to expand its target population to include the "new poor"—that is, those who were pushed into poverty because of a climate shock—to prevent them from slipping deeper into poverty (refer to the special focus section). BOMA in Kenya is an example of a program that scaled up by expanding its reach to several new population groups, making design adjustments as it did so (refer to box 3.1).

> **BOX 3.1   BOMA's REAP Approach for Different Population Groups**
>
> In Kenya, BOMA developed an effective economic inclusion methodology, Rural Entrepreneur Access Project (REAP), that has been used successfully and evaluated in many contexts and countries. BOMA has refined the REAP model over several years, and then women in the program suggested other applications.
>
> After identifying several new groups of people who might find the program beneficial, BOMA adopted variations designed to meet the needs of different groups, including REAP for Nutrition, which enrolls women with children younger than five years old and households that currently or previously have experienced child malnutrition. Other examples are REAP for Refugees, which targets displaced populations (refugees, internally displaced people) and host communities, and another variation, REAP for Youth, which works with pastoralist youth in Kenya. The fundamental program elements—savings groups, business capital, livelihood skills and soft skills training, and coaching—remain the same in these programs, but they are modified to fit the context and needs of the participant groups. New components, such as nutrition training and links to services, have been added to achieve population-specific outcomes.

FIGURE 3.2   Customization of Malawi's Social Support for Resilient Livelihoods Project

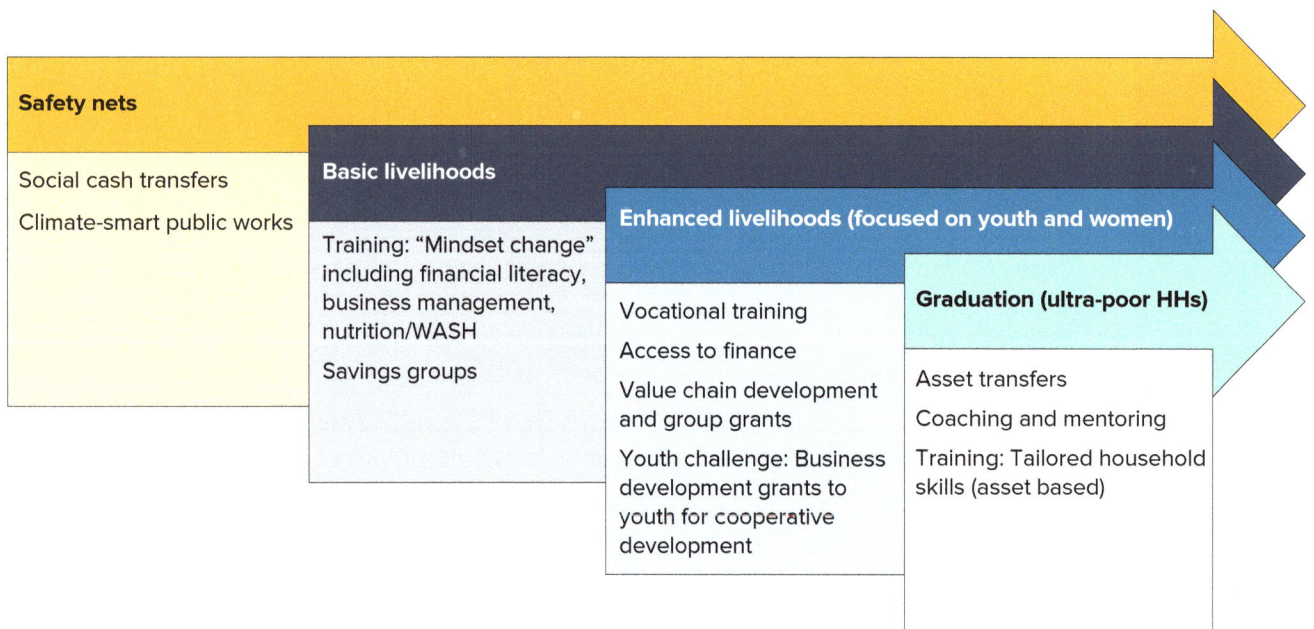

Safety nets

Social cash transfers

Climate-smart public works

Basic livelihoods

Training: "Mindset change" including financial literacy, business management, nutrition/WASH

Savings groups

Enhanced livelihoods (focused on youth and women)

Vocational training

Access to finance

Value chain development and group grants

Youth challenge: Business development grants to youth for cooperative development

Graduation (ultra-poor HHs)

Asset transfers

Coaching and mentoring

Training: Tailored household skills (asset based)

Source: Partnership for Economic Inclusion, World Bank.
Note: WASH = water, sanitation, and hygiene; HHs = households.

The Social Support for Resilient Livelihoods Project in Malawi is a good example of how programs are customized to meet the needs of different participant groups (refer to figure 3.2). This program builds on a core intervention—a safety net—but offers four variations: (1) a regular safety net for people living in poverty who do not have the capacity to work; (2) a basic livelihoods variation for those who are able to work but require additional training; (3) an enhanced livelihood variation to meet the needs of women and youth; and (4) a multidimensional graduation approach for households living in ultra-poverty who do have the capacity to work.

Youth-focused programs are reviewed in spotlight 2, program customizations for climate-affected people are reviewed in the special focus section on climate, and gender-intentional design is reviewed later in the chapter. Further research and documentation are warranted for programs designed for people with disabilities and elderly people, but that is beyond the scope of this report. As for programs wishing to scale up by increasing outreach to displaced people and their hosts, the following sections describe some design features, evidence, and good practices.

Forcibly Displaced People Face Specific Barriers That Programs Can Address

The number of forcibly displaced people has increased markedly as a result of burgeoning instability and conflict, growing from 89 million at the end of 2021 to over 117 million by the end of 2023 (UNHCR 2024). As more of these displacement situations become protracted, countries are moving toward solutions that help build resilience and self-sufficiency. Doing so requires complementing shock-responsive cash transfers and humanitarian interventions with responses—such as economic inclusion programs—that help build the resilience of poor households over time. Refer to chapter 4 for more on global initiatives to address the crisis. Nearly 40 percent of all surveyed programs now target people affected by forced displacement or conflict, an increase over SEI 2021. One-third of all programs operate in settings of fragility and conflict, with a great overlap between the two (57 percent of programs in those settings target people affected by displacement or conflict versus 30 percent elsewhere).

Responding to the needs of conflict-affected and forcibly displaced populations requires understanding the nature of the conflict or the displacement, the level of services and resources available to target populations, and the policies regulating their access to those resources. Forcibly displaced populations may face unique barriers to economic inclusion: psychosocial constraints and trauma; loss of assets; insufficient documentation or skills to work in their new country of residence; or legal and policy barriers that limit their mobility, right to work, or even ability to open bank accounts or receive public services. Furthermore, because most programs that work with displaced populations also target host communities, care must be taken to identify the differentiated needs of both groups and ensure that programs support cohesion building and do not inadvertently exacerbate tensions (Heisey, Arévalo-Sánchez, and Bernagros 2022).

Economic inclusion programs support displaced people in restoring or kickstarting livelihoods or linking them to job opportunities. Surveyed programs that target displacement-affected people are more likely to offer business capital (80 percent) and to facilitate links to markets (78 percent) than programs not targeting this group (75 percent and 72 percent, respectively). Links to wage employment are much more likely to be offered by programs for displacement-affected people (41 percent) than programs not targeting that group (29 percent).

Facilitating access to social services and taking steps to support social cohesion between host and forcibly displaced populations are also relevant (Betts et al. 2022). For example, within the past 2 years, Ethiopia's Urban Productive Safety Net and Jobs Project has reached over 700,000 internally displaced people and 10,000 refugees, along with host community members. This program has done so with custom-made economic inclusion packages combining flexible cash transfers, public works, business development training, livelihood grants, and social cohesion programming.

BOX 3.2   Empowering Displaced People: What Does the Evidence Say?

According to the preliminary impact evaluation of the World Bank–funded Niger Refugees and Host Communities Support Project, economic inclusion programs in the form of entrepreneurship training activities and a lump sum grant of US$200 can have positive effects on displaced and host household income, employment, and economic activities. Thus, economic inclusion programs can have important benefits for the most vulnerable populations (refugees, internally displaced people, and hosts) in highly fragile and volatile contexts.

Early results from Uganda's Graduating to Resilience program targeting both refugee and host communities are promising. The program had significant positive impacts on participants and their households across both the refugee and host communities on key outcomes, including food security, nutrition, and self-reliance (Brune et al., forthcoming).

A recent pilot project explored application of the graduation approach in the forced relocation of a community in Guinea. Lessons learned include the importance of tailoring support to diverse community needs, necessitating segmentation and flexibility. The psychosocial impacts of relocation, such as entitlement expectations, underscored the need for effective communication and trust-building between project staff, the company enforcing relocation, and the community. The project successfully demonstrated the applicability of multifaceted economic inclusion programs beyond extreme poverty, showcasing its potential to address the complex livelihood challenges arising from community relocations in diverse contexts, such as infrastructure projects or climate change impacts (Simanowitz 2024).

The evidence on economic inclusion programs targeting displaced populations is modest but growing. A review compiled by Heisey, Arévalo-Sánchez, and Bernagros (2022), together with the evidence snapshot in box 3.2, reveal the good practices that are emerging.

Programs Expanding Their Reach by Including Different Poverty Segments Must Assess Their Specific Needs

As noted in chapter 2, economic inclusion programs typically target those people at the lower end of the income distribution who have the capacity to engage in economic activities: the ultra-poor (40 percent of surveyed programs), extreme-poor (53 percent), and poor (55 percent) populations. Distinctions between these and other poverty segments are not easy to make in practice, and they are highly contextual. Household-focused programs with a strong mandate to target people in extreme poverty use quite deliberate strategies to do so. Area-focused programs focused on a broader swath of the population are less likely to focus on distinctions within communities.

Yet both household- and area-focused programs report that they target more than one poverty segment. As programs move to scale, some elect to do so by expanding to new poverty segments, often by modifying the program package to meet their differentiated needs. The distinction between household- and area-focused programs that has emerged from the landscape data is important because it highlights a distinction between programs that deliberately target individual households and those that incorporate households into programs with an area- or system-led focus.

Some household- or individual-targeted programs serving additional poverty segments begin, for example, with people living in extreme poverty and then move to include people near or at the poverty line. In some contexts, the distinctions between groups are slight, and a single shock to the household could push those currently above the poverty line into deeper poverty. For example, in Cambodia, the Graduation-based Social Protection Project, co-piloted by the United Nations Development Programme and the government, uses the national Identification of Poor Households (IDPoor) Program to identify program participants. Established in 2007, IDPoor is the main system for identifying and targeting participants for all social protection programs in Cambodia. The IDPoor system has three categories: very poor, poor, and at risk. The pilot targeted the first two categories. The at-risk category may be included if the program is scaled up.

Area-focused programs may include several poverty segments by virtue of targeting by geography. These programs may provide each poverty segment with a unique set of services depending on their needs, with the poorest people receiving the full complement of program components and less poor people receiving a subset of those components. For example, Bangladesh's Sustainable Coastal and Marine Fisheries Project supports economic inclusion by investing in capacity building and vocational training, offering loans, and creating community organizations. It uses a community-driven development approach to strengthen community fisheries management and transform the livelihoods in 450 poor fishing communities by reducing their dependence on fishing. In addition to training and community inputs, the poorest and most vulnerable fishing households receive one-time grants to allow them to purchase key household livelihood assets and reduce their dependence on outside money lenders. Less-poor households can access credit and loan funds through a revolving loan fund to support fisher households to adopt livelihoods outside capture fishing and to establish sustainable fishing practices. Fishing households can benefit from community savings groups, and women's savings groups help ensure that women are the direct recipients of livelihood support.

Some programs manage to include several poverty segments by combining two program approaches and using multiple ministries or organizations. In Uganda and Ethiopia, the Delivering Resilient Enterprises and Market Systems Project emerged from an understanding that, although market system approaches can address some barriers the poorest face when trying to access markets, they cannot provide the "push" needed to enable participants to launch economic activities, begin to save, and to access other benefits from the market (refer to box 3.3).

BOX 3.3   Combining "Push" and "Pull" Programming

The Delivering Resilient Enterprises and Market Systems (DREAMS) Project in Ethiopia and Uganda combines the household-focused approach and market systems development to engage refugee and host households economically. DREAMS integrates the "push" factor from Village Enterprise's graduation model that targets people living in extreme poverty, with the "pull" factor via Mercy Corps' market systems development, promoting inclusive market growth.

DREAMS engages households in poverty graduation activities, including savings, asset transfers, and business training. In doing so, it enhances local value chains, connecting "graduates" to market opportunities for sustained business growth and a reduced reliance on external aid. The program, which is under way, will support 40,000 families over 5 years.

Other programs offer specific packages for poverty segments, depending on need and objective. In one area-focused program in Türkiye, the package of support offered to participants varies based on their dependence on forests for their livelihood. The Forest and Village Relations Program (ORKOY), a national program managed by the General Directorate of Forestry (OGM), builds the socioeconomic development and climate resilience of forest villagers by engaging communities in traditional forest management practices. There are 6.9 million people living in 23,111 forest villages in Türkiye that have been engaged in afforestation, rehabilitation (silviculture), and maintenance and protection of forests since 1974 through OGM's livelihood support programs.

While forest villagers are among the poorest in the country, ORKOY reports that it does not target people directly based on poverty. Instead, the program focuses on diversifying income and employment, especially for vulnerable groups such as women and people with disabilities. In the targeted forest villages, those living in poverty receive grants and microcredit based on a demand-driven approach informed by household surveys taken before and after each grant or microcredit cycle.

The World Bank Climate Resilient Forests Project finances employment opportunities for forest villages in regions highly susceptible to wildfires through the ORKOY program. Grants and microcredit are designed to enhance livelihood opportunities and continuity of enterprises, build climate resilience, contribute to recovery efforts after a series of earthquakes in 2023, and reduce the risk of accelerated rural abandonment of forest areas. The support to forest villagers varies, based on the following criteria: women-led initiatives receive 100 percent grant support; forest village households receive financial support that is 20 percent grant and 80 percent low-interest loan; and in earthquake-affected areas, financial support is 50 percent grant and 50 percent low-interest loan to ensure the continuity of forest-dependent livelihoods and enterprises.

Programs That Scale Up by Expanding to New Geographic Areas May Require Adaptation

Programs can also increase coverage through geographic expansion, including broadening the area served to adjacent sites, such as new districts or regions, or expanding from urban to rural or rural to urban.

As programs incorporate new geographic areas, they must adapt their design to deal with new contexts and to ensure that any differences in the properties of the original program and those of the scale-up have been considered (Gupta et al. 2021). For example, they must consider factors such as differences in population density, barriers to economic inclusion that may be unique to new areas, and different sociopolitical considerations. Programs successfully implemented in one area cannot be assumed to work exactly the same in a new context, even if it is nearby.

The process of choosing new geographic areas can vary, but two factors must be considered: (1) whether the new area is contiguous with a current one to facilitate potential exchange and increase the likelihood of a similar context and (2) the geographic concentration of potential participants (to manage costs in terms of travel time and expenses).

Expanding to New Districts or Regions

Programs may choose new districts based on criteria such as the concentration of poor people. Tanzania's Productive Social Safety Net Project scaled up its livelihood program by gradually expanding to new districts. It began by splitting the districts into three groups ranked by poverty. Several poor districts were given priority for the initial project, and it began to scale up within the poorest 51 districts. Budget constraints, however, forced the project to curtail its scale-up plans for the enhanced livelihood component, and so scale-up has focused almost exclusively on the poorest districts.

Another example is the Improved Household Income Support Program, supported by the National Uganda Social Action Fund 3, which launched its sustainable livelihoods component in 9 districts. Based on success in those districts, it then scaled up first to 31 districts and then added 22 more with additional funding for the component. The project secured political buy-in based on the success of the component, which facilitated a decision to replicate it in other parts of the country.

Expanding into Urban and Rural Areas

Traditionally, economic inclusion programs have focused on rural areas, and PEI's Landscape Survey 2023 once again found that most programs operate in rural areas (84 percent of surveyed programs, 43 percent exclusively), which is similar to the finding in SEI 2021. In 2023, however, there was a slight increase in the percentage of programs operating in urban areas, with 57 percent of surveyed programs serving urban or peri-urban populations, compared with 54 percent in 2021.

Urban areas are the engines of economic growth, typically offering a wide range of economic opportunities, including better access to wage employment and more integration into markets. However, urban poor individuals face multiple constraints, including limited access to public utilities, lack of affordable housing, and lower social cohesion. Programs designed for the urban context must, therefore, consider the specific constraints that negatively affect the livelihoods of the urban poor population (Avalos et al. 2021).

Although many aspects of economic inclusion program design remain the same in urban settings as in rural areas, programs may tweak some of their components to fit the context. For example, because wage job opportunities are often higher in urban areas, the scope of training and coaching may be changed to equip participants with the skills required in the workplace (including basic literacy and numeracy, soft skills, and technical skills). The fact that urban areas are more densely populated than rural areas can have implications for delivery mechanisms, component design, and costs. However, urban areas can offer a greater diversity of livelihood activities and access to more services.

One example of expansion from urban to rural areas is from Senegal. The Yook Koom Koom (YKK) pilot was launched in four urban areas and later expanded to rural zones. It was started in response to rising urbanization, high job insecurity, and labor informality. YKK's package of interventions includes community savings and loan groups, coaching, life skills training, microentrepreneurship training, access to markets, and cash grants. Participants demonstrated a notable resilience to the COVID-19 pandemic, their household consumption increased, and many succeeded in business. The pilot initially focused on 15,000 households in four urban areas, where it had strong impacts on well-being and entrepreneurship. In 2022, the project tripled its goal by reaching 45,000 households in 14 regions, both urban and rural. The program aims to eventually reach 80,000 households across the country over the next 5 years (Bossuroy et al. 2024).

In sparsely-populated rural areas, the delivery of components such as coaching will likely require more time and funds for travel, and, therefore, may be more expensive. Community-oriented activities such as savings groups may also be difficult to support in sparsely-populated areas. Although working in such areas may increase costs, programs can adjust components to offset this risk. For example, YKK's lower-cost community volunteers and local program staff delivered the savings and coaching components, so these program costs were modest (under US$20 per participant). In rural Mauritania, where qualified NGO workers have provided those services with a much higher ratio of participants to providers, the same activities cost US$180 per participant.

Expanding economic inclusion programs into urban areas necessitates a deeper exploration of rural-urban links, which are integral to maximizing program impact and sustainability. Market links serve as a cornerstone of these connections, as rural initiatives often rely on access to urban and peri-urban markets to enhance profitability and scalability. However, rural-urban links extend beyond market connections to include knowledge transfer, innovation diffusion, and labor mobility. Recognizing the multifaceted nature of these links is crucial for designing effective economic inclusion strategies that bridge the rural-urban divide and promote inclusive growth.

Programs Broadening Their Activities Must Balance Participant Needs, Monitoring, Cost, and Complexity

Another way in which programs can increase scale is through functional expansion— that is, increasing the scope of activities to deepen program outcomes. Each program offers a distinct package of program components designed to address the specific barriers faced by participants selected by the program. Almost all programs that responded to the Landscape Survey 2023 reported that they provide participants with three or more program components. Seventy-five percent of government-led programs and 86 percent of nongovernment-led programs use at least five program components (refer to figure 3.3).

FIGURE 3.3 **Distribution of Government- and Nongovernment-Led Programs, by Number of Components**

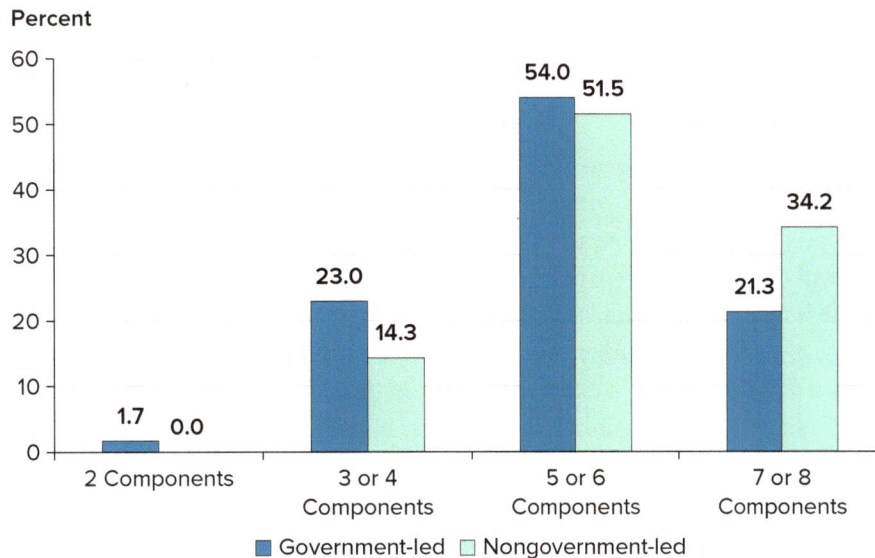

Source: Partnership for Economic Inclusion, World Bank.

Note: Figure shows the percentage of all government- and nongovernment-led programs (N_1 = 174 and N_2 = 231, respectively). By definition, economic inclusion programs provide at least two components.

The following factors play a role in determining whether to add or strengthen a program component for functional expansion:

- *Participant needs.* Programs may add one or more program elements or services, or improve their quality, with the goal of improving participant outcomes. Each component plays a specific role in the development of human, physical, financial, social, or natural capital through assets, savings, coaching, and other support to improve outcomes and build resilience to shocks. The combination of components and the sequence in which they are provided offer just-in-time support to meet participants' needs throughout the course of the program and enable them to continue to participate in program activities.

- *Evaluation results, monitoring feedback, or other data input.* Economic inclusion programs may decide to add a component if diagnostics, monitoring data, or field staff input show that program activities are not succeeding because of a specific barrier. Programs may also consult the evaluation results of other programs in similar contexts or with similar population groups to consider whether, in combination with these other criteria, a program component should be added. Uganda's Graduating to Resilience program illustrates the value of using diagnostics, monitoring, feedback from coaching staff, and a formal evaluation to make changes in component design, both when the program starts and in the course of implementation (refer to box 3.4).

- *Costs.* Designers and program implementers should focus on those participants' needs that must be met for livelihood activities to succeed. Furthermore, although each component brings value to the program package, combining certain components can add outsized value. For example, combining training with coaching can be complementary in two ways. First, coaches can help participants access training services. If they are offered by a third party, poor participants may face challenges in attending that coaches can help them overcome, from solving transport issues to conquering self-confidence barriers stemming from lack of a formal education. Coaches also can help identify childcare options or manage institutional barriers to attendance such as lack of official identification. Second, coaches can help reinforce training messages by enabling participants to apply valuable livelihood, health, or other information provided in the training.

- *Implementation requirements.* The benefits of providing additional or enhanced services must be balanced with the additional implementation requirements placed on the program. New or improved components will require greater coordination and may involve identifying new partners or service providers to deliver them. One way to ease the implementation burden is by customizing program packages and providing a subset of participants rather than all participants with new or more intensive components. This option is explored further in this chapter, and chapter 4 presents more details on managing implementation arrangements.

BOX 3.4   Testing Variations in Program Components in Uganda

Over the course of two participant cohorts and based on monitoring and evaluation data, the Graduating to Resilience program managed by AVSI in Uganda refined its targeting strategy, added a group interpersonal therapy component, adapted its gender and nutrition components, reduced the coaches' caseload, and lowered costs by prioritizing group coaching and shortening the program.

Launched as a 30-month program, AVSI offers a sequenced intervention with components, including coaching, financial inclusion support, transfers for consumption support, livelihood skills training, and asset transfers. A randomized controlled trial (RCT) tested variations in coaching and asset transfers, leading to changes aimed at greater cost-effectiveness. Group and individual coaching, in particular, proved effective, although group coaching was found to be 13 percent more cost-effective than individual coaching. These changes, along with a shorter program timeline (24 months), reduced per-household costs from US$1,400 to approximately US$1,000.

Throughout the program, changes were informed by data collected through monitoring, feedback from community members, surveys, and the RCT. Program adjustments included refining coaching strategies, prioritizing group coaching, and addressing challenges such as rising dropout rates and trauma among participants. The program also tackled gender disparities by engaging male spouses, emphasizing gender equality in coaching, and incorporating individual household touchpoints.

COVID-19 prompted further changes, including the use of remote coaching and modifications of data collection. The program addressed nutrition challenges through home visits and coaching on versatile farming techniques. A gender assessment in 2021 highlighted the role of digital tools in addressing gender inequality, leading to the provision of mobile phones to participants. The introduction of a Digital Skills Training Program showed positive outcomes. Participants in the digital literacy curriculum demonstrated better resilience and business engagement. Changes introduced as part of the program expansion included providing basic phones, which subsequent assessments revealed as having positive impacts on participants' learning, resilience, business engagement, and household dynamics.

BOX 3.5   Building Resilience in Response to COVID-19

Seventy-eight percent of surveyed economic inclusion programs and 95 percent of those under way when the COVID-19 pandemic broke out at the beginning of 2020 were affected by the event. Twenty-six percent of surveyed programs (and 39 percent of programs under way as of early 2020) experienced a major or severe impact. Some economic inclusion programs were temporarily discontinued or deprioritized, as attention shifted to providing immediate responses at the outset of the pandemic.

Because economic inclusion programs are characterized by their flexibility and ability to respond to different contexts, 86 percent of surveyed programs affected by the pandemic took steps to respond to it. Program responses included changes to program design (57 percent of impacted programs) such as reducing the frequency of training or coaching; deploying digital technologies to carry out program activities (43 percent), to transfer payments to participants, or to deliver training or coaching (refer to spotlight 3); changing how in-person components were delivered (26 percent) by ensuring social distancing during training or coaching sessions or reducing group size; or adding new components (25 percent), such as providing business continuity grants, food baskets, or inputs to support home food production. Economic inclusion programs also provided training on how to adapt businesses to the pandemic and raised awareness on how to prevent the spread of the virus and deliver protective equipment such as masks and sanitizers.

Both program and participant resilience were tested during the pandemic, and lessons emerged on the importance of building strong systems and program flexibility to be better prepared to respond to participants' needs (refer to box 3.5). Many programs changed or added program components to respond to the new and changing context of COVID-19, reinforcing the flexibility of economic inclusion programs.

One new element of the Landscape Survey 2023 is that programs were asked to report whether each participant received every program component (refer to figure 3.4). Sixty-five percent of programs reported they are not providing every participant with every component, meaning they are providing different program bundles. This approach may reflect several factors. First, some programs are customizing the package of services to meet the needs of different participants. In Uzbekistan, the Entrepreneurship Support through Business Start-up Subsidies program varies the intensity of coaching or mentoring based on an assessment during the first visit to determine the level of difficulties the participant is facing. Participants who independently start livelihood activities after training do not receive coaching.

Second, some programs are offering different packages of support to participants with different profiles or livelihood activities. Türkiye's Scaling-up Farmers Field Business Schools, which is focused on refugees as a target population, reports that participants are grouped based on their activities and resources, including female small-scale producers (farmers), agricultural laborers, and community health agents, and each is given a specific predetermined set of support packages. Customizing components to match the differentiated needs of a population helps to improve cost-effectiveness, but too much customization can be difficult to administer (refer to chapter 4 for details on institutional coordination).

FIGURE 3.4 **Distribution of Programs Serving All or a Subset of Participants, by Number of Components**

Percent

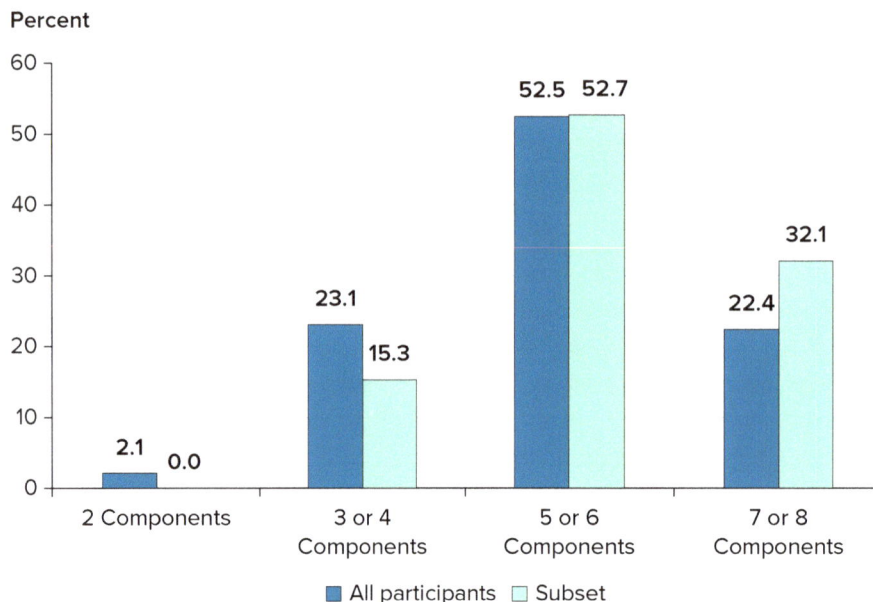

Source: Partnership for Economic Inclusion, World Bank.

Note: Figure shows the percentage of programs providing components to all participants (*N* = 143) and to a subset (*N* = 262) of participants.

Each component added to a program has implications for that program's cost, complexity of implementation, and effectiveness in achieving outcomes. Many programs have experimented with different types of program bundles to help maximize program outcomes and streamline program complexity, while still achieving strong program outcomes. Therefore, it is crucial to understand the relative cost-effectiveness of different packages of interventions to enhance program design for scalability. This involves isolating and analyzing the effects of various program components to determine which combinations yield the best outcomes relative to their costs.

Programs Seek to Achieve Women's Economic Empowerment

According to the Landscape Survey 2023, 90 percent of the programs target women. Although most programs include some measures to support women, one-third of all programs reported women's economic empowerment as one of their core program objectives and that they are deliberate about the strategies they use to strengthen women's economic inclusion. Ninety-three percent of programs in which women's economic empowerment is a core objective—and 84 percent of programs in which it is not—reported that women were the direct recipients of program benefits or components. Furthermore, 72 percent of such programs reported that they measure women's participation or empowerment.

Programs often utilize bundled economic inclusion interventions to address the many constraints poor women face and to empower them in both the economic and social domains. Gendered market assessments can help programs tailor livelihood options that are reasonable given women's time constraints and other responsibilities. These assessments enhance a program's ability to identify the barriers, such as care responsibilities, limited mobility, and gaps in skills, that women face, and can also identify opportunities for livelihood engagement. In the Arab Republic of Egypt, the FORSA (meaning "opportunity" in Arabic) pilot included a gendered rapid market assessment that enabled the program to identify sectors such as ready-made garments and food processing as potential livelihood options for women, as well as the soft and technical skills female participants need to take advantage of these opportunities.

Program design features can help facilitate women's access to livelihoods and also support the early childhood development agenda. Forty-one percent of programs with women's economic empowerment as a core objective reported having specific components for women; 44 percent of programs in which women's economic empowerment is a core objective also had adapted their program design to support women. Only 11 percent of programs that had women's economic empowerment as a core objective reported making provisions for childcare (and only 2 percent made provisions for eldercare), so there is ample room for improvement in how programs adapt their components and designs to support an early childhood agenda.

Seventy percent of programs sensitize communities to the needs of women or use gender-related messaging in their design. Among other things, they raise the awareness of female participants of their legal rights or discuss the importance of gender equality with male participants or spouses and the community at large. Some programs provide partners in the private sector, nongovernmental organizations, or governments with guidance on the specific barriers women face.

Programs often use their training and coaching components to help shift gender norms. For example, in the Democratic Republic of Congo, the Stronger Nations, Stronger Women program, led by Women for Women International, trained participants in the value of women's work, women's rights, and the prevention of violence against women. Female participants then demonstrated higher levels of autonomy and short-term improvements in their ideas about women's role in society. The program even found that intimate partner violence decreased among participants who were at high risk.

Similarly, the Satat Jeevikoparjan Yojana program in India confronted issues facing women by discussing early marriage and family planning. In many of their programs, Concern Worldwide works to change how men view women in their community by employing an "engaging men and boys" component in which coaches discuss with men in the community such issues as gender roles, power, and healthy relationships (Bhari and Laszlo 2020). However, only 28 percent of programs that have women's economic empowerment as a core objective take these interventions a step further and engage in advocacy for governmental policy changes.

Programs have also found that engaging the broader household, especially male spouses, from the beginning helps build trust and reduces backlash from spouses. The Women's Income Generating Support Program in Uganda has included male spouses since the program's inception (Sumanthiran and Roelen 2023). The Supporting Women's Livelihoods initiative under the Girls' Education and Women's Empowerment and Livelihood Project in Zambia holds a joint orientation with male household members to reduce backlash by helping them understand the goals of the project. The program also includes a session called "Family Vision" during which female participants and their male household members can set common goals and negotiate their household contributions.

By acknowledging the intersectionality of women's empowerment, childcare, and nutrition, policy makers and stakeholders can also adopt a holistic approach to fostering economic inclusion. Empowering women to make informed decisions about their own health and that of their children; providing access to nutritious food, health care services, and education; and implementing supportive policies and programs can break the cycle of malnutrition and poverty, unlocking the full potential of individuals and communities to participate in and benefit from economic inclusion programming.

As noted, most of the economic inclusion programs surveyed target women and have demonstrated significant positive impacts on various economic outcomes, including consumption, assets, income, and savings. The SEI 2021 reviewed in a spotlight the evidence (Andrews et al. 2021), and box 3.6 reviews the evidence published since then.

BOX 3.6   **Empowering Women: What Does the Evidence Say?**

Earlier studies of economic inclusion programs have found limited impacts on women's empowerment (Bandiera et al. 2017; Banerjee et al. 2015). However, recent studies using broader measures of empowerment and well-being have found stronger effects (Bedoya Arguelles et al. 2019; Bossuroy et al. 2022), as highlighted in spotlight 1 in chapter 1.

Afghanistan
Government programs are also demonstrating positive impacts on women's empowerment. In Afghanistan, the Targeting the Ultra Poor program induced improvements in women's empowerment such as a 22 percentage points increase in labor force participation and improvement in mental health (Bedoya Arguelles et al. 2019).

Democratic Republic of Congo
One recent study illuminates the impact of a graduation program in eastern Democratic Republic of Congo, implemented by Women for Women International. This program, targeting ultra-poor women in a region facing protracted conflict, pairs the graduation approach with training in women's rights, negotiation, decision-making, civic action, safety nets, and building social connections with other women. In addition to the significant impact on household consumption and assets, the study reveals positive effects on women's participation in household decision-making and locus of control. The improvements in household decision-making are primarily driven by women's increased involvement in decisions about income generation. Furthermore, children's attendance at school increases by 5 percentage points. The overall conclusion is that the positive effects on women in a very poor post-conflict setting are encouraging for policy makers aiming to enhance women's welfare (Angelucci, Heath, and Noble 2023).

(Box continues next page)

BOX 3.6   Empowering Women: What Does the Evidence Say? (*continued*)

Niger and Zambia

Zambia's Supporting Women's Livelihoods program has increased overall consumption by 38 percent, household income by 62 percent, business profits by 80 percent, and savings by 234 percent after three years (Botea et al. forthcoming). The interventions also demonstrated substantial improvements in participants' mental health, including perceived happiness, self-esteem, and a comprehensive mental health index incorporating symptoms such as depression and exhaustion.

Similar positive effects on mental health, including life satisfaction, inner peace, and depression, were observed in Niger. In terms of empowerment, the Niger program showcased significant positive effects on women's social well-being and social capital within their communities, indicating increased financial support, social standing, and collective action. Sustained effects on the index of women's control over their own earnings and productive activities also were noted. However, in both Niger and Zambia, the higher income and business revenue for women did not necessarily translate into enhanced decision-making power over household resources (Bossuroy et al. 2022, Botea et al. 2023). In Zambia, limited evidence of a shift in decision-making power could be attributed to the targeting of women-headed households, which may have already been relatively more empowered.

Effective Scale Up Requires Good Diagnostics

Identifying an approach that works in one area or with one population group does not guarantee similar results if scaling up to new areas or groups. Gupta et al. (2021) has identified four categories of risks a program may face if it scales up: (1) inference, when a program is scaled before there is sufficient evidence of effectiveness; (2) an ill-suited population, when results are not representative because programs are tested on a subset of the population that is, or is perceived to be, more likely to succeed; (3) a challenging situation, when the program design or delivery in the pilot phase does not adequately reflect the broader context; or (4) unanticipated spillover effects, which can make it difficult to assess impacts. Programs moving to national scale should consider the specifics of population, properties, and delivery in designing for new contexts.

Successful programs start with thorough assessments to understand the specific constraints and opportunities facing vulnerable households (Bossuroy et al. 2022), and successfully scaled up programs continue to use them when moving to new locations or serving new population groups. Common constraints at the individual level include limited experience navigating markets, a lack of community connections or networks, and a limited cognitive ability for future planning (Mullainathan and Shafir 2013). Once the overall profile of participants is determined, additional assessments—including context analyses and vulnerability, livelihood, and market assessments—will inform the design of program components.

Program designers should consider that changes in program design, components, program delivery, or other elements may not always be required when working in new areas or with new population groups, particularly when programs were designed with ultimate scale-up in mind. Program planners should design for scale, envisioning how initial program activities can inform future growth so that future participants have the same likelihood of success as those in the pilot project, thereby avoiding a mismatch of the properties of a population (Gupta et al. 2021).

Finally, participants should be involved in the design and delivery of programs to ensure the programs are responsive to needs and participants feel invested. Flexible, demand-driven programs accounted for the success of several efforts in the agrifood area. Research demonstrated that programs with food security objectives were successful because they had a demand-driven model that responded to the different capacity-building needs of participants. Actively engaging participants in the design, providing them with supervision, and monitoring responsibilities contributed to participants' success (World Bank 2022).

References

Andrews, Colin, Aude de Montesquiou, Inés Arévalo-Sánchez, Puja Vasudeva Dutta, Boban Varghese Paul, Sadna Samaranayake, Janet Heisey, Timothy Clay, and Sarang Chaudhary. 2021. *The State of Economic Inclusion Report 2021: The Potential to Scale.* Washington, DC: World Bank. http://hdl.handle.net/10986/34917.

Angelucci, Manuela, Rachel Heath, and Eva Noble. 2023. "Multifaceted Programs Targeting Women in Fragile Settings: Evidence from the Democratic Republic of Congo." *Journal of Development Economics* 164 (103146). https://doi.org/10.1016/j.jdeveco.2023.103146.

Avalos, Jorge, Sarang Chaudhary, Timothy Clay, and Puja Vasudeva Dutta. 2021. *A Path to Jobs for the Urban Poor. PEI in Practice, Volume 1.* Washington, DC: World Bank. http://hdl.handle.net/10986/36594.

Bandiera, Oriana, Robin Burgess, Narayan Das, Selim Gulesci, Imran Rasul, and Munshi Sulaiman. 2017. "Labor Markets and Poverty in Village Economies." *Quarterly Journal of Economics* 132 (2): 811–70. https://doi.org/10.1093/qje/qjx003.

Banerjee, Abhijit, Esther Duflo, Nathaneal Goldberg, Dean Karlan, Robert Osei, William Parienté, Jeremy Shapiro, Bram Thuysbaert, and Christopher Udry. 2015. "A Multifaceted Program Causes Lasting Progress for the Very Poor: Evidence from Six Countries." *Science* 348 (6236): 1260799. https://www.science.org/doi/10.1126/science.1260799.

Bedoya Arguelles, Guadalupe, Aidan Coville, Johannes Haushofer, Mohammad Isaqzadeh, and Jeremy Shapiro. 2019. "No Household Left Behind: Afghanistan Targeting the Ultra Poor Impact Evaluation." Policy Research Working Paper 8877, World Bank, Washington, DC. https://documents.worldbank.org/en/publication/documents-reports/documentdetail/8558 31560172245349/no-household-left-behind-afghanistan-targeting-the-ultra-poor-impact -evaluation.

Betts, Alexander, Maria Flinder Stierna, Naohiko Omata, and Olivier Sterck. 2022. "Social Cohesion and Refugee-Host Interactions: Evidence from East Africa." Policy Research Working Paper 9917, World Bank, Washington, DC. https://openknowledge.worldbank.org /handle/10986/36918.

Bhari, Anoushka, and Sonia Laszlo. 2020. "Policies and Practices to Enhance the Gender Transformative Potential of Multi-Faceted Social Protection Programs." https://www .peiglobal.org/sites/pei/themes/pei/kc_files/Bhari%20and%20Laszlo%202020.pdf.

Bossuroy, Thomas, Markus Goldstein, Bassirou Karimou, Dean Karlan, Harounan Kazianga, William Parienté, Patrick Premand, Catherine C. Thomas, Christopher Udry, Julia Vaillant, and Kelsey A. Wright. 2022. "Tackling Psychosocial and Capital Constraints to Alleviate Poverty." *Nature* 605 (7909): 291–97. https://www.nature.com/articles/s41586-022-04647-8.

Bossuroy, Thomas, Dean Karlan, William Parienté, Patrick Premand, Christopher Udry, Julia Vaillant, and Kelsey Wright. 2024. "Impact des mesures d'inclusion productive du programme Yom Kom Kom au Sénégal." Banque Mondiale, Washington, DC.

Botea, Ioana, Andrew Brudevold-Newman, Markus Goldstein, Corrine Low, and Gareth Roberts, 2023. "Supporting Women's Livelihoods at Scale: Evidence from a Nationwide Multi-Faceted Program." NBER Working Paper No. w31625. National Bureau of Economic Research, Cambridge, MA. https://www.nber.org/system/files/working_papers/w31625/w31625.pdf.

Botea, Ioana, Andrew Brudevold-Newman, Markus Goldstein, Corrine Low, and Gareth Roberts. Forthcoming. "Long-Term Impact of Supporting Women's Livelihoods at Scale." Washington, DC, World Bank.

Brune, Lasse, Nathanael Goldberg, Doug Parkerson, Dean Karlan, and Christopher Udry. Forthcoming. "The Graduating to Resilience Program That Was Designed to Improve Food and Nutrition Security." Kampala, Uganda.

Carter, Becky, Anu Joshi, and Michelle Remme. 2018. *Scaling Up Inclusive Approaches for Marginalised and Vulnerable People*. K4D Emerging Issues Report. Brighton, UK: Institute of Development Studies.

Cooley, Larry, and Johannes F. Linn. 2014. *Taking Innovations to Scale: Methods, Applications and Lessons*. Washington, DC: Results for Development Institute.

Gupta, Snigdha, Lauren Supplee, Dana Suskind, and John List. 2021. "Failed to Scale." In *The Scale-Up Effect in Early Childhood and Public Policy: Why Interventions Lose Impact at Scale and What We Can Do About It*, edited by John List, Dana Suskind, and Lauren Supplee, 1–21. New York: Routledge. https://doi.org/10.4324/9780367822972.

Heisey, Janet, Inés Arévalo-Sánchez, and Alexi Bernagros. 2022. *Working for Inclusion: Economic Inclusion in Contexts of Forced Displacement. PEI in Practice, Volume 4*. Washington, DC: World Bank. https://openknowledge.worldbank.org/server/api/core/bitstreams/f9d7b36b-d436-5c62-9f23-cdd1e0827726/content.

Mullainathan, Sendhil, and Eldar Shafir. 2013. *Scarcity: Why Having Too Little Means So Much*. New York: Times Books/Henry Holt. New York. https://us.macmillan.com/books/9781250056115.

Simanowitz, Anton. 2024. "Lessons from a Livelihoods Pilot in Guinea." *India Development Review.* https://idronline.org/article/programme/lessons-from-a-livelihoods-pilot-in-guinea/.

Sumanthiran, Shilohni, and Keetie Roelen. 2023. *Coaching in Economic Inclusion: Learning from Existing Models and Casting a Way Forward. PEI in Practice, Volume 10*. Washington, DC: World Bank. http://hdl.handle.net/10986/40738.

UNHCR (United Nations High Commissioner for Refugees). 2024. *Refugee Data Finder.* Geneva, Switzerland: UNHCR. https://www.unhcr.org/refugee-statistics/.

World Bank. 2022. *Toward Productive, Inclusive, and Sustainable Farms and Agribusiness Firms: An Evaluation of the World Bank Group's Support for the Development of Agrifood Economies (2010–20)*. Washington, DC: World Bank, Independent Evaluation Group. https://ieg.worldbankgroup.org/evaluations/toward-productive-inclusive-and-sustainable-farms-and-agribusiness-firms.

Adapting Economic Inclusion to a Growing Youth Population

Introduction

The global youth unemployment rate, estimated at 13.3 percent in 2023, is more than three times the adult unemployment rate; 75 million young people of working age are unemployed worldwide (ILO 2023). Young workers are twice as likely as adults to live in extreme poverty and more prone to informal employment, and youth in low- and middle-income countries are more likely to confront these issues. Many young people lack access to quality education and relevant skills training, thus hindering their ability to compete in the formal labor market. Even where education is available, a mismatch between learned skills and market demands persists due to factors such as outdated curricula and limited employer involvement in training programs (World Bank 2019). The informal economy, prevalent in developing nations, does offers jobs, but these often offer low wages, poor conditions, and job insecurity—all of which make it challenging for young people to transition to formal, decent-paying work. The cycle is perpetuated as employers hesitate to hire inexperienced workers, creating hurdles for young people to gain valuable work experience (ILO 2023; World Bank 2019).

Economic inclusion programs offer a testing ground for innovative approaches to tackle job challenges and to integrate young people into the economy. Of the surveyed programs, 65 percent (61 percent of nongovernment-led initiatives and 69 percent of government-led efforts) target youth (so-called "youth-focused programs"). Although most program objectives differ little between youth- and nonyouth-focused programs (refer to figure S2.1, panel a), there is a more pronounced emphasis on climate resilience (73 percent of programs) and greater access to wage employment (40 percent) in youth-focused programs, compared with 53 percent and 22 percent, respectively, for programs that do not explicitly target youth (refer to figure S2.1, panel b).

FIGURE S2.1   Main Program Objectives and Components of Youth-Focused Programs Versus Nonyouth-Focused Programs

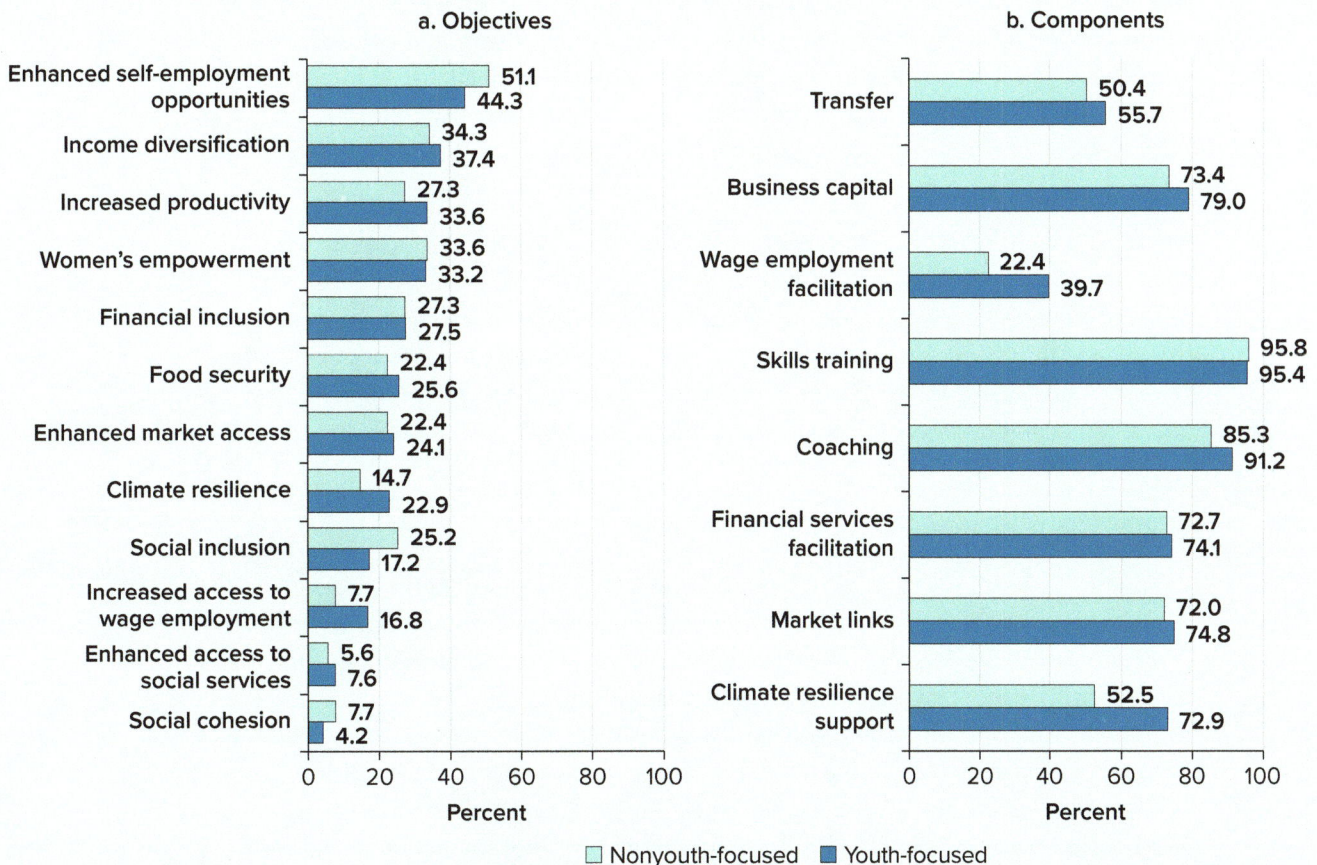

a. Objectives

Objective	Nonyouth-focused	Youth-focused
Enhanced self-employment opportunities	51.1	44.3
Income diversification	34.3	37.4
Increased productivity	27.3	33.6
Women's empowerment	33.6	33.2
Financial inclusion	27.3	27.5
Food security	22.4	25.6
Enhanced market access	22.4	24.1
Climate resilience	14.7	22.9
Social inclusion	25.2	17.2
Increased access to wage employment	7.7	16.8
Enhanced access to social services	5.6	7.6
Social cohesion	7.7	4.2

b. Components

Component	Nonyouth-focused	Youth-focused
Transfer	50.4	55.7
Business capital	73.4	79.0
Wage employment facilitation	22.4	39.7
Skills training	95.8	95.4
Coaching	85.3	91.2
Financial services facilitation	72.7	74.1
Market links	72.0	74.8
Climate resilience support	52.5	72.9

Percent

☐ Nonyouth-focused   ■ Youth-focused

Source: Partnership for Economic Inclusion, World Bank.
Note: Figure shows the percentage of youth- and non youth-focused programs (N_1 = 262 and N_2 = 143, respectively).

Emerging Evidence on Youth-Focused Economic Inclusion Programs

Recent studies have found that government-led economic inclusion programs targeting youth entrepreneurs, specifically programs providing grants and training, have positive impacts. The Small Business Support program in Liberia's Youth Opportunities Project and the Kenya Youth Employment and Opportunities Project have both shown promising results. In Liberia, participants receiving business grants and training experienced a 46 percent increase in income compared with a control group, along with higher rates of business ownership, higher investments in business assets, and better overall satisfaction levels (Gupta, Del Bono, and Jorgensen 2021). Similarly, in Kenya, youth who received grants and business training during the COVID-19 pandemic were twice as likely to have operational businesses in subsequent rounds compared with the control group. The impacts included longer business survival, the initiation of new businesses, a higher likelihood of citing their business as the primary income source, and lower chances of reporting negative income changes (Domenella et al. 2021).

These findings underscore the positive influence of economic inclusion initiatives targeting youth entrepreneurship and economic well-being. Although youth with adequate mobility and a formal education may encounter fewer constraints than youth lacking these benefits, initiating businesses with a combination of training and grants and a more comprehensive economic inclusion package, including access to markets and mentoring, is still recommended. Support for market links to value chains, as well as access to inputs and aggregation of outputs, is critical to ensuring the long-term sustainability of businesses. Mentoring is also a critical factor in addressing behavioral constraints because it can contribute to better decision-making among young entrepreneurs.

Innovative Youth-Focused Design Considerations

Effective economic inclusion programs for youth require tailored, innovative design elements that address their unique needs and aspirations. By incorporating youth-specific approaches, programs can enhance engagement, build relevant skills, and support sustainable livelihoods. This section outlines key considerations for creating innovative youth-focused design.

Fragile, Conflict-Affected, or Violent Context

Programs designed for youth in fragile, conflict-affected, or violent contexts must consider the root causes of conflict and violence. Exemplifying this approach, the Azoli program, part of the Benin Youth Inclusion Project, conducted a vulnerability study to identify both target communities and the factors driving violence. The study revealed that conflict in Benin is linked to issues such as weak governance, resource competition, illegal activities, inadequate protection of income-generating activities, and limited access to education and health. To address these risks, the program emphasizes the professional and economic integration of vulnerable youth, promotes labor market participation for all, and tailors its strategies to meet the specific needs of target groups. The study informed the development of conflict prevention strategies, allowing for targeted investments in at-risk villages (Rougeaux and Mongan Agbeshie 2024).

Market Systems

Understanding the market failures that exclude poor women and youth from accessing job opportunities is critical for an effective design, especially in urban areas where the youth population is growing faster than jobs can be created. The Livelihoods Improvement for Women and Youth (LIWAY) program[1] in Addis Ababa, Ethiopia, has adopted a market systems development approach to address the root causes of market failure hindering poor women and youth from accessing job opportunities in urban areas. The program targets the development of four interconnected market systems—labor, micro and small enterprise, medium and large enterprise, and skills—to improve access to better-paying jobs, reduce barriers to business growth, and improve skills development. By forming strategic partnerships with private companies and public institutions, the program aims to address market failures effectively, ensuring local ownership for sustainable poverty reduction and social stability for youth (LIWAY 2023).

Socioemotional Skills

The gaps in socioemotional skills—skills that enable individuals to accomplish particular tasks, such as recognizing and managing their emotions and coping successfully with conflict—can exacerbate the challenges faced by youth in pursuing job opportunities, particularly in an informal labor market focused on self-employment. A rural Mongolia project addresses the lack of socioemotional skills among vulnerable youth by integrating entrepreneurship-focused socioemotional skills training into school curricula. The initiative collaborates with local secondary schools, lifelong learning centers, and polytechnic colleges to deliver an innovative curriculum that equips youth with essential skills for entering the challenging labor market.

Apprenticeships

Apprenticeship programs are a valuable tool for addressing youth unemployment challenges by offering hands-on learning in real work environments. Participants receive valuable industry-relevant skills and experience, significantly enhancing their employability. The Urban Productive Safety Net and Jobs Project in Ethiopia recently introduced a six-month apprenticeship for unemployed youth with high school diplomas or lower qualifications. The apprenticeships are provided by private and public firms, and the youth are given a stipend during the six-month apprenticeship period and for the subsequent 3 months to support their job search. The program also delivers life, job search, and digital skills training and strengthens the job search intermediary services to help youth find jobs.

Future Directions

Economic inclusion programs specifically designed to tackle youth unemployment have shown promising results in improving access to income through self-employment opportunities. Empowering youth entails addressing capital constraints for starting businesses, providing job market information and career guidance, bridging skills gaps, and leveraging digital tools for skills training. A comprehensive approach is crucial for creating an environment that supports youth in their pursuit of economic opportunities and sustainable livelihoods.

Note

1. LIWAY is a 9-year program (July 2017 to June 2026) funded by Sweden and the Embassy of the Kingdom of the Netherlands.

References

Domenella, Yanina, Julian C. Jamison, Abla Safir, and Bilal Zia. 2021. "Can Business Grants Mitigate a Crisis? Evidence from Youth Entrepreneurs in Kenya during COVID-19." Policy Research Working Paper No. 9874, World Bank, Washington, DC. http://hdl.handle.net/10986/36693.

Gupta, Sarika, Mitja Del Bono, and Erik Jorgensen. 2021. *The Impact of Grants and Skills Training on Youth Employment Outcomes in Liberia.* Washington, DC: World Bank.

ILO (International Labour Organization). 2023. "World Employment and Social Outlook: Trends 2023." ILO Flagship Report, Geneva, Switzerland. https://www.ilo.org/wcmsp5/groups/public/---dgreports/---inst/documents/publication/wcms_865332.pdf.

LIWAY (Livelihoods Improvement for Women and Youth). 2023. "Programme Overview." https://liway.org/shared-files/951/?Programme-Overview-June-2023.pdf.

Rougeaux, Solene, and Saint-Martin Kodjovi Mongan Agbeshie. 2024. "Helping Youth in Benin Find Economic Opportunities." *World Bank Blogs,* January 30, 2024. https://blogs.worldbank.org/africacan/helping-youth-benin-find-economic-opportunities.

World Bank. 2019. *World Development Report 2019: The Changing Nature of Work.* Washington, DC: World Bank. https://www.worldbank.org/en/publication/wdr2019.

CHAPTER 4
Program Delivery at Scale and Policy Integration

KEY MESSAGES

- Effective program delivery depends on well-structured institutional arrangements and organizational frameworks. Fifty-seven percent of the programs surveyed report they have scaled up institutionally. The external service providers, including nongovernmental organizations, engaged by many programs often play a pivotal role in scaling up government-led programs.

- Programs use community structures throughout the delivery chain to build community ownership and enhance cost-effectiveness. Increasing access to digital technologies is also playing a role in innovation and delivery at scale.

- For many programs, embedding economic inclusion in government systems and policies is a priority to achieve sustainability. Securing sustainable financing and improving the understanding of how decisions are made within government structures will help programs scale up to reach all people living in extreme poverty.

Introduction

Because of the multidimensional nature of economic inclusion programs, effective implementation relies on well-structured institutional arrangements and organizational frameworks. The institutional scale-up in the past two years that 57 percent of programs have reported has emerged in various ways, including expanding capacity within implementing organizations and establishing new partnerships or institutions (26 percent); integrating economic inclusion programs into government structures through policy, programming, and systemic changes (16 percent); and operationalizing through building or using delivery systems (45 percent).

Government programs layer their economic inclusion approaches on a wide range of sectoral interventions, including social safety nets, jobs and skills, agriculture, and environment. This trend reveals that economic inclusion programs are not only expanding their reach in coverage but also are embedding themselves within broader institutional frameworks. However, efforts to scale up economic inclusion programs can encounter numerous institutional constraints such as lack of organizational coordination and capacity or the absence of delivery systems. Addressing these challenges is imperative for scale-up (Carter, Joshi, and Remme 2018; Cooley and Linn 2014).

Coordination and managing the interests of a range of stakeholders are key. For government-led programs, creating partnerships within government ministries and departments and collaborating with diverse stakeholders—including community organizations, nongovernmental organizations (NGOs), and the private sector— are critical to mitigating institutional constraints. For nongovernment-led programs, operating within the broader institutional and policy framework of governments requires additional coordination and stakeholder management. To overcome the institutional challenges, these programs must navigate diverse interests and ensure sustained cooperation among stakeholders for building a coalition of support for economic inclusion programs.

Institutional constraints are further shaped by the broader policy frameworks under which programs operate, whether social protection, livelihood, or environmental policies. Establishing an enabling policy environment—which includes providing access to resources, creating regulatory frameworks, and streamlining bureaucratic processes— is an ongoing challenge requiring continual engagement with policy makers to align livelihood strategies and policies with program objectives (Beegle, Coudouel, and Monsalve 2018).

Securing financing brings its own set of challenges, notably the need to ensure sustainability for both government- and nongovernment-led programs. Achieving financial sustainability requires strategically reallocating funding toward cost-effective initiatives and reducing inefficient spending within broader social protection and livelihood programming, particularly for government-led programs. For example, in Kenya and Uganda, the Village Enterprise Development Impact Bond attracted the additional resources needed to scale up a program dedicated to creating and sustaining microenterprises, ultimately helping the extreme-poor population achieve economic self-sufficiency (Njogu-Ndongwe et al. 2022).

This chapter addresses the institutional dimensions of scaling up for economic inclusion programming and examines the diverse arrangements for achieving scale in view of the operational and organizational challenges. It especially examines the strategies used by these programs to leverage existing platforms and systems—such as community structures and digital delivery mechanisms—to reduce costs while upholding quality at scale. It also explores the process of integrating economic inclusion programs into the broader policy and strategic framework of the governments.

Implementation Arrangements Vary Widely to Ensure Effective Delivery

Both government organizations and NGOs lead economic inclusion programs, collaborating with other organizations to deliver program components. Collaboration entails careful consideration of the roles and responsibilities assigned to each organization based on its capacity and expertise. Effective coordination and stakeholder management are critical to ensuring seamless collaboration among the parties for the successful delivery and implementation of diverse elements.

Lead implementation agencies take on diverse roles throughout the delivery chain, including funding, targeting and enrollment, the delivery of program components, and monitoring, as well as grievance and case management (refer to figure 4.1). In addition, NGOs, community members, line ministries, and governments at different levels engage in implementation in different capacities alongside the lead agency.

Ninety percent of government programs are led by line ministries at the national level, and the remaining 10 percent are led by regional or local governments. Even when a ministry at the national level takes the lead, implementation is frequently decentralized to the regional and local levels. When one government agency assumes the lead role,

FIGURE 4.1   Percentage of Programs in Which the Lead Agency Plays Selected Roles

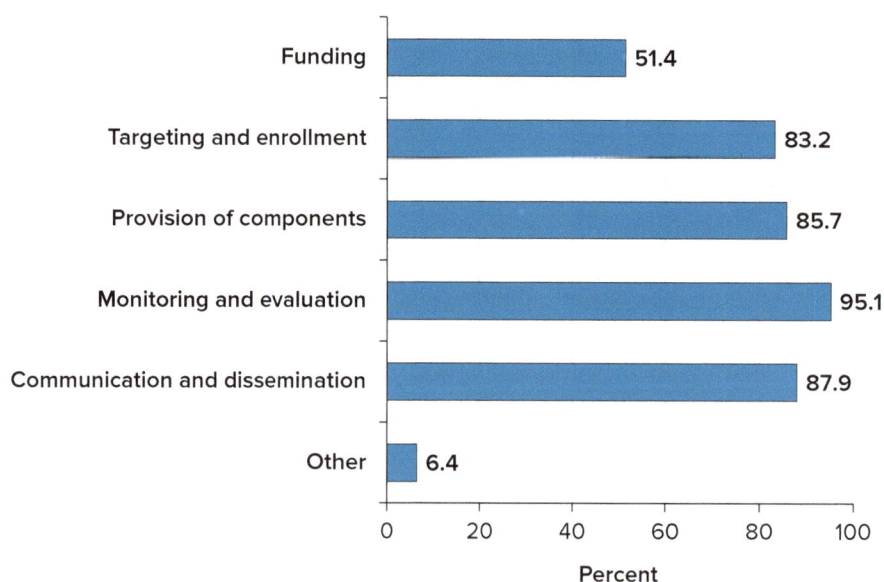

Role	Percent
Funding	51.4
Targeting and enrollment	83.2
Provision of components	85.7
Monitoring and evaluation	95.1
Communication and dissemination	87.9
Other	6.4

Source: Partnership for Economic Inclusion, World Bank.

Note: Figure shows the percentage of all programs (*N* = 405).

implementation involves multiple government agencies or departments in 67 percent of these programs.

Governments also collaborate in 53 percent of nongovernment-led programs and play a critical role in supporting NGOs, especially at the local level. They assist in needs assessments, provide infrastructure such as community centers, and encourage community participation. Local governments also facilitate data-sharing for evidence-based program design, contributing to successful collaboration with NGOs. This intricate interplay of leadership and collaboration reflects the complexity of the governance structure in economic inclusion initiatives.

The complexity of program delivery is further evident in the involvement of a diverse set of institutions beyond the lead implementing agency. For example, different organizations are engaged in targeting and enrollment and monitoring and evaluation in both government- and nongovernment-led programs (refer to figure 4.2). Governments at all levels—national, regional, and local—play roles in these functions. The community's role is particularly pronounced in targeting and enrollment because community engagement ensures that programs reach those who require assistance the most and builds ownership and participation.

FIGURE 4.2   **Percentage of Programs in Which an External Organization Plays Selected Roles, by Role Played**

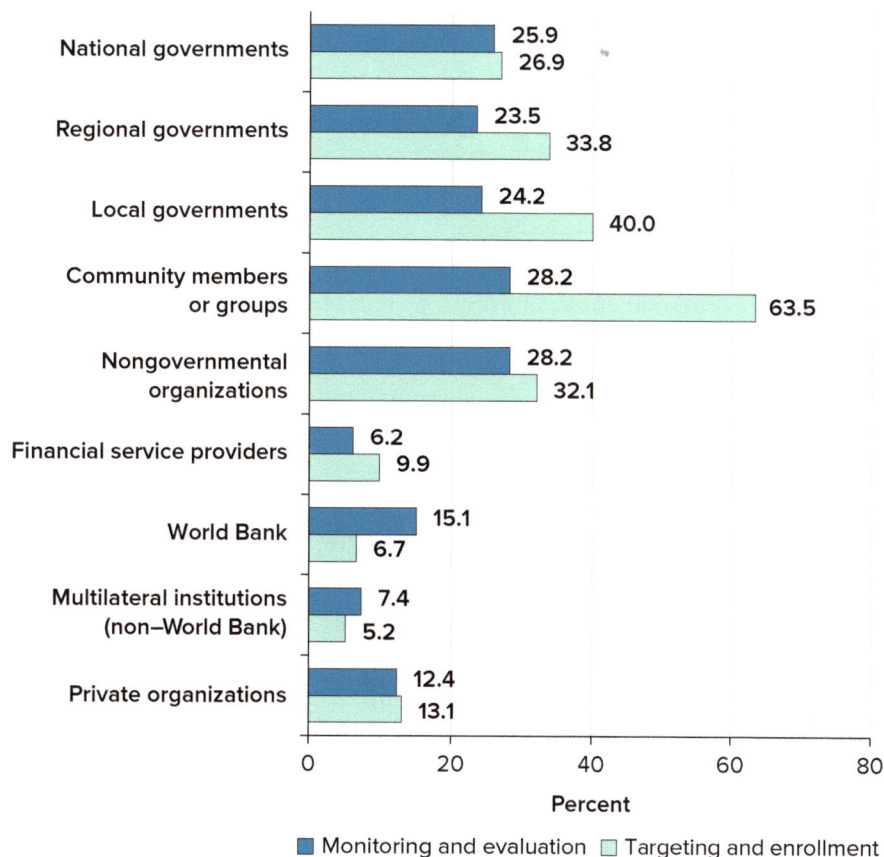

Source: Partnership for Economic Inclusion, World Bank.
Note: Figure shows the percentage of all programs (N = 405).

Because of the intricate and multidimensional attributes of economic inclusion programs, within governmental structures, the institutional frameworks are notably diverse. For government-led programs broadly, three delivery modalities are possible when scaling up, depending on the capacity of the lead implementing agency: (1) *deliver in-house*—that is, execute the program by directly recruiting, overseeing, and managing a substantial cohort of front-line personnel; (2) *deliver through interinstitutional coordination*—that is, engage in collaborative alliances with another governmental institution, line ministry, or departments or agencies within the same ministry; or (3) *deliver by hiring service providers*—that is, enlist the services of an NGO or private sector entity to provide human resource–intensive components, such as training and coaching, or outsource implementation completely to an external agency.

For implementation arrangements, more often nongovernment-led programs deliver a sequenced set of interventions in-house. However, collaboration with governments, especially at the local level, is critical for efficient delivery. In many instances, international NGOs are also collaborating with local NGOs and local governments to implement programs, leveraging collective expertise across organizations, similar to the interinstitutional coordination and delivery using external service providers observed within governments.

In-House Delivery Suits Programs with Existing Institutional Capacity

Government-led programs opt for in-house delivery most often when their institutional capacities are sufficiently robust to provide a package of interventions. This delivery method is common when a scaled-up safety net or livelihood program serves as the basis of interventions. Implementation arrangements are often decentralized, with local government structures assuming responsibility for program staffing and playing a pivotal role in the delivery of interventions. Concurrently, fiduciary and administrative oversight is managed at the regional and national levels of government, establishing a hierarchical structure that ensures effective governance and scrutiny throughout service delivery.

For area-focused programs, the livelihoods protection and rehabilitation activities in the Kenya Locust Response Project exemplifies this approach because it mobilized staffing and administrative capacities built during earlier projects. Led by the National Project Coordination Unit in the Ministry of Agriculture, the project emphasizes climate-smart practices, resilience building, and livelihood support. It builds on the successes of earlier projects, such as the Kenya Climate Smart Agriculture Project and the National Agriculture and Rural Inclusive Growth Project initiated in 2016 and 2017, respectively. Although concluded, these projects played a critical role in building the capacity of the ministry staff and refining procurement and financial management processes. The institutional strengthening arising from these foundational projects contributes significantly to the effective execution of the current economic inclusion initiative.

For programs delivered at the household level, the existing social safety nets serve as a robust institutional setup and delivery mechanism for effectively integrating and scaling up economic inclusion interventions. Existing institutional systems used to implement cash transfers or cash-for-work programs, which are often already at scale, can serve as a foundation for layering economic inclusion programs. The synergy between social safety nets and economic inclusion interventions can enhance the efficiency, reach, and impact of initiatives aimed at empowering individuals and communities economically. Box 4.1 illustrates how safety nets were effectively capitalized to scale up economic inclusion in Nigeria.

Some nongovernment-led programs, while relying on their internal capacity to deliver comprehensive economic inclusion packages by hiring front-line staff, also engage with external agencies, including the government, in the implementation process. Because nongovernment-led programs typically operate in specific geographic locations or target specific groups, they frequently enter into memorandums of understanding (MoUs) with local governments. These MoUs can leverage the expertise and community connections of the government's front-line staff, thereby providing stronger government buy-in and support for nongovernment-led programs.

For example, BOMA's Rural Entrepreneur Access Project (REAP), a gender-focused graduation model in Kenya, implements a sequenced set of interventions through trained front-line staff. These staff members serve as coaches, delivering training and mentoring, while also fulfilling the monitoring function to identify and address operational bottlenecks. BOMA involves stakeholders from county governments in steering committees to oversee the implementation progress, fostering government buy-in and enhancing BOMA's credibility within the community. This collaborative approach ensures that the program aligns with local priorities and policies, facilitating smoother integration and support from government entities.

BOX 4.1   Building on Existing Safety Nets and Delivery Systems in Nigeria

The adaptability and resilience of the foundational social protection systems were critical to the efficient delivery and rapid scale-up of economic inclusion programming in Nigeria.

The National Social Safety Nets Project (NASSP) began in 2016 with the goal of improving the country's social protection delivery systems. The project expanded the access of impoverished households to social safety nets and established a unified National Social Registry. NASSP was meticulously designed to align with an existing economic inclusion program, the Youth Employment and Social Support Operation (YESSO), which was launched in 2013. YESSO primarily concentrated on providing job support to youth through public works and life skills training, achieving significant progress by establishing state coordinating structures and social registries.

Building on the foundation laid by YESSO, NASSP expanded these activities to additional states. It also supported the operation of the National Social Safety Nets Coordinating Office at the federal level to coordinate all social protection interventions. This strategic move enabled the government to target and deliver livelihood programs to poor households. NASSP also introduced an economic inclusion component on top of the existing cash transfers, aiming to build sustainable livelihoods through government structures. A robust foundational safety net system was instrumental to the Nigerian government's swift response to the challenges posed by COVID-19. The COVID-19 Action Recovery and Economic Stimulus Program was designed to expand access to livelihood support, food security services, and grants for poor and vulnerable households and firms.

The use of established delivery platforms simplifies the implementation of program components such as cash transfers for consumption support or business capital and, in some cases, in-kind asset transfers. However, challenges arise when the delivery of human resource–intensive components, such as coaching and training by front-line staff, conflicts with competing responsibilities. Because the effectiveness of these interventions largely depends on the capacity of government personnel, building their capacity to address constraints and priorities is needed to ensure quality of implementation.

Interinstitutional Delivery Is Typical in More-Complex Programs with Diverse Objectives

The Landscape Survey 2023 indicates that in 67 percent of government-led economic inclusion programs, several government agencies are involved in implementation. However, the institutional arrangements vary widely. In some instances, two ministries may co-lead implementation, with one overseeing cash transfers or public works, while the other manages livelihood or job-related components such as training, coaching, and wage employment facilitation. Alternatively, programs may convene a steering committee of stakeholders from various ministries or agencies to provide oversight and administrative support. Bringing together capacity from different institutions to jointly provide program components rather than relying on a single ministry creates opportunities to achieve economies of scale, thereby leading to more impactful, cost-effective services and interventions. Box 4.2 describes how institutional links across ministries are used to scale an area-focused economic inclusion approach.

BOX 4.2 **Building Institutional Linkages in Ghana**

The Ghana Landscape Restoration and Small-Scale Mining Project exemplifies the importance of maintaining institutional memory and good governance mechanisms by bringing together practitioners from various sectors and encouraging joint decision-making to address the complex challenges of natural resources management and adaptation to climate change. The project is a collaborative effort led by two central agencies or ministries: the Environmental Protection Agency (EPA) and the Ministry of Lands and Natural Resources (MLNR). It is designed to deliver sustainable livelihoods through a multisectoral approach, recognizing the interconnectedness of environmental well-being and natural resources sustainability. The EPA takes the lead in investments related to production and forest landscapes, emphasizing the promotion of climate-smart agriculture, conservation efforts, and the establishment of value chains for key commodity crops. In response to the significant impact of mining on forest loss and waterways in Ghana, the MLNR supports appropriate forest landscape restoration opportunities and reclamation of mined-out areas, and it provides miners with alternative livelihood support.

This collaborative project leverages the expertise and engagement of multiple implementing ministries and agencies. It builds on the foundation laid by the Sustainable Land and Water Management Project (SLWMP), the Forest Investment

(Box continues next page)

BOX 4.2   **Building Institutional Linkages in Ghana** *(continued)*

Project, and technical assistance provided by the Natural Resources and Environmental Governance initiative, which reflects decades of World Bank involvement in Ghana's natural resources management sector. SLWMP played a critical role in mainstreaming implementation across various ministries and agencies, equipping government staff with the technical skills and leadership qualities needed to address multisectoral landscape issues and engage diverse stakeholders. SLWMP deliberately engaged technically skilled staff from key agencies at both national and district levels rather than rely solely on project-specific consultants. This approach fostered a higher level of commitment, enabled networking within the agencies, consolidated project gains, and deepened results over the 10-year duration of the project (World Bank 2021a). Retaining key government staff and supplementing them with technical support from consultants as needed are now proving pivotal in achieving the current project's ambitious goals.

Despite good intentions and formalized agreements, achieving effective coordination between different agencies can be difficult. Challenges often arise from the limited operational capacity across departments, a lack of clarity in terms of responsibilities, and the time needed for coordination mechanisms to function effectively. Establishing clear communication channels, defining roles and responsibilities, and streamlining coordination are essential steps toward achieving a successful multisectoral approach.

One example of institutional challenges was the recently concluded Strengthening Social Protection and Inclusion System Project in Panama. Initiated in 2015, it sought to enhance the efficiency of the social protection system and improve the income-generating capacity of poor and vulnerable people. In addition to cash transfers, participants received technical and vocational training and wage employment support. The Ministry of Social Development led the overall project implementation. The National Professional Training Institute (INADEH) in the Ministry of Education and the Ministry of Labor (MITRADEL) led the training and wage employment services, respectively, and acted as technical co-executing agencies.

Collaboration among the three ministries posed significant challenges, however, leading to substantial delays in project implementation. Key contributing factors included the problems encountered in signing interinstitutional agreements with INADEH and MITRADEL to identify their roles and responsibilities in program delivery. Consequently, the project's scope and expected coverage were significantly reduced. Despite the original design featuring a technically sound implementation model with individual agencies assigned service delivery responsibilities, the actual interagency cooperation fell short of expectations, highlighting the complexities involved in coordinating efforts across multiple ministries (World Bank, IEG Review Team 2023).

Economic inclusion programs require robust intra- and interinstitutional coordination. However, achieving effective coordination can be difficult due to institutional rigidities, prioritization of individual objectives over collective goals, and a lack of incentives for joint efforts (box 4.3 describes lessons learned on implementation challenges in Iraq). Some programs have successfully developed political and interagency agreements that clearly define the expected value added from collaboration. Adopting an overarching strategy and promoting a culture of information-sharing through integrated systems can also improve coordination across different entities. These measures can overcome challenges and create a more-cohesive approach to implementing economic inclusion initiatives.

BOX 4.3   **Why Do Some Economic Inclusion Programs Fail? Lessons from Iraq**

Alignment across ministries, institutionalization for sustainability, and a robust fiduciary capacity are important for the delivery of economic inclusion projects, especially in contexts of fragility. The Emergency Social Stabilization and Resilience Project (ESSRP) initiated by the government of Iraq and financed by the World Bank aimed to facilitate recovery in areas liberated from ISIS in 2018. Led by the Ministry of Labor and Social Affairs (MOLSA), the project sought to increase livelihood opportunities, provide psychosocial support, and strengthen social safety nets. However, challenges such as delays in launching activities, procurement issues, and noncompliance with legal covenants led to the project's suspension. Key lessons learned from the ESSRP include the following:

- *Establish a realistic design and implementation timeline.* The project's ambitious three-year timeline proved unrealistic, especially in a context of conflict and violence. Building local capacity takes time, affecting institutional coordination, government ownership, and effective project execution.

- *Ensure alignment with the core responsibilities of the implementing ministries.* The introduction of activities beyond MOLSA's usual scope posed challenges in ownership and commitment to project implementation.

- *Institutionalize a cash-for-work program.* The sustainability of the program relied on integration within MOLSA systems. The limited engagement of MOLSA in implementation and a lack of clarity on institutionalization hindered program sustainability.

- *Establish adequate fiduciary capacity, and eliminate implementation roadblocks.* The inadequate fiduciary capacity of MOLSA emerged as a significant roadblock, and staff turnover in the project management office led to training challenges. Adequate fiduciary capacity is critical to effective implementation, and addressing turnover is essential for maintaining consistency and expertise.

Source: World Bank 2021b.

FIGURE 4.3   **Percentage of Programs in Which External Organizations Are Involved in Program Service Delivery**

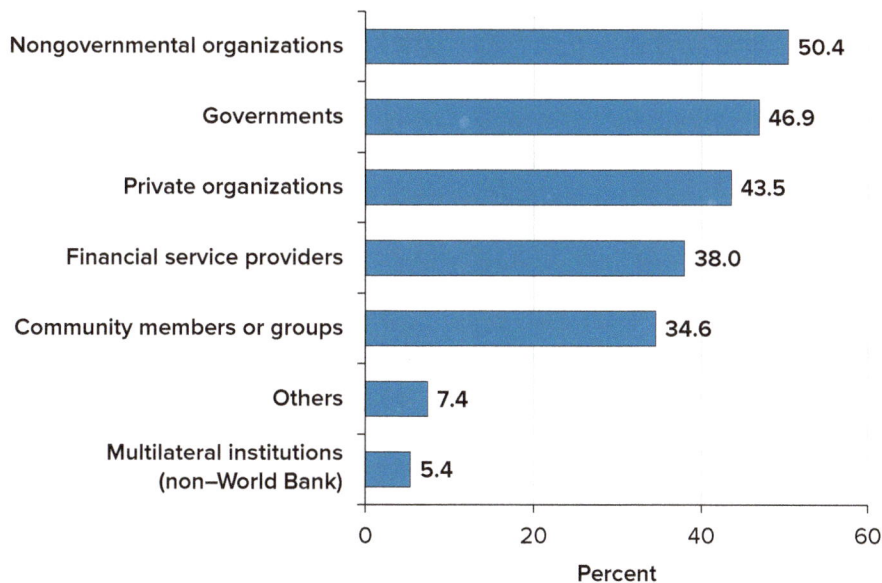

Source: Partnership for Economic Inclusion, World Bank.
Note: Figure shows the percentage of all programs (N = 405).

External Service Providers Can Help Address Capacity Constraints

Both government- and nongovernment-led programs rely extensively on external agencies for service delivery, with NGOs assuming a pivotal role as essential service providers for governments. Globally, 81 percent of surveyed programs collaborate with external agencies to deliver at least one program component. For government-led programs, this figure rises to 91 percent. Figure 4.3 illustrates the percentage of programs in the Landscape Survey 2023 in which external agencies are engaged in the delivery of program components. Governments' reliance on service providers is especially evident in the delivery of wage employment, training, and coaching.

Collaboration enables governments to overcome capacity and expertise constraints. Arrangements with service providers depend on the project design, components, and capacity of the lead implementing agency.

Engaging NGOs as service providers can be an important strategy for scaling up economic inclusion programming through government systems, especially in low-capacity contexts. The Eastern Recovery Project in the Democratic Republic of Congo is an example of a government-led initiative in which local NGOs play a pivotal role. This program provides productive inclusion measures for both labor-intensive public works participants in urban areas and the recipients of unconditional cash transfers in rural areas. Local NGOs are instrumental in the capacity-building of local development committees and training of participants.

Some government programs initiate economic inclusion measures by means of pilot phases with support from NGOs for design and initial implementation, while concurrently building in-house capacity. For example, in the Kenya Social and Economic Inclusion Project, this phased approach allows for a learning-by-doing process, with the government gradually assuming more responsibilities as it develops capacity. This approach also refines implementation tools and systems based on practical experience, contributing to the successful scale-up of multifaceted programs. The sequenced process involves the development of operational guidelines and participant training materials, along with building the capacity of government staff during the initial round of implementation.

Programs aimed at labor market integration also often depend on NGOs and the private sector for technical and vocational skills training, as well as for wage employment and referrals. To ensure long-term sustainability, governments establish formal fee-for-service agreements with external service providers at both the national and regional levels. Implementation is then coordinated by government staff at the local level, fostering collaboration between public and private entities for effective, sustainable labor market integration. For example, Argentina's FOMENTAR active labor market initiative, led by the Ministry of Human Capital, enhances jobs prospects through skills training, internships, and career guidance. Collaborating with NGOs and private training institutions, the decentralized structure ensures delivery at both the national and local levels. Municipal employment offices play a critical role, facilitating access to services, while the centralized Employment Portal streamlines registration. Leveraging Argentina's extensive experience in labor market programs and a competency-based certification system, the program is an example of successful collaboration with an NGO and the private sector to achieve overarching goals.

Some governments adopt a twofold approach to economic inclusion: (1) augment both self-employment and wage employment jobs for poor and vulnerable people, and (2) create an ecosystem of collaboration with NGOs and the private sector for sustainability. Box 4.4 illustrates how a program in the Arab Republic of Egypt is delivered in collaboration with external agencies.

BOX 4.4   Creating an Economic Inclusion Ecosystem in the Arab Republic of Egypt

Led by the Ministry of Social Solidarity, the FORSA (Opportunity) program in Egypt incorporates in its self-employment and wage-focused economic inclusion strategies critical roles for nongovernmental organizations (NGOs) and the private sector in the delivery of the wage and self-employment components. To strengthen the capacity for coordination and oversight, the ministry has built robust institutional structures at both the central and local levels.

The NGOs conduct behavioral change sessions, using content provided by the FORSA team. These sessions guide program beneficiaries toward pathways that align with their profiles, whether wage or self-employment. Rigorously selected NGOs train participants and manage the procurement and transfer of assets for those on the self-employment

(Box continues next page)

BOX 4.4   **Creating an Economic Inclusion Ecosystem in the Arab Republic of Egypt** *(continued)*

track. For those on the wage employment track, the project has signed direct agreements with NGOs for training and facilitating their employment and with private sector companies to provide jobs for FORSA participants. This approach was adopted because of the lower skill levels and limited work experience of the participants. The program has also organized employment fairs to create opportunities for participants within the private sector (World Bank, Partnership for Economic Inclusion 2022).

While collaborating with external agencies is often sought to address capacity constraints, challenges can arise from poor communication and coordination between government agencies and those agencies, hindering the smooth implementation of economic inclusion programs. The inherent complexity and sometimes slow-moving nature of government bureaucracies can delay decision-making and program implementation. As a result, NGOs may face challenges in navigating intricate government systems and critical program delivery timelines can be affected, hindering participant progress.

Engaging the Private Sector in Service Delivery Shows Strong Potential

Nearly 60 percent of surveyed programs acknowledge some level of private sector engagement in the delivery chain. The private sector can bring valuable resources, expertise, and innovation to programs, making them pivotal partners in improving the livelihoods of poor and vulnerable people. Private financial institutions are already playing a critical role in financial inclusion by providing access to credit, facilitating savings, and offering vulnerable populations other financial services, such as insurance. For example, the Strengthening Women's Ability for Productive New Opportunities Project in Bangladesh collaborates with established microfinance institutions such as the Bangladesh Rural Advancement Committee and Grameen Bank to offer tailored financial services.

The private sector also contributes by designing and implementing innovative financial products, such as weather-indexed insurance and crop-specific credit, for smallholder farmers and vulnerable communities. The World Bank's De-risking, Inclusion, and Value Enhancement of Pastoral Economies in the Horn of Africa Project collaborates with a leading private sector reinsurance company to insure livestock losses arising from unpreventable natural disasters and climate risks. The creation of innovation hubs or incubators in collaboration with the private sector is fostering entrepreneurship and supporting the development of new business ventures.

Looking ahead, efforts to capitalize on the private sector's expertise in program delivery are needed. Possibilities are collaborating with private companies to provide technical and vocational training to enhance the employability of target populations; seeking the private sector to help improve access to markets and the value chain integration of smallholder farmers; involving the private sector in fair trade practices and ethical sourcing, thereby ensuring equitable prices for products produced by poor and vulnerable people; and collaborating with private sector companies, often at the forefront of technology development, to introduce innovative solutions for enhancing productivity and improved service delivery. The widespread use of mobile technology for financial transactions and payments, along with the application of precision agriculture techniques to improve agricultural productivity, can benefit vulnerable people in shock-prone areas.

Incorporating Community Structures into Program Delivery Can Facilitate Local Buy-In

Economic inclusion programs rely on community structures and groups across the delivery chain, including for targeting and enrollment, intervention delivery, monitoring, and grievance and case management. By engaging community members, informal community savings and credit groups, local community governance groups, and formalized producer organizations, programs can cultivate trust and acceptance in the community, thereby bolstering social inclusion and participation in developing and implementing programs and empowering local leadership. Integrating complex economic inclusion programs within communities also gives communities a sense of ownership, improving program uptake and sustainability.

Programs that engage community structures for programming can, however, also encounter pitfalls. Elite capture may concentrate benefits among a few, excluding marginalized members. Criteria such as minimum land ownership to join farmer groups may unintentionally exclude vulnerable farmers. Gender, age, and disability biases can also hinder the full participation of certain groups. Limited representation and social capital, cultural barriers, and inadequate empowerment efforts can perpetuate exclusion, impeding the effectiveness of community-based livelihood initiatives. Addressing these pitfalls requires a holistic approach that promotes inclusivity and social equity, ensuring that programs benefit community members regardless of their background or status.

Engagement of Community Members Can Enhance Cost-Effectiveness but May Affect Quality

Some programs formally engage community members in implementation by introducing selection criteria for their participation as facilitators (refer to box 4.5 for examples from Ghana and Tanzania). Facilitators are assigned well-defined roles and responsibilities in program activities at both the individual or household and group levels. Notably, a deliberate emphasis on prioritizing women encourages gender inclusion and augments female participation in program delivery. Scaling up economic inclusion programs using local community individuals for service delivery can also enhance cost-effectiveness and appeal to policy makers.

Quality trade-offs and implementation challenges can arise, however, particularly with intensive components such as coaching. A review of the Adaptive Social Protection program in the Sahel region of Africa revealed different approaches to coaching. In Senegal, nonlocal field agents faced difficulties in building trust, whereas in Niger, the use of coaches from the local communities proved more cost-effective. Challenges in Niger included recruiting adequately educated community coaches and ensuring a uniform understanding of coaching manuals, which relied on pictures because of language and education disparities (Sumanthiran and Roelen 2023). However, these findings are contextual. Programs should invest in diagnostics and monitoring to identify the most effective coaching approaches tailored to context.

BOX 4.5   Engaging Community Facilitators in Ghana and Tanzania

Ghana

The Complementary Livelihood and Assets Support Scheme in Ghana has adopted a structured approach to engage community facilitators in service delivery. These facilitators are selected through a formal process based on criteria such as education level, language proficiency, information and communication technology orientation, proximity to the community, and credibility within the community. Priority is given to female candidates to deepen gender inclusion and female participation in program delivery.

Upon selection, facilitators receive an official appointment letter from the local government that clearly outlines the terms of reference, duration of the assignment, and details of their entitlements. These facilitators play a pivotal role as intermediaries between the local government and the implementation focal points at the community level. Their responsibilities include mobilizing the community and facilitating beneficiary selection, monitoring skills training using biometric-enabled tablets, facilitating grant disbursements, monitoring coaching sessions through a dedicated software application, facilitating grievance redress, and promoting social accountability. The accountability of facilitators is ensured through the submission of monthly monitoring reports.

Tanzania

The Productive Social Safety Net Project in Tanzania has adopted a distinctive approach to community facilitators by selecting them from the communities, specifically targeting those with a certain level of education and those who are locally based. These facilitators, who receive specialized training, are informally invited to contribute to project delivery, leveraging their status as community members to establish trust and a drawing on their nuanced understanding of their peers' challenges. Facilitators promote savings groups, help participants complete business plans and grant application forms, collaborate with local government officers to address these challenges, and support the development of monitoring plans for households and groups. Facilitators also encourage participation in internal monitoring and evaluation of activities, thereby encouraging a sense of ownership and accountability among beneficiaries.

Community-Led Producer Groups Support the Creation of Rural Enterprise Ecosystems

Programs in both the agricultural and nonagricultural sectors collaborate with producer groups within community structures. These programs encourage smallholder farmers to form groups, thereby improving their market access and economic well-being. By acting collectively, groups can pool their resources, share knowledge, and negotiate together with buyers, boosting their bargaining power. Formalizing producer groups empowers economically disadvantaged farmers, addressing access challenges in remote areas. It also improves coordination and access to resources and establishes a structured framework for interventions, enabling the integration of more households into well-managed and monitored producer groups (box 4.6 describes how a program in India has integrated participants into producer groups to create a rural enterprise ecosystem). Finally, collaboration with community organizations extends beyond mere implementation support. These efforts frequently serve as the basis for social and professional networks for program participants—an integral component of a comprehensive support package.

BOX 4.6   **Enterprise Ecosystem Development in India**

Using community structures via a tiered group approach allows projects to seamlessly integrate participants into value chains, thereby contributing to higher income and employment outcomes. In Bihar, India, Satat Jeevikoparjan Yojana (SJY) is a notable government-led scale-up of the graduation approach. Implemented by the Bihar Rural Livelihoods Promotion Society (JEEViKA), SJY uses existing community structures to enhance efficacy.

JEEViKA, as the implementing agency of the National Rural Livelihoods Mission, mobilizes rural women to join community institutions, including self-help groups, village organizations, commodity-specific producer groups, and higher cluster-level federations. Self-help savings and credit groups, facilitated by JEEViKA, operate at the village level, conducting regular meetings and exploring financial savings and internal lending.

JEEViKA's Community Investment Fund stimulates financial activities. Village organizations, composed of multiple self-help groups, act as intermediaries between local banks and member groups. These organizations develop cluster-level federations, which are large financial intermediation platforms. SJY is seamlessly integrated into JEEViKA's community structures, leveraging their strengths and operational capacity. Village organizations and self-help groups play a central role in the SJY beneficiary selection process and key implementation phases, ensuring effective program delivery.

Similarly, the Tamil Nadu Rural Transformation Project has adopted a three-tiered, structured approach emphasizing the formation of collective enterprises. In the first tier, enterprise groups at the community or village level engage up to 30 members in shared farming- and nonfarming-related production directly connected to the market. Producer groups form the second tier, involving producers in aggregation and basic processing and establishing direct links with the market. In the third tier, producer groups are aggregated into higher-order producer collectives, functioning as membership-based organizations representing the groups. The collectives create value for producers through access to inputs, technologies, services, finance, and market links.

Community Savings Groups Promote Financial Inclusion, but Inadvertent Social Exclusion Can Occur

The use of community structures to form new savings groups or rely on existing ones is a common and effective strategy of economic inclusion programs. Community-driven initiatives empower individuals, particularly those in economically vulnerable situations, to save money, access loans, and benefit from financial inclusion. They also have significant nonfinancial benefits, as they can build valuable social networks and elevate the community profile of excluded women and men. Program facilitators work with community members to form small savings groups based on common interests, geographical proximity, or other relevant criteria.

Savings groups often consist of 10–20 members who pool their savings and make collective decisions. Groups establish their own norms, rules, and operational procedures. These guidelines help build trust among group members, ensure transparency and accountability in financial transactions, and are adaptable to allow groups to meet their needs and to fit into different intervention packages.

Box 4.7 demonstrates a structured approach to savings group formation in Malawi. Traditional methods of mobilizing savings groups have inherently tended to exclude the poorest individuals, who may lack common interests or social connections and are perceived as posing a high financial risk to other members. This exclusionary trend is also observed among people with disabilities, Indigenous groups, and marginalized individuals (Fernández-Olit, Paredes-Gázquez, and de la Cuesta-González 2018). Programs should, then, invest in significant efforts to either integrate poor, vulnerable, and marginalized individuals into existing community groups or establish new groups specifically composed of these marginalized members.

BOX 4.7   A Structured Approach to Savings Groups in Malawi

Malawi's Social Support for Resilient Livelihoods Project forms savings and loans groups in collaboration with Malawi's leading cooperative union, COMSIP. Using outcome indicators to measure success, the project unfolds in distinct phases facilitated by extension workers and caseworkers:

- *Mobilization.* Clarify and express collective needs, using recorded discussions and a register of members to help measure success.
- *Formation.* Bring together the group of members seeking benefits, using a group constitution, minutes, initial savings, and a community facilitator to measure success.
- *Group stability.* Maintain a fully functional group whose members actively contribute and adhere to norms, using fewer visits from extension workers, independent decision-making, proper record-keeping, initiation of group businesses, and increased savings as measures of success.
- *Sustainability.* Achieve long-term viability and links with other financial institutions, using stable group businesses and asset creation demonstrating sustainability beyond project phase-out as measures of success.

Although using community structures enhances cost-effectiveness and sustainability in livelihood programs, maintaining program quality requires a balanced approach that incorporates external expertise, accountability mechanisms, and ongoing capacity-building support within the community structures. Community-based delivery relies on peer support, knowledge sharing, and resource pooling; reducing costs associated with program delivery; and monitoring and supervision using external service providers. Although cost-effective resource mobilization at the community level is valuable, providing the proper training and support for community members is essential for effective implementation. Programs should strategically assess where to use the expertise of local NGOs, because these organizations typically have established systems for accountability and monitoring, ensuring adherence to quality standards.

While community models are crucial for engagement, an often-overlooked challenge is the overburdening of these community institutions. These issues can result in decreased program effectiveness and lower community engagement. To mitigate these risks, practitioners should conduct capacity assessments before integrating economic inclusion interventions, prioritize core objectives to maintain focus, and coordinate across programs to prevent duplication and streamline activities. Providing adequate support and training to community leaders and members can help build capacity to deliver effectively.

For community-based approaches that also focus on social inclusion, practitioners implementing economic inclusion programs must carefully balance the dynamics between economic and social inclusion. One key challenge is *sequencing*—ensuring social inclusion is established before introducing economic interventions is critical.

Digital Platforms and Tools Can Significantly Facilitate Service Delivery

Many programs capitalize on digital technologies to deliver components. The increasing accessibility and affordability of digital technologies present a significant opportunity to reach remote communities and tailor interventions to target groups. According to the Landscape Survey 2023, 93 percent of programs use digital technologies. Digital tools are integrated across the delivery chain, with programs using technology for targeting and enrollment and monitoring and evaluation (refer to figure 4.4).

Geospatial data can enhance the targeting of poor and vulnerable populations, and digital platforms can streamline the registration and enrollment processes. Online registration forms and digital databases allow program teams to collect and manage participant information more efficiently. Biometric technologies, such as fingerprint or iris scanning, can play a role in accurate participant identification, preventing duplication, reducing fraud, and ensuring benefits reach the intended recipients.

FIGURE 4.4   Percentage of Programs Using Digital Technology for Program Management and Delivery

a. Program activities undertaken using digital technologies

b. Components delivered using digital technologies

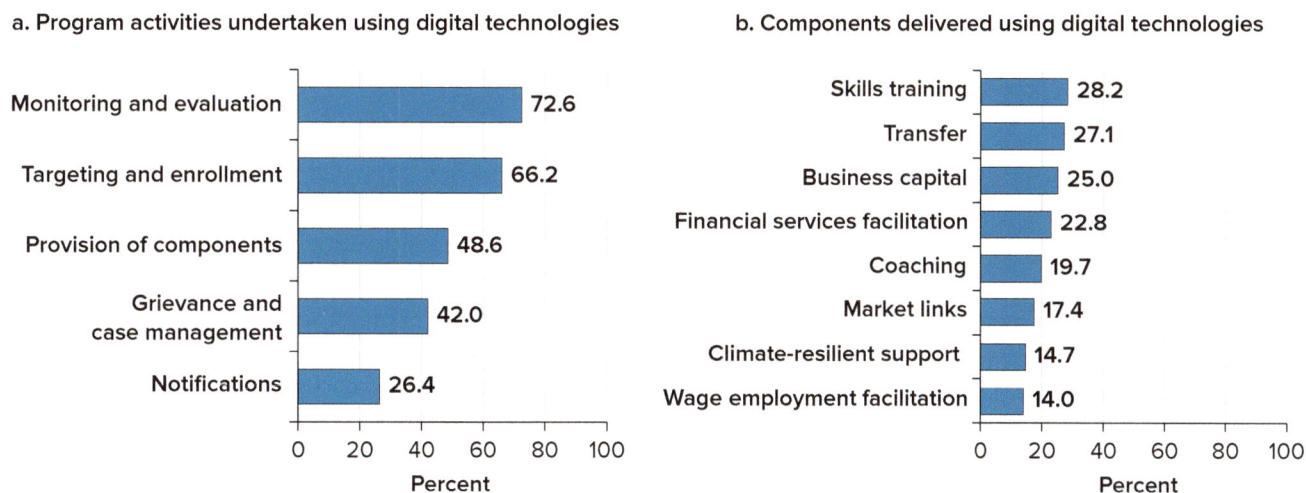

Source: Partnership for Economic Inclusion, World Bank.

Note: Panel a shows the percentage of all programs (*N* = 405). Panel b shows the percentage of programs providing components digitally out of those providing a given component (skills training, *N* = 387; transfer, *N* = 218; business capital, *N* = 312; financial services facilitation, *N* = 298; coaching, *N* = 361; market links, *N* = 299; climate-resilient support, *N* = 266; and wage employment facilitation, *N* = 136). Multiple responses were possible.

Governments are using digital tools to deliver business capital. Digital financial services and electronic payment systems, including mobile money and direct bank transfers, are commonly used to disburse cash. These methods enhance transparency, reduce leakage, and give participants convenient and secure access to funds.

Expansion of the digital government-to-person (G2P) payments model underscores the potential to scale up the cash-based components of economic inclusion interventions. For example, Zambia's Girls' Education and Women's Empowerment and Livelihood Project has provided cash transfers and business grants to approximately 140,000 women to date using G2P, which allows participants to choose from six financial service providers. Short message service (SMS) and automated messaging systems are being used to communicate with participants. Payment updates are sent via text messages to community and district facilitators, ensuring timely and effective communication.

Programs are also using digital technologies for training and coaching, with nongovernment-led programs taking the lead in piloting these innovative solutions for greater cost-effectiveness. Some programs, especially in middle-income contexts, use digital platforms for training and capacity-building of both participants and program staff. For example, the Support to Women Entrepreneurs program in Chile provides online training for refugee women in the basics of entrepreneurship, such as business plans and digital marketing.

In some countries, nongovernment-led programs deliver coaching using computer tablets and mobile phones. In many Latin American countries, including Brazil, Colombia, and Paraguay, Fundación Capital and some of their government partners use digital tools, such as apps and chatbots, to help coaches provide more tailored support and improve responses to participants' needs. Despite the promise shown by digital platforms and apps, it can be challenging to recruit and train sufficiently educated community coaches (Sumanthiran and Roelen 2023). Indeed, although technology offers valuable tools, limitations must be addressed—among them, the availability of qualified coaches or trainers and the need to adapt to varying literacy levels.

Some economic inclusion programs use digital tools and services specifically to enhance women's participation and contribute to their economic empowerment. Direct transfers to women's bank accounts or mobile wallets can expand their ownership of resources, and digital tools such as SMS and mobile apps can ensure that women are well-informed about program details, eligibility criteria, and the timing of benefit transfers. Although not yet widespread, some economic inclusion programs are improving women's access to markets by promoting their products on e-commerce platforms. Women can, then, reach a broader customer base and potentially increase sales, thereby strengthening their overall economic empowerment.

Digital technologies also play a pivotal role in monitoring the quality of service of delivery at scale. Digital tools enable real-time data collection through mobile surveys and applications. Fieldworkers can use mobile devices to collect information on program implementation, gather participant feedback, and acquire other pertinent data that provide timely and accurate insights. The integration of these tools allows programs to establish a more responsive and accountable system for managing grievances and cases, thereby not only streamlining the resolution process but also enhancing the overall effectiveness and credibility of initiatives. Spotlight 3 highlights the emerging innovations in the use of digital technologies in program delivery and the factors that must be considered when integrating digital technologies in programs.

Integrating Programs into National Policies Can Facilitate Political Support and Budget Allocation

Economic inclusion programs often align and sometimes integrate with national policies and strategies. Alignment with broader national objectives supports scalability and long-term sustainability. The integration of economic inclusion programs into government policies provides a legal framework that safeguards the rights of participants, particularly the extremely-poor and vulnerable populations these programs serve. Policy integration clearly delineates the responsibilities of implementing agencies and helps governments prioritize and allocate budgetary resources more effectively, ensuring that programs are funded adequately for optimal impact. Policy integration also improves coordination and collaboration among various government departments, leading to better-synchronized efforts and more-efficient use of resources.

The official recognition of economic inclusion programs in national policies can also generate political support, improving the navigation of political transitions and maintaining momentum. Integration further extends to data collection, monitoring, and evaluation, enabling policy makers to assess impacts and make informed decisions that will lead to more-effective programs. However, as discussed in *The State of Economic Inclusion Report 2021*, political economy also plays a role in program adoption and scale-up (Andrews et al. 2021).

In the context of climate change, policy makers in developing countries, where fiscal capacity is limited, may grapple with the challenge of balancing poverty reduction efforts with the imperative for climate change mitigation and adaptation. This balancing act requires thoughtful resource allocation between environmentally sustainable projects and poverty alleviation programs, recognizing potential trade-offs. Although well-designed climate policies can generate new job opportunities in sectors such as renewable energy, energy efficiency, and sustainable agriculture, they also may lead to job losses in traditional industries. Because poor and vulnerable populations often bear the brunt of climate change impacts, climate policies should prioritize building resilience in these communities, addressing both immediate poverty concerns and long-term climate-related challenges.

Sustainable Financing Is Critical for Piloting, Scale-Up, and Long-Term Success

Several pilot projects, initially funded by donors and spearheaded by NGOs, have informed the adoption and scale-up of government-led initiatives. These projects are underpinned by government policies and at least some financing from government budgets. However, external financing often remains essential. This reliance is unlikely to change substantially, especially in low-income settings where fiscal constraints prevail, and the situation may only intensify in the medium term due to ongoing and overlapping crises.

Because economic inclusion programs are designed to tackle enduring challenges such as poverty, inequality, and vulnerability, adequate and consistent funding is essential for long-lasting impacts. Sustainable financing provides predictability and facilitates better planning, ensuring that benefits and services are delivered consistently to poor and vulnerable populations. By contrast, unpredictable funding can result in interruptions and undermine the effectiveness of these programs, jeopardizing the intended positive outcomes. A stable, sustained financial framework is thus essential for the resilience and long-term success of economic inclusion initiatives.

Although most governments are funding economic inclusion programs to some extent, most programs still rely primarily on donors for funding and sustainability (refer to figure 4.5).[1] However, information on the share of government financing of programs is limited. Country-specific reviews of government expenditures in specific sectors are needed for a deeper understanding of government versus external funding. For nongovernment-led programs, bilateral agencies, the private sector, and regional multilateral institutions remain the key donors.

FIGURE 4.5   Percentage of Government- and Nongovernment-Led Programs Financed by External Institutions

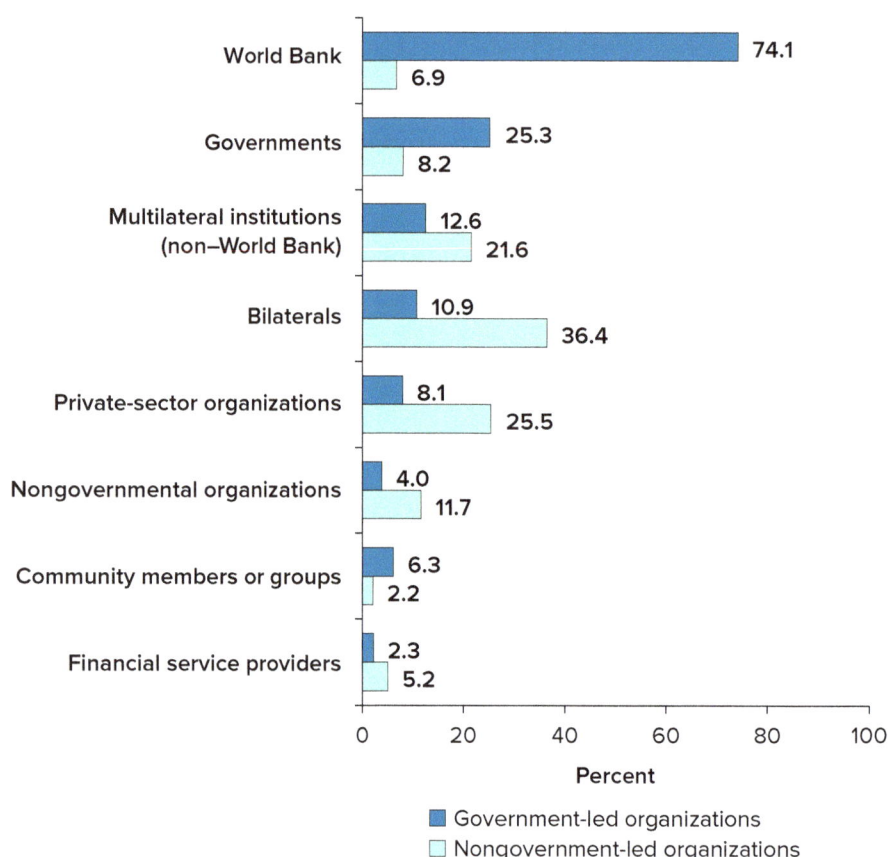

World Bank: 74.1 / 6.9
Governments: 25.3 / 8.2
Multilateral institutions (non–World Bank): 12.6 / 21.6
Bilaterals: 10.9 / 36.4
Private-sector organizations: 8.1 / 25.5
Nongovernmental organizations: 4.0 / 11.7
Community members or groups: 6.3 / 2.2
Financial service providers: 2.3 / 5.2

Percent (0, 20, 40, 60, 80, 100)

■ Government-led organizations
□ Nongovernment-led organizations

Source: Partnership for Economic Inclusion, World Bank.

Note: Figure shows the percentage of government- and nongovernment-led programs (N_1 = 174 and N_2 = 231).

After a substantial surge in programming, a primary concern is securing sustainable financing for sustained scale-up, particularly given the shifting donor-funding patterns arising from overlapping crises. In the aftermath of events such as the COVID-19 pandemic and the Russian Federation's invasion of Ukraine, which led to a food security crisis, donors prioritized humanitarian responses and scaled up cash transfers to address basic needs (Gentilini 2022). Many donors have offered emergency funding and embraced flexible approaches to help countries respond to the dynamic and evolving nature of these crises.

As illustrated by the expansion in economic inclusion programming, donors recognize the importance of sustaining economic inclusion efforts to build long-term resilience and address the broader socioeconomic impacts of such crises. Balancing the urgent needs of a humanitarian response with the imperative of sustaining economic inclusion initiatives becomes a critical consideration in ensuring comprehensive, enduring support in crisis-affected contexts. Philanthropic donors are also supporting the scale-up of government-led programming (refer to box 4.8).

BOX 4.8   Philanthropic Donors Supporting Government-Led Programs

Evolving collaboration among philanthropic donors, nongovernmental organizations, and government-led initiatives offers a promising avenue for donor funding to play a catalytic role in advancing economic inclusion while simultaneously leveraging existing government investments.

Co-Impact, a global organization that brings together philanthropists, foundations, and private sector partners, illustrates this approach. It offers funding that allows governments to access technical assistance from organizations such as Fundación Capital, which works with government agencies to design, implement, and integrate economic inclusion programs into larger successful initiatives, such as Tenonderã in Paraguay and Prospera Familia in São Paulo, Brazil. BRAC International recently signed a memorandum of understanding with the National Rural Livelihood Promotion Society in India to include the poorest communities in the Deendayal Antyodaya Yojana National Rural Livelihoods Mission, a flagship program of the Ministry of Rural Development devoted to uplifting rural livelihoods and reducing poverty.

Similarly, ideas42 collaborates with many country governments—including the Democratic Republic of Congo, Ethiopia, Ghana, Sierra Leone, South Sudan, and Tanzania—to address behavioral barriers related to saving and investment by program participants. The support from ideas42, funded by bilateral and philanthropic donors such as the Global Innovation Fund, comes at no cost to the governments. Similarly, the Bill and Melinda Gates Foundation is supporting Village Enterprise in Kenya, which is collaborating with county and national governments on scaling up graduation approaches.

Impact bonds are another emerging innovation reshaping the financing landscape for programs. The Village Enterprise Development Impact Bond (DIB), the first for poverty alleviation in Africa, involved partners such as the United States Agency for International Development, Foreign, Commonwealth & Development Office (formerly the Department for International Development); Village Enterprise; Instiglio; and the Global Development Incubator. The DIB's structure linked outcome payments to an impact evaluation when Village Enterprise received funds tied to an increase in household income. This model paid approximately US$1 for every US$1 increase in income.

Subsequently, projects will aim to streamline the model, making it an effective blueprint for results-based financing in efforts to reduce extreme poverty. Plans for an outcomes fund call for supporting more experiments, and engaging future outcome payers and service providers in order to scale outcomes funding in poverty alleviation.

Examples of Successful Policy Integration Are Emerging

Programs can be fully integrated into government policy only if they are also included in the broader framework of governmental plans. This strategic alignment ensures that economic inclusion becomes a central and coordinated aspect of decision-making, resource allocation, and long-term planning. Sustainable financing, measurable outcomes, stakeholder involvement, and adaptability are key components of cultivating policy integration.

Pathways for integration into national policies span various sectors, including food security, social protection and labor, skills development, rural transformation, and climate resilience. Although most government-led economic inclusion programs are aligned with broader sectoral policies, they are not always formally integrated at the policy level. Aligning economic inclusion initiatives with overarching national policies across diverse sectors not only enhances their impact but also ensures their continued relevance and effectiveness in addressing the multiple constraints facing poor and vulnerable people. If carried out well, this integration could facilitate a holistic and coordinated approach, leading to the long-term sustainability of economic inclusion efforts within the larger national development agenda.

Some economic inclusion programs are becoming a key feature of livelihood policies. For example, India's National Rural Livelihoods Mission, a flagship program funded by the national and state governments to promote economic inclusion among poor rural households, is integrated into the country's overall livelihood strategy (refer to boxes 4.6 and 4.8).

Following years of technical assistance from and policy dialogue with partners such as Fundación Capital, the Tenonderã Project in Paraguay has evolved into a multifaceted program focused on self-employment. The government institutionalized the project in 2017 by including it in its legal framework, which reflects the government's commitment to its funding and sustainability. Since 2014, the project has been fully funded by the government, with a dedicated line in the annual budget of the Ministry of Social Development. From 2014 to 2019, the annual expenditure of the project rose substantially, from US$0.66 million to approximately US$6 million (ECLAC n.d.). In 2022, the government approved a redesign of Tenonderã, adapting it to a more-classical poverty graduation approach (Resolutions 889/2022 and 128/2024).

BRAC is partnering with several governments to scale graduation and recently signed an MOU with the National Rural Livelihood Promotion Society in India to include the communities furthest behind under the Deendayal Antyodaya Yojana National Rural Livelihoods Mission, a flagship program of the Ministry of Rural Development, focused on building rural livelihoods and reducing poverty. In addition, Rwanda, under the Ministry of Local Government, launched a National Strategy for Sustainable Graduation in 2022 to scale graduation with BRAC's support and empower people in more than 900,000 households in poverty to develop sustainable, long-term livelihoods, as part of a broader strategy to eradicate extreme poverty by 2030. Box 4.9 demonstrates how the government of Rwanda is integrating graduation into social protection policy.

BOX 4.9   **Evolution of a National Strategy of Sustainable Graduation in Rwanda**

Rwanda has made significant strides in integrating the graduation approach into its social protection policy and programs, emphasizing continual monitoring and adaptive management for a sustained impact.

Implementation of the Vision Umurenge Program as a flagship social protection program since 2008 generated valuable lessons that influenced development of the National Social Protection Strategy in 2011. Guidelines on graduation within the program were formalized in 2012.

The commitment to graduation approach gained momentum with the 2013–18 National Social Protection Strategy, featuring specific outcomes related to graduation. Introduction of the Minimum Package for Graduation (MPG) in 2015 marked a practical step toward translating graduation rhetoric into action. The National Strategy for Transformation 1 (2017–24) elevated the importance of graduation from extreme poverty, making it a prominent feature of the social transformation pillar, with priority given to promoting resilience and enhancing graduation from poverty or extreme poverty.

Graduation was formally defined for the first time in the 2020 National Social Protection Policy for Rwanda as "A situation whereby a previously poor household increases their household productivity and resilience to the extent that their consumption permanently remains over and above the official poverty line" (Rwanda Ministry of Local Government 2020, iv).

The recently cabinet-approved National Strategy for Sustainable Graduation (November 2022) draws lessons from the evaluations of earlier graduation initiatives in the country, which are guided by the MPG. The key changes introduced in the strategy encompass a shift from social protection as a sector-focused initiative to a multisectoral undertaking, with graduation seen as an agenda for the entire government and its partners. The importance of the enabling environment, including access to markets and service delivery systems, is acknowledged and requires cross-sector coordination.

Economic inclusion programs are also aligning with government policies at the subnational level. An excellent example is the implementation of Prospera Familia by the government of the state of São Paulo in Brazil. Integrated with the national safety net program Bolsa Familia and leveraging the national social registry, Prospera Familia is fully funded by the state of São Paulo. With a current enrollment of 7,500 participants and cumulative coverage reaching 18,000 households, this program demonstrates that in large countries where states possess both funding and institutional capacity, economic inclusion programs can be seamlessly integrated into subnational policies. In Guatemala, Trickle Up has collaborated with four municipal governments over the past 5 years to seek adoption of livelihood programming tailored to Indigenous women living in extreme poverty. Initially, Trickle Up provided funding for the programs at the municipal level. However, as the programs gained traction and produced results, the total investment in specific municipalities increased, and the financial contribution from municipalities largely replaced Trickle Up's initial investment.

Economic Inclusion Is Embraced as a Key Strategy to Address Forced Displacement

With the marked increase in the number of people facing forcible displacement, global initiatives to both promote an effective policy response and improve coordination among stakeholders is a key priority to address the immediate needs of displaced people and their hosts. To help global coordination efforts to this end, the Global Compact on Refugees seeks to improve the global response to refugee needs. In December 2023, governments, UN agencies, donors, private sector actors, NGOs, and displaced people convened at the Global Refugee Forum to discuss progress on the compact. Economic inclusion programs emerged as a practical approach that combines elements of humanitarian response, often in the form of cash relief, with development strategies to engage displaced people and host communities in livelihood activities and link them to social services, where possible.[2]

Multiple organizations and governments joined a multistakeholder pledge to support 1 million refugees and their hosts, and economic inclusion initiatives were among them. Forty-seven governments offered pledges to support economic inclusion, as did all members of the Poverty Alleviation Coalition,[3] a global alliance to reduce poverty for refugee and host communities, led by the United Nations High Commissioner for Refugees (UNHCR). To advance achievement of these goals, the coalition, led by the Refugee-Self-Reliance Initiative and UNHCR, will support at least 15 governments to strengthen laws and policies supporting economic inclusion to reach refugees, forcibly displaced and stateless people, and members of host communities with jobs and social services and expand quality data and evidence to promote effective programs and policies.

Notes

1. According to the Landscape Survey 2023, 74 percent of the surveyed government-led programs are funded by the World Bank and 6 percent by other multilateral or bilateral donors. However, the coverage of the survey is biased toward the World Bank because most of its programs responded to the survey, and programs funded by bilateral or other multilateral institutions are not fully represented.
2. Refer to International Network on Conflict and Fragility 2023.
3. A coalition of UNHCR, the World Bank's Partnership for Economic Inclusion, and 16 NGOs; refer to https://alleviate-poverty.org/about.

References

Andrews, Colin, Aude de Montesquiou, Inés Arévalo-Sánchez, Puja Vasudeva Dutta, Boban Varghese Paul, Sadna Samaranayake, Janet Heisey, Timothy Clay, and Sarang Chaudhary. 2021. *The State of Economic Inclusion Report 2021: The Potential to Scale.* Washington, DC: World Bank. http://hdl.handle.net/10986/34917.

Beegle, Kathleen, Aline Coudouel, and Emma Monsalve. 2018. *Realizing the Full Potential of Social Safety Nets in Africa.* Africa Development Forum. Washington, DC: World Bank. http://documents.worldbank.org/curated/en/657581531930611436 /Realizing-the-Full-Potential-of-Social-Safety-Nets-in-Africa.

Carter, Becky, Anuradha Joshi, and Michelle Remme. 2018. "Scaling Up Inclusive Approaches for Marginalised and Vulnerable People." *K4D Emerging Issues Report,* Institute of Development Studies, Brighton, UK.

Cooley, Larry, and Johannes F. Linn. 2014. *Taking Innovations to Scale: Methods, Applications and Lessons.* Washington, DC: Results for Development Institute. https://2012-2017.usaid.gov/sites/default/files/documents/1865/v5web_R4D_MSI -BrookingsSynthPaper0914-3.pdf.

ECLAC (Economic Commission for Latin America and the Caribbean). n.d. "Tenonderã." ECLAC, Washington, DC. https://dds.cepal.org/bpsnc/programme?id=98.

Fernández-Olit, Beatriz, Juan Diego Paredes-Gázquez, and Marta de la Cuesta-González. 2018. "Are Social and Financial Exclusion Two Sides of the Same Coin? An Analysis of the Financial Integration of Vulnerable People." *Social Indicators Research* 135: 245–68. https://doi .org/10.1007/s11205-016-1479-y.

Gentilini, Ugo. 2022. *Cash Transfers in Pandemic Times: Evidence, Practices, and Implications from the Largest Scale Up in History.* Washington, DC: World Bank. http://documents.worldbank.org/curated/en/099800007112236655/P17658505ca 3820930a254018e229a30bf8.

International Network on Conflict and Fragility. 2023. *Addressing Forced Displacement with a Humanitarian-Development-Peace Nexus Approach. Policy Roundtable Summary.* Paris: Organization for Economic Cooperation and Development. https://one.oecd.org/document /DCD/DAC/INCAF(2023)4/en/pdf.

Njogu-Ndongwe, Frida, Jeff McManus, Miguel Angel Jimenez Gallardo, Winfred Kanan Ntonjira, Christy Lazicky, and Pignon Cassandre. 2022. "IDinsight, Nairobi." Village Enterprise Development Impact Bond Evaluation Findings. https://www.idinsight.org/publication /village-enterprise-development-impact-bond-evaluation-findings/.

Rwanda Ministry of Local Government. 2020. *National Social Protection Policy (NSPP).* https:// www.minaloc.gov.rw/fileadmin/user_upload/Minaloc/Publications/Policies/Social_Protection _Policy_Adopted__1_.pdf.

Sumanthiran, Shilohni, and Keetie Roelen. 2023. *Coaching in Economic Inclusion: Learning from Existing Models and Casting a Way Forward. PEI in Practice, Volume 10.* Washington, DC: World Bank. http://hdl.handle.net/10986/40738 License: CC BY-NC 3.0 IGO.

World Bank. 2021a. *Ghana—Sustainable Land and Water Management Project.* Implementation Completion and Results Report. Washington, DC: World Bank. http://documents.worldbank.org/curated/en/320281638846629890/Ghana -Sustainable-Land-and-Water-Management-Project.

World Bank. 2021b. *Iraq—Emergency Social Stabilization Project.* Washington, DC: World Bank. http://documents.worldbank.org/curated/en/414431639055793718/Iraq -Emergency-Social-Stabilization-Project.

World Bank, IEG Review Team. 2023. *Panama—PA Strengthening SP and Inclusion System* (English). Washington, DC: World Bank. http://documents.worldbank.org/curated/en /099193003142313829/P1550970ff58d90f60a17c007ad5c990122.

World Bank, Partnership for Economic Inclusion. 2022. "Moving from Protection to Production in Egypt." PEI Results Stories. World Bank, Washington, DC. https://www.peiglobal.org/sites/pei /files/2022-10/RS_EGYPT_Final_0.pdf.

Economic Inclusion in an Increasingly Digital World

Introduction

Digital tools and technologies are increasingly contributing to the enhanced efficiency, accessibility, and effectiveness of economic inclusion programs. The emergence of innovative digital technologies holds promising implications for scaling up these programs and improving cost-effectiveness. Nongovernmental organizations are taking the lead in developing and testing these digital innovations to optimize program operations, but several governments are also pursuing opportunities to connect poor and vulnerable people to increasingly available digital and digitally enabled job opportunities. Although the digital delivery of cash and business capital grants has been widely adopted by both government- and nongovernment-led programs, other digital innovations have emerged in recent years. What follows are some noteworthy examples.

Delivering Training

AppTitude, developed by Fundación Capital, is a mobile application leveraging digital technology to train program participants in entrepreneurship, financial education, and life skills. The app delivers through its five modules practical lessons via engaging mobile lessons, games, and videos. Tailored to individual learning styles, the app includes self-assessments and quizzes to ensure efficient progress. Data dashboards and reports enable participants and managers to track individual and group progress. AppTitude not only adapts content to specific needs and cultural contexts, it also encourages collaboration and knowledge sharing within communities, strengthening social networks. With more than 30,000 households in Latin America benefiting from its training, the app shows significant potential for reaching a large number of participants.

Improving Access to Information and Market Linkages

Digifarm, created by Safaricom with support from Mercy Corps's AgriFin program, improves farmers' access to discounted inputs and credit options for seeds and fertilizers. The platform directly connects farmers to buyers, eliminating intermediaries and ensuring fair prices for their produce. Digifarm provides agricultural advice, weather updates, and best practices, empowering farmers to make informed decisions and improve their techniques. It also promotes financial inclusion and independence by offering access to small loans and financial services. Currently, more than 1 million farmers in East Africa are registered with Digifarm.

Conducting Data Collection, Monitoring, and Analysis

Village Enterprise uses an adaptive management system, using digital tools such as the TaroWorks App for real-time data collection on businesses, savings groups, and program progress. This approach eliminates paper-based processes. The collected data are stored centrally in the Salesforce Database, facilitating analysis and visualization. Custom dashboards and reports are generated from the data, offering valuable insights into program performance. This streamlined approach enhances decision-making, saving time and resources while allowing cost-effective program implementation. The system is adaptable and scalable to support Village Enterprise's expanding reach and programs in Sub-Saharan Africa.

Improving Savings and Financial Inclusion

Many programs are piloting the use of digital savings group solutions such as SAVE, DreamSave, Jamii.one, Chomoka (powered by the Cooperative for Assistance and Relief Everywhere), Maximus, and LedgerLink. These mobile-based applications support savings and credit groups in managing their finances effectively. They enable the electronic recording of individual and group savings and loan transactions, ensuring accuracy and transparency. In addition, they automate loan calculations, disbursement, and repayment tracking, reducing errors and streamlining the process. Applications operate offline, with automatic data synchronization upon reestablishing connectivity. They are designed for ease of use, making them suitable for groups with limited literacy and no prior digital experience.

Government-led programs are also harnessing the potential of digitalization to boost job opportunities for program participants. In Rwanda, the Priority Skills for Growth Program equips participants with market-ready digital skills through technical and vocational education and training, providing both short- and long-term training programs. Some governments are pursuing a comprehensive strategy by building a digital ecosystem addressing both supply- and demand-side constraints to more-inclusive digital development. Box S3.1 describes how the government of Jordan is creating a digital ecosystem focusing on youth and women.

BOX S3.1   **Digital Ecosystem for Job Creation in Jordan**

The Youth, Technology and Jobs (YTJ) Project addresses the challenge of youth unemployment in Jordan by promoting digital skills development; creating job opportunities in the information, communications, and technology sectors; and expanding access to technology-driven services.

Supported by the World Bank and implemented by the Ministry of Digital Economy and Entrepreneurship (MoDEE), the YTJ Project is seeking to improve digitally enabled income opportunities and expand digitized government services in Jordan

(Box continues next page)

BOX S3.1   Digital Ecosystem for Job Creation in Jordan *(continued)*

through interventions that address specific constraints and opportunities in both the supply and demand sides of the economy. To address supply-side challenges, the project is integrating digital skills into public school curricula for grades 7–12, reaching approximately 300,000 students. It is also providing digital skills training and certifications through programs in coding, data analysis, and digital marketing. Finally, the initiative is establishing three to five technology hubs in underserved communities, offering co-working spaces, training, and mentorship to support tech start-ups and entrepreneurs. On the demand side, the project is boosting the digital economy by digitizing government services and nurturing growth of the gig economy.

Meanwhile, MoDEE is collaborating with the relevant ministries to improve the quality and accessibility of selected e-government services, and it is also partnering with freelance platforms to integrate Jordanian youth and women into the digital workforce.

The use of digital technologies in economic inclusion programming holds great promise, but careful consideration of design and delivery factors is essential, including assessing the digital literacy levels of both program implementers and participants and providing the appropriate training for effective implementation. Understanding the local digital divide is critical, especially in rural areas with limited access to smartphones and the internet and where innovative solutions will be needed for inclusion. Digital tools must prioritize accessibility and inclusivity, considering local language, context, and cultural sensitivities. To ensure widespread, equitable access, tools should work offline or with low connectivity and should accommodate individuals with disabilities.

Many organizations are beginning to explore the use of artificial intelligence (AI) technologies in economic inclusion programs—a move that poses both immense promise and significant challenges. AI could dramatically improve the efficiency and effectiveness of economic inclusion programs. By integrating AI-driven tools, these programs can increase their cost-efficiency, particularly in traditionally resource-intensive areas such as personalized coaching. AI can provide tailored learning experiences, automate complex financial services, and adapt to the specific needs of individuals.

That said, the deployment of AI in this context must be approached with caution, ensuring that its benefits are accessible to all, particularly the poor or marginalized populations that stand to gain the most from economic inclusion efforts. The effectiveness of AI technologies in strengthening economic inclusion critically depends on access to dependable data, a resource often in short supply in developing regions. In addition, the ethical landscape surrounding AI—encompassing privacy, data security, and the potential for algorithmic bias—demands meticulous attention to avoid deepening existing societal disparities. Therefore, although AI holds the potential to revolutionize economic inclusion, its implementation must be thoughtfully managed to navigate these limitations and ensure it serves as a tool for empowerment rather than exclusion.

SPECIAL FOCUS
Climate-Resilient Economic Inclusion

KEY MESSAGES

- Two-thirds of economic inclusion programs build climate resilience. The climate change and poverty agenda presents an opportunity for collaboration across diverse sectors, ministries, and implementers.

- Climate-resilient economic inclusion programs introduce adaptations and innovations in three key areas: (1) adaptive safety nets, (2) food and ecological systems, and (3) green jobs and the green transition.

- Although interest in climate-resilient economic inclusion is growing, the number of programs that comprehensively address issues at the intersection of climate and poverty is limited, and the results have not yet been fully assessed.

Introduction

Ensuring sustainable livelihoods by building climate resilience is emerging as the next frontier for economic inclusion programming. Programs are helping participants become better able to adapt to and recover from multiple and recurrent shocks, such as pandemics and natural disasters, by building their resilience. The evidence for these initiatives is strong (refer to box SF.1), suggesting a positive impact on generic adaptive capacity, such as improvements in income security, asset accumulation, food security and nutrition, and diversification of economic activities (Andrews et al. 2021; Bhalla et al. 2024).

However, there is growing recognition that programs need to be designed to also address the medium- to long-term threat to economic inclusion posed by climate change. A new generation of climate-resilient economic inclusion (CREI) programs is needed to build specific adaptive capacity (Bhalla et al. 2024) to directly contribute to climate mitigation, to reduce the negative—sometimes unintended—impacts of climate mitigation policies, or both.

People living in extreme poverty face many environmental and natural resources management challenges, with climate change being an accelerating factor in the medium to long term. They tend to rely more heavily on climate-sensitive livelihoods, such as agriculture in rural areas and unskilled sectors such as construction in urban areas. They also commonly reside in regions more exposed to extreme events and have less-resilient or more-exposed infrastructure. These areas are also projected to be most impacted by climate change (Hallegatte et al. 2017; IPCC 2022).

In the medium to long term, environmental degradation and climate change amplify risks and exacerbate the "poverty trap," by introducing an additional layer of stressors (refer to box SF.2). By 2030, climate change could increase the number of people living in extreme poverty by 122 million (IPCC 2022), reversing some of the progress in poverty reduction in recent decades. Climate change leads to more-frequent extreme events (for example, storms, floods, and droughts). Gradual changes or slow-onset events and inadequate natural resources management also affect lives and livelihoods (for example, sea level rise, desertification, and ecosystem degradation). Furthermore, negative spillovers can result in food insecurity among the most vulnerable populations.

Climate change also requires societies to transition to greener, less-carbon-intensive economies, sometimes called a "green transition." This transition is necessary and desirable, but it can leave some people behind—especially those who lack the opportunities and skills to move to new, higher-skilled jobs (IPCC 2022).

Thus, governments are increasingly recognizing the need to adopt climate-resilient development strategies that holistically address the intertwined challenges of poverty and the impacts of climate change. The world's poorest people typically lack the resources (money, physical assets, and human capital) to cope with the direct and indirect short- and long-term shocks and livelihood changes that accompany climate change. They often must cope with shocks in ways that further deteriorate their surrounding natural environment, reinforcing a vicious cycle of poverty and environmental degradation. Women in particular bear a disproportionate impact from the climate crisis, which exacerbates existing gender inequalities (refer to box SF.3). In this context, economic inclusion approaches can play an important role in addressing the challenges at the intersection of climate resilience and poverty reduction.

BOX SF.1   Economic Inclusion and Climate Resilience: What Does the Evidence Say?

The State of Economic Inclusion Report 2021 conducted a thorough examination of impact evaluations across 80 programs in 37 countries. The findings highlighted the significant role played by economic inclusion initiatives in bolstering household resilience to various shocks. These programs achieved this by diversifying livelihoods and sources of income, facilitating savings and access to affordable credit, and building social networks (Andrews et al. 2021). More recent evidence also suggests positive impacts on resilience to shocks, including for women (Bedoya Arguelles et al. 2023).

Furthermore, a recent review of a broad range of rural social protection programs (including several that include economic inclusion programs) found evidence that these programs facilitate climate adaptation, mainly through improved natural resources management and ecosystem restoration. Evidence of impact through the adoption of climate-adaptive agricultural practices and through income diversification to less-climate-sensitive livelihoods is more limited, with mixed results. Some evidence also shows that these programs contribute to climate change mitigation targets through a reduction in greenhouse gas emissions and in the easing the negative impacts of climate mitigation policies (such as fuel subsidy reform) (Bhalla et al. 2024).

BOX SF.2   The Climate-Poverty Nexus

The intersection of poverty constraints and climate impacts presents a complex array of challenges.

Unless addressed, the consequences for the poor population of the climate-poverty nexus are significant. As depicted in the center of figure BSF2.1, two forces—poverty constraints and climate impacts—intersect in ways that can amplify or compound each other, giving rise to a set of limiting conditions for poor people:

FIGURE BSF2.1   The Climate-Poverty Nexus

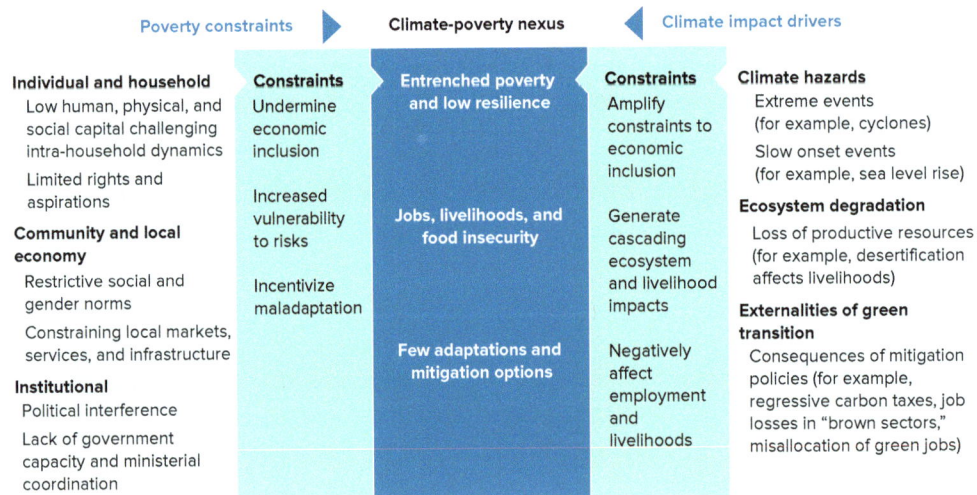

Source: Costella et al. 2023.

(Box continues next page)

BOX SF.2   The Climate-Poverty Nexus *(continued)*

- *Entrenched poverty and a lack of climate resilience,* in which poverty has become a fixed condition and opportunities for developing more-resilient livelihoods are scarce or nonexistent.

- *Greater job and livelihood insecurity,* characterized by a lack of consistency, predictability, and opportunities for better employment and livelihoods. This situation is exacerbated by more-widespread food insecurity arising from, among other things, more-frequent heat waves, heavy rainfall, and drought.

- *Limited opportunities for adaptation and mitigation* that do not require adopting drastic and risky changes to livelihoods, which may exacerbate poverty.

This special focus section details this emerging agenda of designing economic inclusion programs to enhance the long-term climate resilience of poor and vulnerable individuals and communities. The 2023 Landscape Survey revealed that nearly two-thirds of the surveyed programs can be loosely categorized as CREI. Despite these seemingly large numbers, however, this is still a nascent agenda, and cumulative experience with respect to positive climate-resilient outcomes is quite limited within economic inclusion programs. This section examines the landscape of CREI programs, presenting emerging experience from programs intentionally supporting climate-resilient development. As this is still an emerging area for programming, the section also draws on approaches that address other aspects of environmental or natural resources management challenges, not necessarily only those induced by climate change.

BOX SF.3   Climate Resilience and Women's Economic Empowerment

Women bear a disproportionate impact from the climate crisis, which exacerbates existing gender inequalities. These existing inequalities are often tied to women's context, agency, and access to resources (Cunningham and Gupta 2023).

Social and institutional barriers contribute to the exclusion of women from sectors such as energy, manufacturing, construction, and transport, all of which are expected to experience growth in response to climate change. Even within sectors with high female participation, women encounter barriers such as limited access to markets and value chains, disparities in credit, insurance, and savings, as well as stringent requirements for debt financing and collateral (Notta 2022).

For example, in the agriculture sector—a primary employment sector for women (UN Women 2022)—women often lack agency, depriving them of the opportunity to adopt sustainable agricultural practices that could enhance sector resilience (Erman et al. 2021). Consequently, women earn significantly lower incomes from agricultural labor compared to men. Female-headed households are especially vulnerable, with studies indicating that they experience a significantly greater income reduction than male-headed households during

(Box continues next page)

BOX SF.3   Climate Resilience and Women's Economic Empowerment *(continued)*

extreme weather events (FAO 2024). Not only do women have less access to resources, they also shoulder the responsibility of finding food and water for their households. The climate crisis exacerbates this burden as securing food and water becomes increasingly challenging (UN Women 2022). Furthermore, girls are disproportionately affected by climate disasters, as household coping mechanisms often involve withdrawing girls from school or arranging early marriages (Doherty, Rao, and Radney 2023).

Economic inclusion interventions aimed at enhancing women's economic inclusion and climate resilience target barriers related to their context, agency, and resource accessibility. For instance, initiatives led by the International Fund for Agricultural Development and the Food and Agriculture Organization address harmful context-related social norms, attitudes, and behaviors through guided dialogues within families and communities as part of climate change interventions (Quisumbing et al. 2023). Similarly, Women's World Banking and the Grameen Shakti program help diversify women's livelihoods and increase their resilience to climate shocks (Liao, Barrett, and Kassam 2014). In addition, women's agency has been found to improve through self-help groups and community structures by increasing their access to information and finance (Huyer and Chanana 2021; Kumar et al. 2021; Mittal 2016). Improving women's access to financial services has also helped women invest in risk reduction, adapt to climate-resilient livelihoods, and support their recovery after climate disasters (Ubfal 2023).

Economic Inclusion Programs as Enablers of Climate-Resilient Development

Economic inclusion programs are well placed to enable climate-resilient development by supporting climate adaptation and, in certain instances, mitigation. These programs extend beyond short-term shock responsiveness, aiming to enhance resilience over the long term, and are particularly well suited to addressing challenges posed by climate change in the following ways:

- *By targeting poor and vulnerable groups.* In both rural and urban areas, economic inclusion programs target disadvantaged and vulnerable groups, especially women, who often face greater exposure to risk and loss of livelihoods (Avalos et al. 2021). At the same time, rural poor people are often also environmental stewards, with the potential to manage natural resources effectively and sustainably (Charles, Kalikoski, and Macnaughton 2019). However, their potential for environmental stewardship is frequently undermined by systemic barriers such as lack of access to education, financial resources, and political power. Overcoming these barriers requires a multifaceted economic inclusion approach that addresses socioeconomic inequities while empowering poor communities to engage in sustainable natural resources management practices. In particular, the strong focus on community engagement makes it possible to protect and promote local, traditional, and Indigenous knowledge as a strong foundation for environmental stewardship (IPCC 2022).

- *By helping people prepare for climate shocks and reducing their vulnerability to shocks when they occur.* Programs do so by building financial and social capital through bundled, multisectoral interventions such as cash or in-kind transfers, business grants, skills training, coaching, and access to finance, including microinsurance. These interventions can help people acquire assets and savings and diversify their incomes in ways that make them better prepared to cope with and recover from shocks (Andrews et al. 2021).

- *By enhancing adaptive capacity[1] or natural resources–based livelihoods.* This approach includes programs that promote sustainable farming practices as well as a wide range of ecosystem management activities. Economic inclusion programs support adaptive capacity for households and communities through activities such as livestock restocking, seed transfers, training and skills development, microfinance initiatives, and grants to support the adoption of green technologies.

- *By directly building climate resilience through livelihood diversification and support for alternative income-generating activities.* As climate change reduces the productivity of natural resources–based livelihoods, those engaged in these livelihoods will need help to diversify or transition to new ones. Establishing tangible economic and social benefits is essential to increasing the uptake of climate-sensitive activities. Many of the CREI programs (a subset of economic inclusion programs) support alternative income-generating activities to encourage livelihood diversification, particularly in areas where ecosystems are under pressure from overuse (for example, nontimber forest products).

- *By helping facilitate a just transition.* An equitable and just transition focuses on a set of principles, processes, and practices that aim to ensure that no people, workers, places, sectors, countries, or regions are left behind in the transition from a high-carbon to a low-carbon economy (IPCC 2022). Economic inclusion approaches and just transitions emphasize the need to create resilient economies that address the impacts of climate change while enabling fair and inclusive transitions, protecting vulnerable communities, and fostering sustainable livelihoods for all. Cash transfers, skills development and retraining, and business capital are critical to facilitating an equitable and just transition (ILO 2023).

A Growing Body of CREI Programs

This is a growing agenda, and many economic inclusion programs are already contributing to climate-resilient development. According to the Landscape Survey 2023, 20 percent of programs cite enhancing climate resilience as a core objective, while 28 percent of programs target people affected by climate change or environmental risks. Overall, 66 percent of programs, benefiting more than 58 million individuals, incorporate some design element to help participants build climate resilience. These elements help participants prepare for, cope with, and adapt to climate risks or contribute to ecosystem conservation and climate change mitigation efforts. Geographically, 65 percent of CREI programs are in Sub-Saharan Africa, 14 percent in South Asia, and 10 percent in Latin America and the Caribbean (refer to map SF.1).

Despite these seemingly large numbers, cumulative experience with respect to positive climate resilience outcomes is still limited. In particular, following the CREI framework (refer to figure SF.1), there is considerable variation in (1) the degree to which programs incorporate the core principles underpinning the framework and (2) how effectively they incorporate climate-resilient activities and outcomes in program design (Costella et al. 2023).

MAP SF.1   CREI Programs and Climate Vulnerability

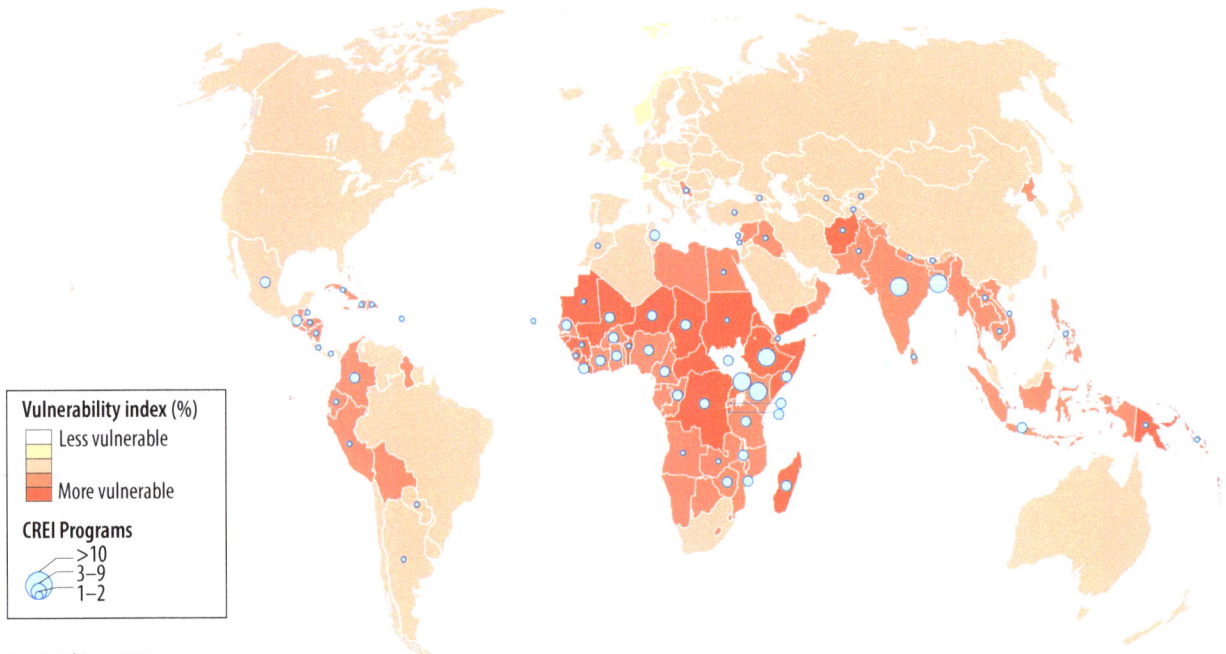

Vulnerability index (%)
Less vulnerable

More vulnerable

CREI Programs
>10
3–9
1–2

IBRD 48228 | June 2024

Sources: University of Notre Dame 2023; Partnership for Economic Inclusion, World Bank.

Note: Climate data measure a country's level of vulnerability and readiness to adapt. On the map, the darker the color, the more vulnerable a country is to climate impacts and the less prepared it is. Blue dots indicate the locations of World Bank–financed CREI projects.

FIGURE SF.1   The CREI Framework

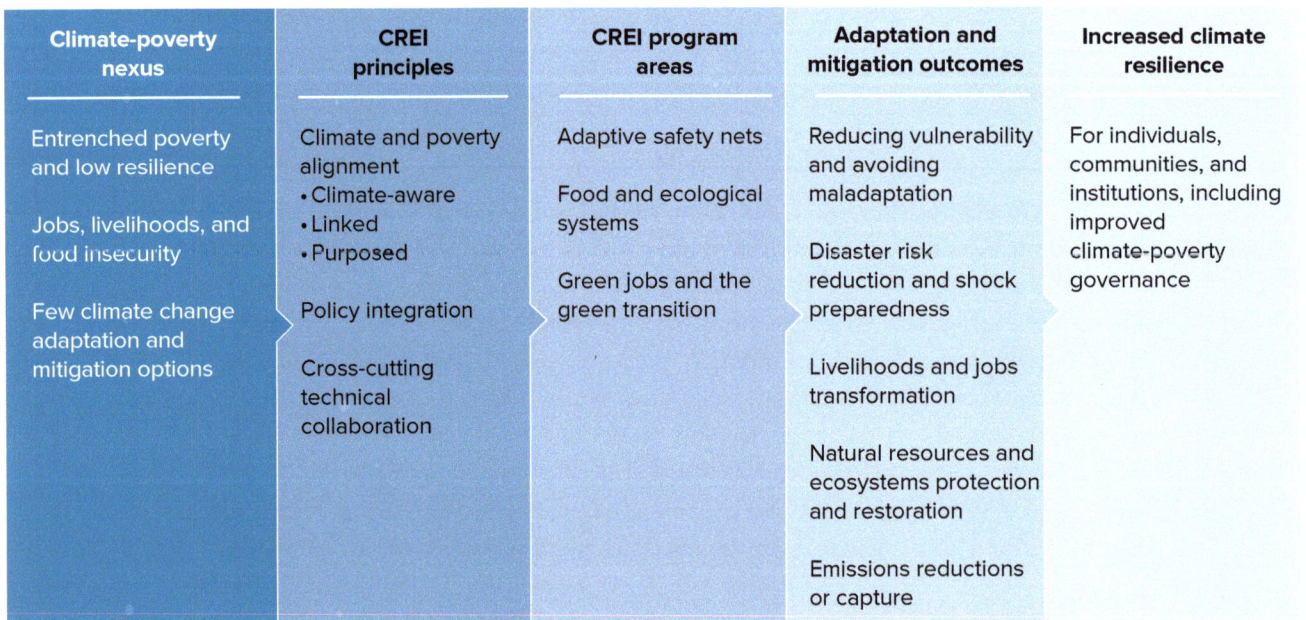

Climate-poverty nexus	CREI principles	CREI program areas	Adaptation and mitigation outcomes	Increased climate resilience
Entrenched poverty and low resilience	Climate and poverty alignment	Adaptive safety nets	Reducing vulnerability and avoiding maladaptation	For individuals, communities, and institutions, including improved climate-poverty governance
Jobs, livelihoods, and food insecurity	• Climate-aware • Linked • Purposed	Food and ecological systems	Disaster risk reduction and shock preparedness	
Few climate change adaptation and mitigation options	Policy integration	Green jobs and the green transition	Livelihoods and jobs transformation	
	Cross-cutting technical collaboration		Natural resources and ecosystems protection and restoration	
			Emissions reductions or capture	

Source: Costella et al. 2023.

Note: CREI = climate-resilient economic inclusion.

First, the CREI framework identifies three core *principles*: (1) climate and poverty alignment, (2) policy integration, and (3) cross-cutting technical collaboration (refer to figure SF.1). Adherence to these principles helps ensure that economic inclusion interventions reduce vulnerability by enabling targeted populations to navigate the climate and poverty risks and avoid contributing to maladaptation. At this early stage, however, only a few of the surveyed programs comprehensively incorporate all three principles.

For the first principle, CREI programs align climate and poverty objectives with varying levels of intensity. Some programs acknowledge the intersection of climate change and policy, some establish a link to climate-affected groups, and others systematically address the interaction between climate change and poverty through concrete objectives and components. CREI programs can thus be categorized as climate aware, climate linked, or climate purposed.[2]

- *Climate-aware programs* (53 percent) acknowledge climate risks but do not comprehensively integrate climate and poverty considerations into their objectives, components, or targeting.

- *Climate-linked programs* (25 percent) acknowledge climate risks and target those people affected by climate change. However, addressing climate and poverty considerations is not a primary objective and is not fully aligned with project outcomes.

- *Climate-purposed programs* (22 percent) have the highest level of climate-poverty alignment. They comprehensively assess and address the intersection of climate and poverty by explicitly incorporating climate objectives into their activities and targeting.

At a minimum, adhering to the alignment principle would signify that programs avoid maladaptive outcomes. *Maladaptation* refers to actions that, often unintentionally, may lead now or in the future to an increased risk of adverse climate-related outcomes, including through higher greenhouse gas emissions, a greater or shifted vulnerability to climate change, more inequitable outcomes, or diminished welfare. For example, interventions that aim to increase agricultural production by poor people must consider potential environmental impacts such as soil contamination or degradation, overexploitation of water aquifers, deforestation, and biodiversity loss. However, avoiding maladaptation is not enough to be considered climate purposed. Climate-purposed programs are capable of transformational change and reduce the risk of unintended consequences or maladaptation.

Second, the CREI framework also recognizes that programs vary in how they incorporate climate-resilient activities and outcomes. Programs can be loosely categorized into three *program areas:* (1) adaptive safety nets, (2) food and ecological systems, and (3) green jobs and the green transition (all described in box SF.4). These program areas draw on the World Bank's portfolio of economic inclusion programs and are motivated by the recent Intergovernmental Panel on Climate Change report (IPCC 2022). CREI programs may fall into more than one program area because of the multidimensional nature of economic inclusion programs and the interplay between climate and poverty risks.

BOX SF.4   **Climate-Resilient Economic Inclusion Program Areas**

Of the three Climate-Resilient Economic Inclusion (CREI) program areas, 38 percent focus on adaptive safety nets, 86 percent on food and ecological systems, and 35 percent on green jobs and the green transition.

- *Adaptive safety net programs* build resilience by helping poor and vulnerable households prepare for, adapt to, and cope with climate-related shocks. These programs bring together social protection, disaster risk management, and climate change adaptation to build household resilience to both extreme and slow-onset climate events (Bowen et al. 2020). Typical economic inclusion programs in this area include interventions that combine anticipatory cash transfers related to specific shocks, access to climate risk information (including early warning systems), access to disaster insurance, and public works programs with a focus on disaster risk reduction. These interventions can be combined with those that help build a savings and asset base (for example, skills training, livelihoods diversification, and financial services).

- *Food and ecological systems programs* reduce the vulnerability and exposure of people with climate-dependent livelihoods (for example, crop production, forestry, and fisheries), especially to gradual environmental changes such as drought and rising temperatures. These programs promote practices that preserve and restore natural resources and help shift employment toward diversified nonagricultural job opportunities. Typical interventions include technical and financial support for sustainable and enhanced value chains in climate-dependent sectors, such as climate-smart agriculture and agroforestry. Other interventions are "nature-based solutions" that promote the use of natural features and processes to tackle socioenvironmental issues, such as the planting of mangroves, which reduces the impact of storms and supports biodiversity (refer to box SF.6). CREI interventions in this program area often include training, livelihood diversification, business capital and financial services, access to climate risk information relevant to economic activity, and access to cleaner energy sources.

- *Green jobs and the green transition programs* can help households move from extractive or climate-sensitive work to greener sectors and cope with the transition. Typical interventions are training, coaching, mentoring, and other forms of skills development; access to wage employment in green (or climate neutral) jobs, including job search and placement; access to financial services and business capital; access to cleaner energy and technologies for cooking and transportation; and compensation of households affected by the shift away from carbon-intensive industries. These programs stress the need for a just transition to ensure that no people, places, sectors, countries, or regions are left behind in the transition from a high-carbon to a low-carbon economy.

Climate-Resilient Programs Tackle Climate Change and Poverty by Design

A new frontier is emerging across the social protection, environment, and agriculture sectors. Several programs, both government- and nongovernment-led, are moving in the direction of climate-purposed programming. Building specific adaptive capacity (Bhalla et al. 2024) requires critical adaptations. This section describes program-level insights on targeting approaches, adaptations to core economic inclusion components, and innovations with respect to new components.

These insights can play a role in how CREI programs build stronger climate-poverty alignment across all three program areas, moving from programming that simply acknowledges climate challenges to programming that actively facilitates climate change adaptation and mitigation. As this is still an emerging area for programming, this special focus section also draws on approaches that address aspects of environmental or natural resources management challenges, and not necessarily only those induced by climate change.

Targeting Strategies Incorporate Both Poverty- and Climate-Related Measures

The flexibility inherent in economic inclusion programs is important because it enables CREI programs to serve diverse target groups in a variety of contexts, showcasing their ability to address evolving challenges posed by the climate-poverty nexus.

When targeting program participants, CREI programs typically incorporate both poverty- and climate-related criteria. Specific targeting approaches may depend on whether programs are household- or area-focused, as discussed in chapter 2. As outlined in table SF.1, adaptive safety nets and green jobs and green transition programs take a household-focused approach, whereas food and ecological systems programs adopt an area-focused approach.

- *Household-focused CREI programs* commonly target households that are both poor, or at risk of falling into poverty, and vulnerable to climate-related shocks. For example, in Djibouti the Social Protection Emergency Crisis Response Project relies on a combination of community-based and proxy-means-targeting mechanisms to target poor and vulnerable households affected by overlapping crises, such as drought and food and fuel price increases, and those affected by conflict. Although traditionally focused on extremely poor and vulnerable people, some economic inclusion programs address the impacts of climate change by expanding to include the "near-poor"—individuals or communities teetering on the brink of extreme poverty due to climate-related effects. Workers who may be transitioning out of extractive industries may be targeted as well.

- *Area-focused CREI programs,* typically centered on food and ecological systems, often adopt targeting strategies that are geographic and natural resources based. Environmental programs, in particular, often use watershed- or landscape-based approaches in which targeting entails careful identification of populations in regions aligned with conservation objectives related to soil and land, forest resources, groundwater, and small-scale fishing. Area-focused programs tend to consider all people residing in a targeted geographic area as eligible for participation. When a program has conservation or restoration objectives, it may also extend eligibility to communities that reside just outside of the targeted geographic area. This approach is evident in programs seeking to protect and restore mangroves in the Mangroves for Coastal Resilience Project in Indonesia, forests in the Natural Resources Management Project in Senegal, reserve grasslands in the Local Development and Adaptation Project in Chad, and coastal communities in the Forest Sector Modernization Project in Viet Nam. In all of these countries, local populations often depend on protected areas for their economic needs, thereby exerting direct pressure on the ecosystem.

TABLE SF.1 Targeting Criteria for CREI Programs

Targeting criteria	Household-focused programs	Area-focused programs
CREI program area	Adaptive safety nets Green jobs and green transition	Food and ecological systems
Target population	Poor (or near-poor) households that are vulnerable to disasters or climate-related risks	All household residents in a geographic area, identified from a landscape, natural resources management, or ecological system perspective
Targeting mechanisms	Means-testing, proxy means-test, community based, self-targeting (many programs will also overlay geographic criteria)	Geographic (including watershed- or landscape-based approaches), community based, self-selection, categorical

Source: Original table for this publication.

FIGURE SF.2 Design Adaptations of CREI Programs

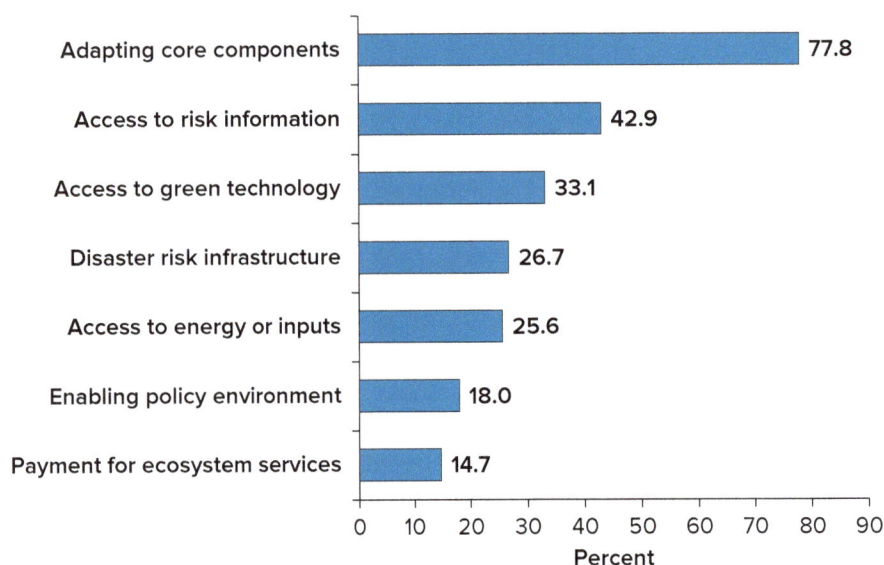

Adapting core components: 77.8
Access to risk information: 42.9
Access to green technology: 33.1
Disaster risk infrastructure: 26.7
Access to energy or inputs: 25.6
Enabling policy environment: 18.0
Payment for ecosystem services: 14.7

Source: Partnership for Economic Inclusion, World Bank.
Note: Figure shows the percentage of CREI programs (*N* = 266).

In some programs, especially disaster risk reduction programs that focus on preparedness efforts in disaster-prone communities, both household- and geographic-targeting approaches are used to understand climate exposure and distinguish the temporarily poor from the chronically poor populations. Such targeting requires incorporating poverty, disaster, or other climate-related vulnerabilities in the criteria for selecting beneficiaries. For example, programs in Burkina Faso, northern Cameroon, Chad, Mali, Niger, and Senegal have used both proxy means-testing and community-based targeting once geographical targeting had been applied.

Programs Adapt Core Components and Introduce New Innovations

Seventy-eight percent of CREI programs either modify existing components or introduce new elements to address specific climate-poverty constraints (refer to figure SF.2). They may also integrate innovations tailored to pursue climate-resilient outcomes, with the approach depending on the program area. As the survey does not provide sufficient information to identify how comprehensively these adaptations align climate and poverty objectives or how effective these are in achieving positive climate outcomes, this section draws on a qualitative review of selected programs to highlight interesting cases.

Adapting Core Components for Climate Resilience

Among CREI programs, 78 percent modify some of the core components of economic inclusion programs, such as transfers, training and coaching, business capital, group formation (savings groups and producer organizations), and market links (refer to chapter 2), in order to help participants better adapt to climate change and, in some cases, advance climate mitigation.

- *Transfers.* Most economic inclusion programs include a cash transfer component (52 percent of CREI programs); the adaptation in CREI programs is to introduce emergency cash transfers or top-ups associated with child nutrition and food insecurity challenges. Cash is one of the most effective ways to reduce vulnerability and increase the agency of people affected by crises. Weather-responsive anticipatory cash transfers—using forecasting models, remote sensing, and mobile banking to deliver cash to affected households—are proactive measures in anticipation of disasters such as floods. Growing evidence indicates that anticipatory cash transfers can boost food security and resilience and can be more cost-effective than humanitarian assistance after a climate event (Balana et al. 2023; IRC and IFPRI 2023; Pople et al. 2021). Furthermore, cash-for-work and other public works programs are increasingly incorporating natural resources interventions to reduce the risk of a climate disaster. For example, Ethiopia's Productive Safety Net Program, one of the largest social protection programs in Sub-Saharan Africa, includes a public works component that employs food-insecure farmers during the slack season. This component has successfully integrated activities such as tree planting and soil and water conservation measures to mitigate the impacts of climatic and food insecurity risks (Andersson, Mekonnen, and Stage 2011).

- *Training and coaching.* Training and coaching are fundamental components of nearly all economic inclusion programs; CREI programs tweak these to build climate resilience. In adaptive safety net programs, the integration of climate messaging into training sessions for front-line coaches and program participants is a key focus. This effort can extend to psychosocial training, in which behavioral interventions empower individuals to recognize both the causes and consequences of climate change, facilitating a shift in norms. In Chad, for example, the Local Development and Adaptation Project promotes literacy courses paired with environmental education on biodiversity to increase behavioral change in the management of natural resources. In food and ecological systems programs, training and coaching help participants move toward more-sustainable farming practices as well as alternative income-generating activities (refer to box SF.5). In Côte d'Ivoire, the Forest Investment Project and in Benin, the Gazetted Forests Management Project, successfully trained participants in developing jobs in nontimber forest products, including beekeeping and shea and mushroom production, effectively reducing deforestation among forest-dependent communities. Furthermore, Concern Worldwide's Graduation Program in Malawi provides training in climate-smart agriculture, home gardening, and food budgeting, thereby reducing food insecurity challenges.

BOX SF.5   **Farmer Field Schools Build Climate Resilience**

CREI programs in agriculture often target farmers, youth, and unemployed individuals, offering climate-smart agriculture practices at subsistence levels or across the value chain. Training may be facilitated through farmer field schools, producer groups, and traditional vocational training centers.

In Morocco, the government's Green Generation Strategy uses farmer field schools to provide technical assistance to groups of 15–30 farmers through hands-on learning and problem-solving sessions in local contexts using demonstration plots. This training streamlines climate-smart practices by emphasizing modern irrigation techniques, proper seed selection, and the rational use of fertilizers and agrochemical treatments for maize farmers, resulting in yield increases, and by promoting conservation agriculture or no-till systems, which have substantially improved cereal yields. Training also targets female farmers to improve bean cultivation by reducing insecticide use; increasing awareness of the importance of pollinators; and enhancing goat's milk production practices and establishing cheese-processing units for women's cooperatives, thereby improving both the quantity and quality of milk produced. Those designing such training should tailor information, content, and priorities to the local gender-specific needs (Chocholata 2020).

Farmer field school-style training can also be found in environment programs, such as in Indonesia, where a program opened mangrove rehabilitation field schools in each village to build community skills, knowledge, and critical thinking around mangrove rehabilitation.

- *Business capital.* By offering business capital and support for business plan development, CREI programs promote sustainable, local, and "green" or "blue" businesses. For example, the Resilient Landscape Restoration Project in the Kyrgyz Republic supports farmers, small entrepreneurs, and vulnerable community members in regions prone to climate-induced mudflows, offering entrepreneurial training, business plan development assistance, and the establishment of market links to produce climate-smart and natural resources–based products using locally available and leftover raw materials. CREI programs may also combine business grants with skills training to enable participants to invest in sustainable or green income-generating activities or away from traditional livelihoods. For example, the Communal Climate Action and Landscape Management Project in Burkina Faso promotes entrepreneurship and sustainable technology in green economy value chains such as shea, moringa, baobab, néré, and medicinal plants. The program directly supports producer organizations, often comprised mostly of women, to strengthen their capacities to capitalize, transform, and market high-quality products. This support includes training and acquiring inputs and equipment (such as production kits, modern irrigation systems, storage capacity, and clean energy solutions). For select value chains, the program also facilitates dialogue with financial institutions and the certification of products.

- *Savings groups and producer organizations.* These components are also being adapted to bolster climate resilience. Savings groups such as Village Savings and Loan Associations can provide a buffer against the impacts of climate shocks on household finances and livelihoods (SEEP 2021). Savings groups also support adaptation and livelihood diversification. For example, some groups have helped their members invest directly in productive agricultural technologies and solar energy products to improve food and energy security. Producer organizations have a distinct advantage because they can offer a coordinated, quick, efficient, long-term response to the impacts of climate change largely due to the close cooperation of farmers, enabling effective resource management. Producer organizations can also facilitate the adoption of sustainable production practices (Groot-Kormelinck et al. 2022). For example, in Bolivia, from 2012 to 2023, the Rural Alliances II Project, PAR II, encouraged small-scale farmers to participate in more than 1,700 rural producer organizations to enhance food security, market access, and the adoption of climate-smart agricultural practices to improve soil health, enhance irrigation efficiency, and rehabilitate degraded lands. In a similar effort, the Corredor Seco Food Security Project in Honduras supports small-scale rural producer organizations by providing extension services and introducing high-value crops, environmental management techniques, and climate-smart technologies. These efforts have resulted in the adoption of climate-smart technologies by almost 8,000 farmers.

- *Market links.* Market-based approaches, which play an important role in promoting the diversification of sustainable livelihoods, are integrated into several CREI programs. Communities are more likely to endorse climate resilience and conservation objectives when they are supported by income-generating activities linked to local value chain investments. For many CREI programs, this work entails incorporating value chain and localized market assessments into project design. For example, in Indonesia, the Mangroves for Coastal Resilience Project conducts rapid local market assessments to inform the design of training and equip participants for engaging in livelihood activities aligned with mangrove conservation and rehabilitation. In Côte d'Ivoire, to promote climate-friendly beekeeping and honey production, the Forest Investment Project conducted a market study to identify sources of demand, explore packaging and labeling options, and assess certification possibilities. Some programs go a step further by conducting specific "green" value chain assessments. Such assessments are increasingly important for identifying sustainable and unsustainable practices, prioritizing skills training needs, assessing economic viability, recognizing stakeholders, addressing gendered aspects, establishing links to service providers, and evaluating climate risks.

BOX SF.6   Potential for Nature-Based Solutions within CREI Programs

Nature-based solutions (NBSs) have gained traction in recent years due to their potential to promote sustainable development and reduce disaster risks (Van Zanten et al. 2023). NBSs leverage or mimic natural processes, often in combination with gray infrastructure, with the objective of strengthening climate resilience while providing environmental and socioeconomic benefits (Trohanis et al. 2023). NBS projects include urban forests or green roofs, the natural restoration of inland wetlands, living shorelines, agroforestry, and the restoration of mangroves and coral reefs.

Economic inclusion programs in coastal, forest, and farmland settings can adopt inclusive NBS approaches to integrate marginalized groups into sustainable resource management and livelihood activities. These groups often depend on the local livelihood benefits of NBS, such as the provision of food and raw materials, skills training, and job creation. For example, the Mangroves for Coastal Resilience Project in Indonesia aims to rehabilitate and manage mangroves through a cash-for-work program that includes training, enterprise support, and access to finance and markets to diversify livelihoods coupled with policy and institution strengthening, the promotion of sustainable mangrove management, and mangrove rehabilitation field schools. Mangroves play a vital role in coastal ecosystems by providing an essential habitat for various species, safeguarding coastlines from erosion and storm damage, sequestering carbon, and bolstering local economies through fisheries and tourism.

Introducing New Components and Innovations

Increasingly, CREI programs are incorporating new components and innovations that support both adaptation to climate change and mitigation of climate change. Among these are access to risk information, climate risk insurance, payment for ecosystem services, green technology, and land tenure access:

- *Access to risk information.* Providing information about impending risks, including through early warning systems, is becoming a more-prominent element of CREI programs (43 percent). In the Sahel, the Pastoral Early Warning System regularly tracks drought in West Africa using satellite images and geospatial technologies. Adaptive safety net programs use information from early warning systems to trigger a scale-up in social protection as a response to or in anticipation of a climate shock, depending on its expected severity. In Malawi, the Social Support for Resilient Livelihoods Project introduced a disaster-risk-financing mechanism based on remote-sensing data to scale up its Social Cash Transfers Program in the event of extreme weather-related shocks, initially drought.

- *Climate risk insurance.* Twenty percent of CREI programs use climate risk insurance mechanisms to help households and communities recover from the effects of natural catastrophes. Parametric insurance, also known as "index-based insurance" (refer to box SF.7), is gaining in popularity. For parametric insurance, payouts are based on a set of predefined parameters such as level of rainfall, temperature, humidity, or crop yield. Because payouts are based on these parameters rather than actual loss or physical damage, payouts can be made more quickly, avoiding a distress sale of assets and deepening poverty following a disaster (Hermann, Köferl, and Mairhöfer 2016). Parametric policies are being introduced at the microinsurance level and sold directly to the consumer via mobile technologies.

BOX SF.7   A Rise in the Use of Parametric Insurance

Parametric insurance is rising in popularity across economic inclusion programs. For example, in Ethiopia, Oxfam and the World Food Programme are targeting households enrolled in the Productive Safety Net Program (PSNP) to participate in the Rural Resilience Initiative (R4), a donor-funded, index-based microinsurance program (World Bank 2013). Complementing the PSNP's public works focus, the R4 program has introduced an "insurance-for-work" scheme into its operations. This scheme gives poor farmers the option to pay for insurance through public work projects that build climate resilience and agricultural productivity.

In the event of a seasonal drought, automatic insurance payouts (currently donor funded) are triggered if rainfall drops below a predetermined threshold. These payouts enable farmers to afford the seeds and inputs needed to plant in the following season and protects them from having to sell off productive assets to survive. As parametric insurance gains popularity, several nongovernmental organizations are exploring ways to incorporate climate risk microinsurance components into their economic inclusion programs.

- *Payment for ecosystem services.* Fifteen percent of CREI programs have components related to payments for ecosystem services (PES). In PES schemes, governments and donors use financial incentives to compensate landowners for managing land and natural resources sustainably, providing global public goods and positive externalities that benefit others. PES plays an important role in financing restoration, reforestation, and soil and water conservation activities in various countries, addressing challenges such as climate change, land degradation, desertification, and food insecurity (Adjognon, van Soest, and Guthoff 2021; Tirivayi 2017). For example, in the Support Forest Conservation and Sustainable Livelihoods Project in Mozambique, the PES scheme led to the adoption of more-sustainable practices such as beekeeping and agroforestry, reducing overall levels of deforestation (FAO 2023b). Commonly applied in agriculture, forestry, and fisheries, PES schemes often extend beyond environmental goals to include social protection and sectoral objectives by, for example, providing income support and compensation to help the rural poor and other vulnerable households transition to more-sustainable agricultural or conservation practices. In Burkina Faso, the Gazetted Forests Participatory Management Project for REDD+ uses a PES scheme to support forest communities and farmers with cash transfers conditioned on afforestation and reforestation initiatives. This program has brought immediate food security benefits with potential long-term benefits in income-generating opportunities.

- *Green technology.* Thirty-three percent of CREI projects introduce green technologies into program interventions, especially in the food and ecological systems program areas. These initiatives contribute to environmental sustainability, especially in lowering emissions from farming and other climate-intensive sectors. For example, the Local Development and Adaptation Project incorporated solar panels to power water pumps in deep wells, providing clean drinking water for vulnerable women, youth, and pastoralists in and around Chad's Ouadi Rimé-Ouadi Achim Wildlife Reserve. For example, in Viet Nam, the Forest Sector Modernization and Coastal Resilience Enhancement Project included the adoption of advanced spatial planning tools as well as the modernization of seedling production using advanced technology such as tissue culture to produce high-quality seedlings, both common fast-growing species and native species. As the costs of low-carbon green technologies decline, there is increased potential to increase the adoption of this component into CREI programs.

- *Land tenure access.* Several CREI programs are addressing the role of land tenure and resource use rights in providing incentives for sustainable land management. Often, the resource-dependent poor lack voice and agency, do not have access to information about their land and resource rights, and are not represented in resource-related decision-making processes (Cotula 2021). This issue is particularly relevant in Africa, where conflicting land rights undermine incentives for land-based investments, especially for women. For example, in Burundi, the Landscape Restoration and Resilience Project issued more than 100,000 land certificates, with more than 70 percent going to women. Legal ownership of land has allowed women to obtain more-equitable access to project activities, such as training in climate-smart agriculture techniques such as terracing, the use of improved seeds, and nature-based solutions that respond to flooding. Land titles have also helped women secure loans for income-generating activities.

For Successful Program Delivery, Collaboration Is Needed Across Diverse Sectors, Ministries, and Implementers

In implementing CREI programs, effectively addressing the intertwined challenges of poverty and climate change depends on integrating strategic programs; collaborating across diverse sectors, government levels, and stakeholders; and emphasizing localized delivery strategies. While these challenges are common to all economic inclusion programs (refer to chapter 4), these are pronounced for CREI programs.

Program Convergence to Achieve Poverty and Climate Objectives

Program convergence, or the integration of two or more programs, is important for strengthening the climate resilience of poor and vulnerable people.[3] When two or more programs overlap in objectives, targeting criteria, participants, or geographic scope, it may be appropriate to either integrate or align their program components. For example, there is opportunity to improve links between food and ecosystem activities and adaptive safety net schemes in many contexts (FAO 2017). Although adaptive safety nets are usually designed to reduce poverty and food insecurity in rural areas, they could be further developed to stimulate both productive investments in agriculture and the protection and sustainable management of natural resources. Examples of successful joint programs include social protection and forestry initiatives in India, Paraguay, and Rwanda (FAO 2023a), where existing programs merged to reduce the vulnerability of forest-dependent communities, enhance economic inclusion, and promote sustainable development.

At times, aligning separate programs may prove more beneficial than designing a joint program. Aligning programs typically involves coordinating and harmonizing different initiatives delivered in the same location. An example is in Tanzania, where the Tanzania Social Action Fund is cooperating with the Private Forestry Program to support tree growers and vulnerable groups through the fund's conditional cash transfers and public works programs (FAO 2023a).

Collaboration to Facilitate Integration Across Sectors

As discussed in chapter 4, economic inclusion programs require strong collaboration across sectors, levels of government, and different stakeholders, including NGOs, civil society organizations, and the private sector. This collaboration is especially important for CREI programs, where more collaboration is needed to bring together social, environmental, agricultural, and climate-related actors to address the climate-poverty nexus. Cooperating and co-learning across sectors and organizations will help speed the integration of climate resilience and economic inclusion objectives and help ensure that outcomes are sustained. A common finding emerging from case studies (Costella et al. 2023) is that a broad network of partnerships is needed to carry out climate action that mitigates vulnerability.

To overcome the climate-poverty challenge, ministries and their respective stakeholders responsible for social protection, agriculture, environment, risk management, and energy, among other sectors, must work together. Creating space for dialogue is an important first step in cultivating interministerial and cross-sectoral collaboration. Several CREI programs encourage collaboration among ministries or agencies (refer to box SF.8). For example, in South Sudan, the Productive Safety Net for Socioeconomic Opportunities Project is implemented by the Ministry of Agriculture and Food Security and by the Ministry of Gender, Child, and Social Welfare. This collaboration reinforces the links between food security and social protection and strengthens the policy dialogue on climate adaptation and mitigation. Institutionalized inter- and cross-sectoral ministerial coordination mechanisms are needed to promote this level of collaboration.

The climate-poverty agenda also emphasizes the need to leverage broader networks of partners. For NGOs and members of the private sector engaged in CREI programming, climate resilience has become an explicit part of their strategies and, in many cases, a fundamental aspect of program design. At the same time, many NGOs engaged in these programs are relatively new to this domain and are in the early stages of building in-house capacity or collaborating with partners with expertise across sectoral areas. These partnerships can yield unintended but significant spillovers. For example, in Rwanda a program led by Concern engaged a climate-focused implementer for an agroforestry activity. Not only was the implementer better equipped for this task, but they also had strong ties with the Ministry of Environment and were able to generate additional interest in the economic inclusion approach.

BOX SF.8   **Building Climate Resilience through Partnership: An Example from Burundi**

The Landscape Restoration and Resilience Project in Burundi works to alleviate pressure on forests through better land use planning, higher land productivity, and erosion control measures. The project, which uses a community-led participatory approach, involves all major stakeholders in decentralized decision-making, thereby ensuring the participation of local communities, including women, youth, and Indigenous Batwa people, in resource-related decisions. Aligned with the government's long-term development strategy, the project collaborates with strategic development partners to scale up agricultural innovation and improve local delivery.

In addition, Alliance Bioversity International provides improved seeds that are resistant to climate change and with a higher nutritional value. Meanwhile, the Food and Agriculture Organization helps establish farmer field schools and provides the expertise needed to improve land productivity and integrate agriculture-nutrition initiatives.

Finally, the University of Burundi supports training initiatives for establishing terracing, bioresource engineering measures, and water-harvesting technology. This comprehensive collaboration exemplifies a government-led program that harnesses the expertise of various international cooperation agencies.

Localized Delivery for Long-Term Sustainability

Addressing challenges to climate resilience requires leveraging Indigenous and local knowledge by engaging local leaders and communities deeply rooted in their local contexts. These actors best understand the prevailing vulnerabilities and their drivers, as well as how climate change may be influencing them. However, local leaders have not been consistently involved in existing adaptation efforts (IPCC 2022). In recent years, the Global Center on Adaptation developed a set of principles to strengthen locally led adaptation (LLA), which has been endorsed by more than 100 organizations (GCA 2021). Under LLA, authority and control over resources are devolved to local actors, and local institutions are strengthened so they are inclusive, agile, and responsive in view of the uncertainties of climate change. Ensuring the participation of marginalized and climate-vulnerable groups in the design, planning, and implementation of CREI initiatives can foster program ownership and long-term sustainability.

A proponent of LLA, BOMA and its REAP for Climate Resilience program tailor graduation interventions to address climate and poverty challenges in Africa's drylands, including Ethiopia and northern Kenya. REAP for Climate Resilience is locally developed and managed, empowering participants to establish green businesses, actively contribute to local conservation efforts, and engage in climate mitigation strategies, including the establishment of tree nurseries. Successful programming also relies on integrating Indigenous knowledge, such as in Ecuador and Guatemala, emphasizing the importance of local wisdom, such as traditional forest management practices, in strengthening the effectiveness of climate-resilient initiatives.

What Will It Take to Scale Up Climate-Resilient Economic Inclusion?

To realize the full potential of economic inclusion programs for climate-related development, adjustments in program design and implementation are essential, supported by a robust innovation and learning agenda and with scale-up made possible through sustainable financing.

The design and delivery of CREI programs should aim to incorporate the core principles of integrating climate and poverty objectives and fostering cross-sectoral collaboration, as follows:

- *Climate and poverty alignment.* Policy makers should prioritize programs and interventions that directly target the climate-poverty nexus. Ideally, programs should be climate purposed, explicitly incorporating climate-poverty objectives into their targeting and activities (including by adapting components typically used in economic inclusion or introducing new and innovative components to build specific tools and skills to adapt to or mitigate climatic threats).

- *Cross-cutting collaboration.* Effective collaboration mechanisms among the relevant departments, partners, and ministries (such as social protection, agriculture, and environment) are necessary to design and implement effective CREI integration at the policy and program levels. The following aspects are important:

- *Program convergence.* Explore opportunities for greater convergence in CREI programming, especially where synergies exist among programs with overlapping objectives, targeting criteria, participants, or geographic scopes.

- *Local partnerships.* Engage local communities, NGOs, and private sector implementers with expertise in addressing climate and poverty challenges.

- *Inclusive planning and implementation.* Ensure the active participation of marginalized and climate-vulnerable groups in the design, planning, and implementation of CREI initiatives. This approach fosters program ownership and contributes to long-term sustainability by reinstating these groups as environmental stewards.

Scale-up will require addressing both technical and political considerations. Although not always feasible, program sustainability is more likely when activities align with national climate, environmental, and social protection policies. Some CREI programs are moving in this direction.[4] Managing the political economy of introducing, adapting, and scaling up these programs would require managing expectations given the long time frame of many interventions, resolving differences of views about competing policies,[5] and building a broad coalition of support.[6] A key aspect of CREI programs is the potential for, and challenge to, international policy coordination, especially for countries affected by regional climate shocks or the environmental decisions made by other nations (for example, territorial disputes over water management).[7]

Scale-up also requires a solid evidence base. A dual-track learning agenda is required to inform this growing agenda, with respect to both operational guidance and a deeper understanding of the impact of CREI programming. This dual track agenda includes the following:

- *Knowledge sharing.* Obtain operational insights from different strategies for integrating climate and poverty objectives in various contexts, such as urban versus rural areas, and for specific vulnerable groups, such as women and internally displaced people. Involve knowledge sharing across actors with different primary objectives. For example, actors in social protection can share lessons on targeting vulnerable groups and measuring vulnerability-reducing effects. Similarly, actors in the environment and agriculture sectors should share knowledge on the most appropriate resource management practices and how to apply and measure their effects in the relevant socioecological systems (World Bank, Independent Evaluation Group 2021).

- *Evidence of impact.* Investigate specific responses and activities that achieve climate objectives within economic inclusion programs. Develop robust criteria for evaluating program success, including indicators for poverty reduction, climate resilience, and sustainable development.

Notes

1. *Adaptive capacity* is the ability of systems, institutions, humans, and other organisms to adjust to potential damage, take advantage of opportunities, or respond to consequences (IPCC 2022).

2. The CREI categories are based on a qualitative review of CREI programs (Costella et al. 2023). A similar level of categorization can be found in the World Health Organization's Gender Responsiveness Assessment Scale (WHO 2010).

3. SEI 2021 examined the challenge of complementary programs, especially those at the intersection of agriculture and social protection (Andrews et al. 2021).

4. For example, the Lowlands Livelihood Resilience Project in Ethiopia aligns with the country's Climate-Resilient Green Economy Strategy in improving the resilience of pastoral and agropastoral communities. Similarly, the Innovation for Resilient Food Systems Project (Rural Alliances Project, PAR III) in Bolivia aligns with the national policy framework outlined in Bolivia's Economic and Social Development Plan (PDES 2021–25) to achieve food sovereignty and greater participation of small-scale farmers in domestic food markets.

5. For example, some programs seeking to promote more-sustainable fisheries or forestry management have met with resistance stemming from deep traditional and societal roots or vested interests.

6. For instance, the Natural Resources Management Project in Senegal takes a pragmatic, flexible approach to strengthening citizen engagement to build political buy-in.

7. For instance, Central Asia's RESILAND CA+ Program, serving Kazakhstan, the Kyrgyz Republic, Tajikistan, Turkmenistan, and Uzbekistan, implemented a regional platform, with the Regional Environmental Centre for Central Asia as the executing organization, to support rural communities in affected transboundary corridors by introducing nature-based solutions for restoring landscapes, safeguarding lives and livelihoods, and enhancing resilience against desertification, landscape degradation, and climate change.

References

Adjognon, Guigonan Serge, Daan van Soest, and Jonas Guthoff. 2021. "Reducing Hunger with Payments for Environmental Services (PES): Experimental Evidence from Burkina Faso." *American Journal of Agricultural Economics* 103 (3): 831–57. https://doi.org/10.1111/ajae.12150.

Andersson, Camilla, Alemu Mekonnen, and Jesper Stage. 2011. "Impacts of the Productive Safety Net Program in Ethiopia on Livestock and Tree Holdings of Rural Households." *Journal of Development Economics* 94 (1): 119–26. https://doi.org/10.1016/j.jdeveco.2009.12.002.

Andrews, Colin, Aude de Montesquiou, Inés Arévalo-Sánchez, Puja Vasudeva Dutta, Boban Varghese Paul, Sadna Samaranayake, Janet Heisey, Timothy Clay, and Sarang Chaudhary. 2021. *The State of Economic Inclusion Report 2021: The Potential to Scale.* Washington, DC: World Bank. https://openknowledge.worldbank.org/entities /publication/b12f8624-c03d-5f1d-a7e3-8bb857e733b7.

Avalos, Jorge, Sarang Chaudhary, Timothy Clay, and Puja Vasudeva Dutta. 2021. *A Path to Jobs for the Urban Poor. PEI in Practice, Volume 1.* Washington, DC: World Bank. https:// openknowledge.worldbank.org/server/api/core/bitstreams/c3072017-bb5d-599b-806f-05c4 d79ddbd2/content.

Balana, Bedru, Dolapo Adeyanju, Clare Clingain, Kwaw S. Andam, Alan de Brauw, Ishaku Yohanna, Olukunbi Olarewaju, and Molly Schneider. 2023. "Anticipatory Cash Transfers for Climate Resilience: Findings from a Randomized Experiment in Northeast Nigeria." NSSP Working Paper 69, Washington, DC: International Food Policy Research Institute. https://doi .org/10.2499/p15738coll2.136812.

Bedoya Arguelles, Guadalupe, Yulia Belyakova, Aidan Coville, Thomas Escande, Mohammad Isaqzadeh, and Aminata Ndiaye. 2023. "The Enduring Impacts of a Big Push during

Multiple Crises: Experimental Evidence from Afghanistan (English)." Policy Research Working Paper No. WPS 10596, Impact Evaluation Series. World Bank, Washington, DC. http://documents.worldbank.org/curated/en/099837211062311087/IDU1e486b8e d1e7a114d231a60d1848c87baeeb1.

Bhalla, Garima, Marco Knowles, Gala Dahlet, and Mahima Poudel. 2024. *Scoping Review on the Role of Social Protection in Facilitating Climate Change Adaptation and Mitigation for Economic Inclusion among Rural Populations.* Rome: Food and Agriculture Organization. https://doi.org/10.4060/cd0287en.

Bowen, Thomas Vaughan, Carlo Del Ninno, Colin Andrews, Sarah Coll-Black, Ugo Gentilini, Kelly Johnson, Yasuhiro Kawasoe, Adea Kryeziu, Barry Patrick Maher, and Asha M. Williams. 2020. *Adaptive Social Protection: Building Resilience to Shocks.* International Development in Focus. Washington, DC: World Bank. https://documents1.worldbank.org/curated /en/579641590038388922/pdf/Adaptive-Social-Protection-Building-Resilience-to-Shocks.pdf.

Charles, Anthony, Daniela Kalikoski, and Alison Macnaughton. 2019. *Addressing the Climate Change and Poverty Nexus: A Coordinated Approach in the Context of the 2030 Agenda and the Paris Agreement.* Rome: Food and Agriculture Organization. https://openknowledge.fao .org/handle/20.500.14283/ca6968en.

Chocholata, Lucie. 2020. *Farmer Field Schools, Gender Equality, Social Inclusion and Community Empowerment—Experiences from Uganda—Karamoja Sub-region, Case Study.* Rome: Food and Agriculture Organization. https://doi.org/10.4060/cb0709en.

Costella, Cecilia Valentina, Timothy Joseph Peter Clay, Manann Donoghoe, and Liz De Los Milagros Giron Pena. 2023. *Pathways to Climate-Resilient Economic Inclusion: A Framework for Integrating Climate Action in Economic Inclusion Programs. PEI in Practice, Volume 9.* Washington, DC: World Bank. http://documents.worldbank.org/curated /en/099140310302341355/IDU0f03fdb360cc560472a09279051ebddeb9e6a.

Cotula, Lorenzo. 2021. "Tenure Rights and Obligations—Towards a More Holistic Approach to Land Governance." FAO Legal Papers No. 106, Food and Agriculture Organization, Rome. https://doi.org/10.4060/cb5191en.

Cunningham, Wendy, and Sarika Gupta. 2023. *An Operational Approach to Enhancing Women's and Girls' Empowerment in World Bank Projects.* Washington, DC: World Bank. https://documents1.worldbank.org/curated/en/099071023114028973/pdf/P1731270b31 c3106b095510c0d44786f951.pdf.

Doherty, Fiona C., Smitha Rao, and Angelise R. Radney. 2023. "Association between Child, Early, and Forced Marriage and Extreme Weather Events: A Mixed-Methods Systematic Review." *International Social Work* 67 (3), 1–19. https://journals.sagepub.com/doi /abs/10.1177/00208728231186006.

Erman, Alvina, Sophie Anne De Vries Robbe, Stephan Fabian Thies, Kayenat Kabir, and Mirai Maruo. 2021. *Gender Dimensions of Disaster Risk and Resilience: Existing Evidence.* Washington, DC: World Bank. http://hdl.handle.net/10986/35202.

FAO (Food and Agriculture Organization). 2017. *Watershed Management in Action—Lessons Learned from FAO Field Projects.* Rome: FAO. http://www.fao.org/3/a-i8087e.pdf.

FAO (Food and Agriculture Organization). 2023a. *Strengthening Coherence between Forestry and Social Protection for Sustainable Agrifood Systems Transformation—Framework for Analysis and Action.* Rome. FAO. https://doi.org/10.4060/cc8648en.

FAO (Food and Agriculture Organization). 2023b. "Terminal Evaluation of the Project 'Payments for Ecosystem Services to Support Forest Conservation and Sustainable Livelihoods.' Project Evaluation Series, 25/2023, FAO, Rome. https://doi.org/10.4060/cc7817en.

FAO (Food and Agriculture Organization). 2024. *The Unjust Climate—Measuring the Impacts of Climate Change on Rural Poor, Women and Youth.* Rome: FAO. https://doi.org/10.4060 /cc9680en.

GCA (Global Center on Adaptation). 2021. *Principles for Locally Led Adaptation Action.* The Netherlands: CGA. https://gca.org/programs/locally-led-adaptation/.

Groot-Kormelinck, Annemarie, Jos Bijman, Jacques Trienekens, and Laurens Klerkx. 2022. "Producer Organizations as Transition Intermediaries? Insights from Organic and Conventional Vegetable Systems in Uruguay." *Agriculture and Human Values* 39: 1277–1300. https://doi.org/10.1007/s10460-022-10316-3.

Hallegatte, Stephane, Adrien Vogt-Schilb, Mook Bangalore, and Julie Rozenberg. 2017. *Unbreakable: Building the Resilience of the Poor in the Face of Natural Disasters.* Climate Change and Development. Washington, DC: World Bank. https://hdl.handle .net/10986/25335.

Hermann, Alexandra, Peter Köferl, and Jan Philip Mairhöfer. 2016. "Climate Risk Insurance: New Approaches and Schemes." Economic Research Working Paper, Allianz, Germany. https:// www.allianz.com/content/dam/onemarketing/azcom/Allianz_com/migration/media/economic _research/publications/working_papers/en/ClimateRisk.pdf.

Huyer, Sophia, and Nitya Chanana. 2021. "Gender-Smart Agriculture: An Agenda for Gender and Socially Inclusive Climate-Resilient Agriculture." CCAFS Working Paper No. 404, CGIAR Research Program on Climate Change, Agriculture and Food Security (CCAFS), Wageningen, The Netherlands. https://hdl.handle.net/10568/117523.

ILO (International Labour Organization). 2023. *Social Protection for a Just Transition.* Geneva, Switzerland: ILO. https://www.ilo.org/publications/social-protection-just-transition.

IPCC (Intergovernmental Panel on Climate Change). 2022. "Summary for Policymakers." In *Climate Change 2022: Impacts, Adaptation and Vulnerability. Contribution of Working Group II to the Sixth Assessment Report of the Intergovernmental Panel on Climate Change,* edited by H.-O. Pörtner, D.C. Roberts, E.S. Poloczanska, K. Mintenbeck, M. Tignor, A. Alegría, M. Craig, S. Langsdorf, S. Löschke, V. Möller, A. Okem, 3–33. Cambridge, UK: Cambridge University Press. https://doi.org/10.1017/9781009325844.001.

IRC (International Rescue Committee), and IFPRI (International Food Policy Research Institute). 2023. *Acting before Disaster Strikes: The Impacts of Anticipatory Cash Transfers on Climate Resilience in Northeast Nigeria. Research Brief.* New York: IRC and IFPRI. https://rescue.app .box.com/s/17e0avdz5uzoal1gkr7v92i44zc563o0.

Kumar, Neha, Kalyani Raghunathan, Alejandra Arrieta, Amir Jilani, and Shinjini Pandey. 2021. "The Power of the Collective Empowers Women: Evidence from Self-Help Groups in India." *World Development* 146. https://doi.org/10.1016/j.worlddev.2021.105579.

Liao, Chuan, Christopher B. Barrett, and Karim-Aly S. Kassam. 2014. *Does Diversification Translate into Improved Livelihoods? Evidence from Pastoral Households in the Altay and Tianshan Mountains of Xinjiang.* Ithaca, NY: Cornell University. https://doi.org/10.2139 /ssrn.2628701.

Mittal, Surabhi. 2016. "Role of Mobile Phone-Enabled Climate Information Services in Gender-Inclusive Agriculture." *Gender, Technology and Development* 20 (2): 200–17. https://doi .org/10.1177/0971852416639772.

Notta, Sabaa. 2022. "State of the Climate-Responsive Financial Product Landscape." *CGAP Blog.* https://www.cgap.org/blog/state-of-climate-responsive-financial-product-landscape.

Pople, Ashley, Ruth Hill, Stefan Dercon, and Ben Brunckhorst. 2021. "Anticipatory Cash Transfers in Climate Disaster Response." CSAE Working Paper Series 2021-07, Centre for the Study of African Economies, University of Oxford, Oxford, UK. https://ora.ox.ac.uk/objects /uuid:12ea16b2-edc0-4af5-8824-132aba4557bd.

Quisumbing, Agnes, Beatrice Gerli, Simone Faas, Jessica Heckert, Hazel Malapit, Catherine McCarron, Ruth Meinzen-Dick, and Florencia Paz. 2023. "Assessing Multicountry Programs through a 'Reach, Benefit, Empower, Transform' lens." *Global Food Security* 37. https://doi .org/10.1016/j.gfs.2023.100685.

SEEP (Small Enterprise Evaluation Project) Network. 2021. *Driving Climate Resilience through Savings Groups.* Washington, DC: SEEP. https://seepnetwork.org/Webinar-Post/Driving -Climate-Resilience-through-Savings-Groups-exist.

Tirivayi, Nyasha. 2017. "Social Protection for Building the Resilience of Forest-Dependent People: Evidence, Linkages, Practices and Potential Applications." Social Protection and

Forestry Working Paper No. 1. Rome, FAO. https://openknowledge.fao.org/items/d2dc0c1d -ed70-445f-a720-85959cde0506.

Trohanis, Zoe Elena, Brenden Jongman, Escobar Saenz, and Mirtha Liliana. 2023. *Integrating Gender and Social Inclusion in Nature-Based Solutions: Guidance Note.* Washington, DC: World Bank.

Ubfal, Diego Javier. 2023. "What Works in Supporting Women-led Businesses?" World Bank, Washington, DC. http://hdl.handle.net/10986/38564.

University of Notre Dame. 2023. *Notre Dame Global Adaptation Initiative (ND-GAIN).* Notre Dame, IN: University of Notre Dame.

UN Women. 2022. "Explainer: How Gender Inequality and Climate Change Are Interconnected." UN Women, New York. https://www.unwomen.org/en/news-stories/explainer/2022/02/explainer -how-gender-inequality-and-climate-change-are-interconnected.

Van Zanten, Boris Ton, Gonzalo Gutierrez Goizueta, Luke Mckinnon Brander, Borja Gonzalez Reguero, Robert Griffin, Kavita Kapur Macleod, Alida Ivana Alves Beloqui, Amelia Midgley, Luis Diego Herrera Garcia, and Brenden Jongman. 2023. *Assessing the Benefits and Costs of Nature-Based Solutions for Climate Resilience: A Guideline for Project Developers.* Washington, DC: World Bank. http://hdl.handle.net/10986/39811.

WHO (World Health Organization). 2010. *WHO Gender Responsive Assessment Scale: Criteria for Assessing Programmes and Policies—Mental Health, Men and Culture: How Do Sociocultural Constructions of Masculinities Relate to Men's Mental Health Help-Seeking Behaviour in the WHO European Region?* NCBI Bookshelf. Geneva: WHO. https://www .ncbi.nlm.nih.gov/books/NBK559709/table/ch2.t1/?report=objectonly.

World Bank. 2013. "Ethiopia—Using a Social Safety Net to Deliver Disaster Insurance to the Poor: Case Study." World Bank, Washington, DC. http://documents.worldbank.org/curated /en/252531468158380847/Ethiopia-Using-a-socialsafety-net-to-deliver-disaster-insurance-t.

World Bank, Independent Evaluation Group. 2021. *The Natural Resource Degradation and Vulnerability Nexus: An Evaluation of the World Bank's Support for Sustainable and Inclusive Natural Resource Management (2009–2019).* Washington, DC: World Bank. https:// ieg.worldbankgroup.org/evaluations/natural-resource-degradation-and-vulnerability-nexus /chapter-5-conclusions-and.

Policy Recommendations

Introduction

This report illustrates the potential of economic inclusion programs to unlock the productive potential of poor and vulnerable populations. The evidence clearly reveals that these programs play a critical role in building resilience to shocks, including those exacerbated by climate change. In the current context of overlapping crises, these programs are more relevant than ever before.

Through a multidimensional approach, these programs address multiple constraints faced by poor and vulnerable individuals, households, and communities, thereby increasing their incomes and assets. Initially driven by evidence from nongovernment-led programs, a growing body of evidence from government-led programs now demonstrates robust impacts on key economic outcomes among poor and vulnerable populations, including improvements in food security, consumption, income, business revenues, and asset accumulation. There is also evidence of increased resilience to shocks over the long run, as well as greater diversification of women's economic activities, which is a key pathway to resilience. Although the evidence is limited to a few studies, these programs have been shown to be very cost-effective, high-return investments.

Scaling up programs that empower poor and vulnerable populations to access economic opportunities, enhance food security, and build both short- and long-term resilience can contribute to more inclusive and sustainable growth that leaves no one behind. Based on an in-depth review of the current landscape of economic inclusion programs, this report provides the following five key policy recommendations.

1. Continue to Expand Coverage to Reach Those Most in Need

Poor and vulnerable populations face a complex web of challenges such as lack of access to education, health care, financial services, and employment opportunities. These constraints are often interlinked, reinforce each other, and create a cycle of poverty and exclusion. Without comprehensive economic inclusion programs, there is a considerable risk of leaving these populations behind as countries progress economically.

This report highlights a promising trend of increasing coverage of economic inclusion programs. These programs currently reach more than 15 million households and benefit more than 70 million individuals, directly or indirectly, in 88 countries globally. These figures represent an increase of more than 50 percent in the number of individuals participating in these programs since 2021. Despite this expansion, these programs cover only a small proportion of the overall population living in poverty. Millions more poor and vulnerable people remain economically and socially excluded.

As the report shows, expanding coverage means not only increasing the number of participants but also ensuring that the most marginalized and hard-to-reach people are included. This work requires a multifaceted approach involving improved data collection for better targeting, increased financial and administrative resources, and enhanced coordination between government agencies and nongovernmental organizations. Scaling up involves replicating successful models while adapting them to local contexts, ensuring sustainability, and continuously evaluating and refining approaches. By doing so, economic inclusion programs can more effectively address the complex and varied needs of poor and vulnerable individuals, building their long-term resilience and creating job opportunities.

2. Strengthen Outcomes for Women and Youth through More Intentional Design and Delivery and for Youth by Connecting Them to Wage Employment Opportunities

It is especially important to focus on women and youth in the expansion of economic inclusion programs. As illustrated in the report, these groups are a priority for most economic inclusion programs: 90 percent of programs target women, and 65 percent target youth. In regions experiencing a youth bulge, a much larger share of programs focuses on supporting the access of youth to better economic opportunities (86 percent of programs in the Middle East and North Africa and 70 percent of programs in Sub-Saharan Africa). However, targeting these groups is just the first step. Although these vulnerable groups share some of the same constraints to economic inclusion, understanding specific barriers to engaging in income-generating activities is key to supporting them effectively. There has been progress on this front in recent years, but more programs must take an evidence-based approach to customizing design and delivery for these groups.

Many more programs could adopt gender-intentional design and delivery that actively considers and addresses the different needs, experiences, and challenges of all women, particularly focusing on reducing gender inequalities. Emerging lessons stress the importance of addressing social norms, tailoring the timing and nature of program activities, and including components to reduce the burden of unpaid care work on women, which often limits their time and opportunities for economic participation. Beyond programmatic interventions, a critical dimension to scaling up also requires policy-level engagement, at a minimum to take advantage of any enabling policy frameworks (such as decent work provisions for childcare or community-based care) and, at best, to gradually influence legislative and regulatory barriers that women might face.

Similarly, economic inclusion programs offer a testing ground for innovative approaches to tackle job challenges and integrate young people into the economy, especially those hardest to reach. In contexts where labor demand is extremely low, these programs typically promote self-employment opportunities for poor and vulnerable youth. The prevailing trends of increasing urbanization and demographic shifts, such as the youth bulge in developing economies, present an opportunity to promote more access to wage employment for youth. By focusing on comprehensive provision of skills training, job placement services, and referrals, these programs can boost labor market participation of youth and promote their economic self-sufficiency. However, it is essential to integrate demand-side measures into such programs, and practitioners should better understand constraints such as skills mismatches, employer biases, regulatory barriers, and economic instability, all of which may dampen demand for labor. Building strong partnerships with employers, developing skills training programs aligned with market needs, and offering job-matching services can help connect young job seekers with suitable employment opportunities.

3. Maintain Program Quality While Scaling Up

This report highlights the opportunities and challenges in scaling up both individual programs and establishing systematic links across programs for a more coherent economic inclusion policy framework. At the program level, it is important to prioritize the quality of program implementation as these programs scale up. Effective program delivery at scale will require well-structured institutional arrangements and organizational frameworks. Fifty-seven percent of the programs surveyed in the report indicate that they have scaled up institutionally by forming new partnerships or becoming more integrated with government structures. As government-led programs move to scale, collaborating with external organizations such as NGOs, community-based organizations, and the private sector is critical to overcoming capacity constraints. Leveraging existing delivery systems and digital technologies also plays a role in innovation and cost-effective delivery at scale.

At the policy level, as programs move to scale, a coherent approach toward an overall economic inclusion strategy is needed. The report underscores the diversity of economic inclusion programs across different countries and contexts, particularly within government institutions. While these programs often utilize distinct strategies and target various geographic areas and populations, fragmentation remains a substantial risk. To address this issue, it is crucial to develop national economic inclusion strategies that provide a coordinated approach, in particular by understanding the interplay between household- and area-focused interventions to catalyze sector-wide transformation. Enhancing interagency coordination, streamlining program design and implementation, and leveraging technology for integration are essential steps to reduce fragmentation. These actions can help create a unified, scalable approach to economic inclusion, ensuring programs work synergistically to maximize their impact on poverty reduction.

4. Continue to Build an Evidence Base to Inform Scale-Up and Enhance Government Capacity for Implementation

Scaling up involves replicating successful models while adapting them to local contexts, ensuring sustainability, and continuously evaluating and refining approaches. However, current evidence from government-led economic inclusion programs primarily comes from a few household-focused programs, which do not fully capture the variety of programs across different regions and contexts. A broader evidence base and a more comprehensive research agenda are needed to evaluate the impact and cost-effectiveness of large-scale government-led programs in diverse settings. Critical learning gaps must be addressed, specifically for optimal program design for achieving scalability, impact, and cost-effectiveness. So far, most evaluations have measured impact in the short term, 1–3 years after program completion. To assess the long-term sustainability of these programs, more evaluations of at least 7–10 years after program completion are needed. Going forward, it is also crucial to better understand the impact of area-focused programs on poverty and the broader economy and their potential synergies with household-focused interventions.

Beyond building the evidence base, the research and evaluation agenda at the country level can help national governments build capacity for implementation. Research teams should work hand-in-hand with national governments and implementing agencies to establish robust monitoring and evaluation frameworks. Embedding impact evaluations during program rollout and scale-up can ensure the production and use of high-quality, operationally relevant data to inform decision-making. Engaging all stakeholders in the evaluation process can create a dynamic learning environment that improves program outcomes in real time.

Throughout the program cycle, a strong case exists for establishing comprehensive data systems, incorporating real-time monitoring and beneficiary feedback, and systematizing operational learning. In the design phase, expanding to new populations or geographies while ensuring strong program quality requires adopting good diagnostics, tailoring program components, and sequencing components. During implementation, monitoring participant progress, making real-time adjustments, and refining program design are hallmarks of success. Programs should balance participant needs, costs, complexity, and feedback from monitoring data to inform design refinements.

5. Design for Sustainable Impacts

Economic inclusion programs have demonstrated their effectiveness in boosting income and assets by creating household enterprises or by diversifying income sources and occupational choices. The next generation of economic inclusion programming should focus on enhancing the sustainability of these impacts, for example, by integrating their participants into local and international markets and value chains to the extent feasible. Achieving this outcome requires a thorough understanding of market systems and the constraints specific to each context, followed by the development of tailored interventions to create strong market linkages. Thus, conducting detailed market assessments to identify opportunities and challenges, understanding consumer preferences, and analyzing competitive landscapes are needed. By doing so, programs can better align their interventions with market demands, enhancing the viability and profitability of household enterprises or the employability of their participants.

For many programs, securing sustainable financing and embedding economic inclusion in government systems and policies is a priority to achieve sustainability. It is also important to calibrate expectations—many participants of economic inclusion programs will make continued efforts to sustain household enterprises. As such, while economic inclusion programs typically provide a time-bound, sequenced set of components, referrals to other services or support will likely be necessary to sustain the positive impacts on incomes, assets, and occupational choices, especially due to the increasing frequency of economic and climate-related shocks.

Going forward, economic inclusion programs must retain their flexibility in responding to broader development challenges, most notably building climate resilience, as illustrated in this report's special focus.

APPENDIXES

Survey Methodology

Introduction

This appendix provides an overview of the methodology used in executing the Landscape Survey 2023 and the analysis underpinning this report.

Mapping the Economic Inclusion Program Universe

The Partnership for Economic Inclusion (PEI) Landscape Survey 2023, which builds on the 2020 round of the survey, is a comprehensive inventory of ongoing economic inclusion programs.[1] For both rounds of the survey, the PEI team defined economic inclusion programs as multidimensional interventions that support and enable individuals, households, and communities to achieve sustainable livelihoods and increase their incomes and assets, while building human capital and promoting social inclusion.

To map the universe of economic inclusion programs, the PEI team reviewed the World Bank's lending portfolio and external sources. In mapping World Bank projects, PEI conducted its annual 2023 World Bank portfolio review. The team scanned both active and pipeline projects (listed in the World Bank Operations Portal) across all geographic regions led by the following seven Global Practices (GPs): (1) Agriculture and Food; (2) Education; (3) Environment, Natural Resources, and Blue Economy; (4) Finance, Competitiveness, and Innovation; (5) Social Protection and Jobs; (6) Social Sustainability and Inclusion; and (7) Urban Resilience and Land.

The portfolio review was conducted in two stages. In the first stage, the team updated the list of economic inclusion programs identified from the previous year's portfolio review.[2] This work involved removing closed projects and documenting project restructuring, additional financing, and other general information updates to the portfolio of pipeline and active projects. Project information was updated using key project documents such as implementation status and results, reports, and project papers (PPs).

The second stage involved identifying new economic inclusion programs that emerged over the past year since the previous 2022 portfolio review. To speed up the mapping process, the PEI team collaborated with the Text and Data Analytics (TDA) team within the Information Technology and Knowledge Solutions Department of the World Bank to compile a list of all new World Bank projects that aligned with the definition of economic inclusion. Using a predefined set of economic inclusion keywords,[3] the TDA team applied advanced text analytics across project documents including project appraisal documents (PADs) or, when a PAD was not available, its project information document, PP, or project information and integrated safeguards data sheet. The TDA team applied this technique to both active and pipeline projects in all geographical regions and across the seven GPs.

Once completed, the PEI team was then provided with a matrix of projects that included a text analysis ranking based on the taxonomy of keywords as well as prepopulated project information, including relevant keywords, project summaries, and specific thematic information. As part of the second stage review process, the PEI team manually assessed the matrix of projects provided by the TDA team. The team evaluated whether each project aligned with PEI's definition of economic inclusion programming by examining prepopulated project information and relevant keywords, including keyword frequency. When the information provided by the TDA team was insufficient, the PEI team manually reviewed PADs and other project documents to reach a final decision.

To complete the mapping of World Bank–financed economic inclusion programs, once the final list of new projects was confirmed, it was merged with the original updated list of projects from the first-stage review, accounting for any overlaps. Overall, these methods allowed the PEI team to map 321 World Bank economic inclusion programs, representing 239 individual programs in 83 countries.[4]

Surveys were sent to these 239 unique identified programs, and responses were received from 175 of them (refer to table A.1).

To map projects outside of World Bank operations, the PEI team used the PEI Landscape Survey 2020 data set to identify both ongoing projects and partner organizations, including governments, nongovernmental organizations (NGOs), regional organizations, multilaterals, and other development partners involved in economic inclusion programming. Organizations were approached to self-identify programs that met a prescribed set of criteria based on the working definition of an economic inclusion program.[5] The PEI team also mapped other relevant economic inclusion interventions by scanning existing databases and inventories of social protection and productive inclusion programs, including the Economic Commission for Latin America and the Caribbean database on productive inclusion programs and the Atlas of Social Protection Indicators of Resilience and Equity. The PEI team identified 357 projects outside the World Bank portfolio, of which 331 responses were expected and 230 responses were received (refer to table A.1).[6]

Despite efforts to map the entire universe of economic inclusion interventions, additional programs spearheaded by some United Nations agencies, including the International Fund for Agricultural Development and the Food and Agriculture Organization, as well as by some NGOs, were not mapped as comprehensively as for the World Bank. Therefore, the sample is dominated by World Bank operations and PEI partnership organizations.

There are 165 missing responses both within and outside World Bank operations (102 from nongovernment programs and 63 from government programs). Because of insufficient information, it is not possible to assess whether programs not included in the survey are substantially different in nature from the surveyed programs.

TABLE A.1 **Response Rate for the Partnership for Economic Inclusion Landscape Survey 2023**

Project	Mapped projects	Expected responses	Received responses	Survey response rate
World Bank	321	239	175	73%
External	357	331	230	69%
Total	**678**	**570**	**405**	**71%**

Source: Partnership for Economic Inclusion, World Bank, 2023.

Although the survey sample does not fully represent the entire universe of economic inclusion programs, by having captured responses from 405 programs in 88 countries and 6 geographical regions and led by more than 200 organizations, the survey still captures a sufficiently strong variation across regions and institutional setups to provide a comprehensive overview of economic inclusion programming worldwide.

The Survey Tool

The questionnaire for the Landscape Survey 2023 builds on the survey questionnaire that was used in the Landscape Survey 2020. The questionnaire for the Landscape Survey 2023 included some minor changes from the questionnaire used in 2020 to add clarity and granularity to some of the questions. The 2023 survey was also expanded slightly to capture information on design and implementation features on PEI's priority topics: women's economic empowerment and climate resilience. Consultations with PEI's technical partners and World Bank staff informed the revisions to the questionnaire. The 2023 survey questionnaire has 54 questions, which were divided into nine sections: (1) basic information on the program, (2) program objectives, (3) target beneficiaries and coverage, (4) design and implementation features, (5) institutional arrangements, (6) research and evaluation plans, (7) scaling up, (8) COVID-19 impact and responses, and (9) additional information.

The survey was completed by staff from the lead implementing agency, implementing partners, or other organizations supporting programs. It was made available in English, French, and Spanish through an online platform.[7] Each returned survey represented a unique program. Organizations that were involved in more than one economic inclusion program filled out several surveys.

The survey was administered between February and June 2023. This process involved reaching out to economic inclusion program representatives, soliciting survey responses, following up with emails and phone calls, and assisting with survey completion as needed.

Because data were self-reported, data quality relied primarily on respondents' knowledge of the program and understanding of the survey questions. To ensure overall quality, several quality control features were embedded in the design of the survey tool, and, to further improve data accuracy, the PEI team undertook a full quality review of all of the forms, checked the completeness and consistency of survey responses during the survey data collection process, and followed up with survey respondents to request clarifications or additional information wherever data were missing or inconsistencies were found.

Analysis of Survey Data

The analysis presented in the report is a statistical summary of the survey results and does not attempt to draw inferences about the universe of economic inclusion programs because this is unknown. For this reason, and in line with the approach followed in the Landscape Survey 2020, the PEI team decided not to apply weights to the data. Additional analysis, including cross-tabulations, was performed to illuminate factors that may help explain the differences across programs.

The Landscape Survey 2023 provides a holistic inventory of economic inclusion programs worldwide. Despite changes to the questionnaire, the Landscape Survey 2023 remains comparable to the 2020 survey round, allowing for the analysis of trends between these two years for most survey questions. Where comparisons are not possible, this is noted in the text.

The following seven indicators were added to the survey data to support the analysis: (1) countries' income group; (2) region; (3) lending category; (4) poverty headcount ratio at the extreme poverty line (US$2.15 per day at 2017 purchasing power parity, PPP), lower-middle-income poverty line (US$3.65 per day in 2017, PPP), and upper-middle-income poverty line (US$6.85 per day in 2017, PPP), as well as population size (most recent data from the World Bank Open Data portal); (5) headcount ratio using the Oxford Poverty and Human Development Initiative's Multidimensional Poverty Index; (6) average household size (various sources); and (7) whether a country is included in the World Bank's Classification of Fragile and Conflict-Affected Situations.[8]

Analysis of Coverage Data

The survey asked for the number of participants currently enrolled, number of participants reached to date, and target participants for the respective programs. Programs could report the number of participants as the number of households or the number of individuals. Of the 405 programs reporting overall, for the coverage analysis the sample is limited to 333 programs from 78 countries because 72 programs did not report the coverage numbers.[9] Coverage estimates are likely to be biased with the likely exclusions of several programs outside of the World Bank Group and PEI's partnership organizations, as noted earlier.

The estimates provided in this report delineate coverage in terms of households (direct participants) and individuals (direct participants plus indirect beneficiaries). The individual figure is determined by multiplying direct participants by average household size in the country. This approach follows an accepted estimation approach across social protection programs globally (Beegle et al. 2018; Milazzo and Grosh 2008) and is the process followed for the Landscape Survey 2020. The programs for which coverage data are reported currently cover more than 70 million individuals as both direct recipients and indirect beneficiaries, which corresponds to over 15 million households.

Estimates do not account for the potential spillover and community effects of an intervention. Because, in some programs, different members of the same household are direct recipients of economic inclusion program components, in aggregating coverage figures it was not possible to distinguish between direct participants and indirect beneficiaries. Coverage data reported as the number of individuals thus include both direct participants and indirect beneficiaries. There may be overlap in program coverage within countries, where different programs serve the same population groups, but the extent to which this happens is unknown.

Because of the tailored nature of economic inclusion programs, the PEI team considered coverage equivalents, defined as the number of direct participants plus indirect beneficiaries reached by a program relative to the national poverty line. This consideration is in line with the approach followed in Andrews et al. (2021) and World Bank (2022). These equivalent measures provide important illustrations of the potential coverage of programs that have a strong focus on poverty. They also recognize a wider debate on poverty measurement thresholds (refer to box 4.1 in Andrews et al. 2021). For this report, the analysis of coverage equivalents did not consider other poverty lines.

Calculation of the coverage equivalent at the country level began by adding up the number of individual beneficiaries for all the programs in a given country. The number of individual beneficiaries (direct and indirect) per country was then compared with the poor population calculated using the total population of the country and the poverty headcount ratio at the national poverty line (percentage of population). The most recent data on poverty headcount ratio were retrieved from each country's database.[10] In addition, the most recent population estimates were taken from the World Bank Open Data portal.

Notes

1. To review the methodology of PEI's Landscape Survey 2020, refer to Andrews et al. 2021.
2. The PEI team reviews the portfolio of World Bank financing every year with the purpose of identifying operations that support economic inclusion programming.
3. Keywords include the following: access to finance; access to market; accompanying; accompanying measures; adaptive social protection; cash plus; cash transfer; climate adaptation; climate change; climate mitigation; climate smart; community-driven; coordinated intervention; CSA; disabilities; disaster risk; displaced populations; economic empowerment; economic inclusion; economic opportunities; ecosystem service; employment opportunities; extremely poor; financial services; graduation; food system; green economy; green job; green recovery; green transition; IDP; inclusion; Indigenous; integrated livelihood package; integrated package; just transition; livelihood; livelihood enhancement; livelihood enhancing; livelihood opportunities; marginal; marginalized; market access; multidimensional; multifaceted; multi-faceted; poorest; producer group; producer organization; productive; productive inclusion; productive safety net; productive social safety net; promotion; refugees; safety net; self-help group; SHG; social inclusion; socio-economic inclusion; targeted; targeting criteria; ultra-poor; vulnerable; WEE; women's economic empowerment; value chain.
4. The list of 239 programs excludes operations in the pipeline, additional financing projects, and other projects recently closed that are included in the list of 321 projects.
5. Programs targeted by the survey had to be under way and meet the following criteria: (1) Projects support individuals, households, and communities to achieve sustainable livelihoods and increase the assets and income of participants, while building human capital and promoting social inclusion; (2) projects are either targeted to or at least benefit extreme-poor or otherwise vulnerable households or people within the household or community; and (3) projects seek to address several sources of vulnerability through a mix of at least two different types of interventions (that is, they are multidimensional interventions).
6. The list of 331 programs excludes programs in the pipeline as well as programs for which information on implementation status could not be obtained.
7. The online tool is available at the SEI 2024 landing page at peiglobal.org/state-of-economic-inclusion-report.
8. The sources of additional indicators used to analyze survey data were the following: World Bank Country and Lending Groups and Income, https://datahelpdesk.worldbank.org/knowledgebase/articles/906519-world-bank-country-and-lending-groups; poverty, https://databank.worldbank.org/source/world-development-indicators#, World Bank. 2023. "Macro Poverty Outlook: Country-by-Country Analysis and Projections for the Developing World 2023," https://thedocs.worldbank.org/en/doc/77351105a334213c64122e44c2ef e523-0500072021/related/mpo-am23.pdf; Harmonized List of Fragile Situations FY24,

https://thedocs.worldbank.org/en/doc/608a53dd83f21ef6712b5dfef050b00b-0090082023
/original/FCSListFY24-final.pdf; Household size: Afghanistan Central Statistics Organization
(CSO)—Afghanistan Living Conditions Survey 2016–2017, https://adsp.ngo/wp-content
/uploads/2018/12/PS-24_AFGHANISTAN-LIVING-CONDITIONS-SURVEY-2016-2017
.pdf; Albania Household Budget Survey 2020; Angola Demographic and Health Surveys
(DHS) 2016; National Institute of Statistics and Census of Argentina (INDEC)—Continuous
Household Survey, Annual Results 2020; Armenia Stats 2022; Aruba, United Nations
Demographic Yearbook 2010; The State Statistical Committee of Azerbaijan 2018; Bangladesh
Bureau of Statistics (BBS)—"Bangladesh Household Income and Expenditure Survey 2016";
Belize, Michael Bauer Research 2020; Benin Demographic and Health Surveys (DHS) 2018;
Bhutan Living Standards Survey 2017; Bolivia Population and Housing Census 2012; Bosnia
and Herzegovina, World Bank, ECAPOV (2015); Botswana Demographic Survey (BDS)
2017; Brazilian National Household Sample Survey 2019; Bulgaria Labour Force Survey
2020; Burkina Faso Demographic and Health Survey 2017-2018; Burundi Demographic and
Health Surveys (DHS) 2016; Cambodia Socio-Economic Survey 2019; Cameroon Household
Consumption Survey 2014; Cape Verde Population and Housing Census 2010; Central African
Republic National Household Survey 2019; Chad Demographic and Health Surveys (DHS)
2015; Chile Census of Population and Housing 2017; China National Bureau of Statistics,
CEIC 2020; Colombia National Population and Housing Census 2018; Comoros Demographic
and Health Surveys (DHS) 2012; Congo, Democratic Republic Demographic and Health
Surveys (DHS) 2013; Congo, Republic Demographic and Health Surveys (DHS) 2011; Costa
Rica Continuous Household Survey 2020; Côte d'Ivoire Demographic and Health Surveys
(DHS) 2017; Cyprus, Labour Force Surveys (LFS) of the European Union 2011; Cuba, Global
Data Lab 2019, https://globaldatalab.org/areadata/table/hhsize/CUB/?levels=1; Djiboutian
Household Survey for Social Indicators (EDAM4—IS) 2017; Dominica 2011 Population
and Housing Census, https://stats.gov.dm/wp-content/uploads/2020/04/2011-Population-and
-Housing-Census.pdf; Dominican Republic Demographic and Health Surveys (DHS) 2018;
Ecuador Continuous National Survey of Employment, Unemployment, and Underemployment
2020; Egypt, Arab Rep. Demographic and Health Surveys (DHS) 2014; El Salvador, Michael
Bauer Research 2018; Eswatini National Household Survey 2015; Ethiopia Demographic
and Health Surveys (DHS) 2016; Fiji, IPUMS-International Minnesota Population Center
2014; Gabon National Household Survey 2015; Gambia Demographic and Health Surveys
(DHS) 2019; Georgia, UNICEF GEOSTAT 2018; Ghana Demographic and Health Surveys
(DHS) 2014; Guatemala Demographic and Health Surveys (DHS) 2015; Guinea, Global Data
Lab 2018, https://globaldatalab.org/areadata/table/hhsize/GIN/; Guinea-Bissau Demographic
and Health Surveys (DHS) 2012; Statistics Guyana 2019; Haiti Demographic and Health
Surveys (DHS) 2017; Honduras Living Conditions Survey 2018; India Demographic and
Health Surveys (DHS) 2015; Indonesia Demographic and Health Surveys (DHS) 2017; Iraq
Household Socio-Economic Survey 2018; Israel Central Bureau of Statistics 2016; Jamaica,
ESRI 2020; Jordan Demographic and Health Surveys (DHS) 2017; Kenya Demographic
and Health Surveys (DHS) 2015; Kiribati Household Income and Expenditure Survey 2021;
Kosovo Population and Housing Census 2011; Kyrgyz Republic Demographic and Health
Surveys (DHS) 2012; Lao PDR Population and Housing Census 2015; Lebanon Household
Living Conditions Survey 2019-2020; Lesotho National Survey 2015; Liberia Demographic
and Health Surveys (DHS) 2019; Libya Census 2012; Madagascar Demographic and
Health Surveys (DHS) 2019; Malawi Demographic and Health Surveys (DHS) 2015; Mali
Demographic and Health Surveys (DHS) 2015; Mauritania Census 2013; Mexico, IPUMS-
International Minnesota Population Center 2015; Moldova Census 2014; National Statistics
Office of Mongolia 2017; Morocco High Commission for Planning 2017; Mozambique
Demographic and Health Surveys (DHS) 2011; Myanmar Demographic and Health Surveys
(DHS) 2016; Namibia Demographic and Health Surveys (DHS) 2013; Nepal Annual
Household Survey 2015; Nicaragua Annual Household Survey 2021; Niger Demographic and
Health Surveys (DHS) 2012; Nigeria Demographic and Health Surveys (DHS) 2015; Pakistan

6th National Population and Housing Census 2017; Panama, IPUMS-International Minnesota Population Center 2010; Papua New Guinea National Population and Housing Census 2011; Paraguay Permanent Household Survey 2019; Peru National Household Survey 2020; Philippines Demographic and Health Surveys (DHS) 2017; Romania National Household Survey 2017; Rwanda Integrated Household Living Conditions Survey 2016/2017; São Tomé and Principe National Household Survey 2018; Senegal National Household Survey 2017; Serbia National Household Survey 2017; the Seychelles Demographic and Health Surveys (DHS) 2010; Sierra Leone Demographic and Health Surveys (DHS) 2019; Sint Maarten (Dutch) Central Bureau of Statistics 2021; Solomon Islands Census 2009; Somalia Population Estimation Survey 2014, UNFPA; High Frequency South Sudan Survey, World Bank 2015; Sri Lanka Household Income and Expenditure Survey, Department of Census and Statistics 2016; St Maarten, Demographic Yearbook (DYB) of the United Nations 2011; St. Lucia National Household Survey 2017; Sudan, IPUMS-International Minnesota Population Center 2008; Syrian Arab Republic, UNDP 2005 Poverty in Syria: 1996-2004 Diagnosis and Pro-Poor Policy Considerations; Tajikistan Demographic and Health Surveys (DHS) 2017; Tanzania 2012 Population and Housing Census, NBS; Thailand National Household Survey 2022; Timor-Leste Demographic and Health Surveys (DHS) 2016; Togo Demographic and Health Surveys (DHS) 2014; Tonga Census of Population and Housing 2011; Tunisia Data Atlas 31st December 2014; Türkiye Household Budget Survey 2019; Uganda Demographic and Health Surveys (DHS) 2016; Ukraine National Household Survey 2017; Uruguay, IPUMS-International Minnesota Population Center 2011; Uzbekistan Living Standards and Welfare Survey, Statistics Committee 2016; Vanuatu Census 2020; Viet Nam Household Living Standard Survey (HSS), General Statistics Office 2016; West Bank and Gaza, Palestinian Central Bureau of Statistics (PCBS) 2017; Yemen, Republic of Demographic and Health Surveys (DHS) 2013; Zambia Demographic and Health Surveys (DHS) 2013; Zimbabwe Demographic and Health Surveys (DHS) 2015.

9. As noted in chapter 2, the 72 programs for which beneficiary data is missing had not started actual implementation, that is, the economic inclusion components were yet to be delivered to participants at the time of the survey.

10. Refer to the World Bank Global Poverty Working Group's (ID: SI.POV.NAHC) Poverty and Inequality Platform, in which data are compiled from official government sources or are computed by World Bank staff using national (that is, country specific) poverty lines.

References

Andrews, Colin, Aude de Montesquiou, Inés Arévalo-Sánchez, Puja Vasudeva Dutta, Boban Varghese Paul, Sadna Samaranayake, Janet Heisey, Timothy Clay, and Sarang Chaudhary. 2021. *The State of Economic Inclusion Report 2021: The Potential to Scale.* Washington, DC: World Bank. http://hdl.handle.net/10986/34917.

Beegle, Kathleen G., Aline Coudouel, and Emma Monsalve, eds. 2018. *Realizing the Full Potential of Social Safety Nets in Africa.* Washington, DC: World Bank. https://documents1.worldbank .org/curated/en/657581531930611436/pdf/128594-PUB-PUBLIC.pdf.

Milazzo, Annamaria, and Margaret Grosh. 2008. "Social Safety Nets in World Bank Lending and Analytical Work: FY2002–2007." Social Protection Discussion Paper No. SP 0810, World Bank, Washington, DC. http://documents.worldbank.org/curated/en/920421468155739339 /Social-safety-nets-in-World-Bank-lending-and-analytical-work-FY2002-2007.

World Bank. 2022. *Poverty and Shared Prosperity 2022: Correcting Course.* Washington, DC: World Bank. https://openknowledge.worldbank.org/server/api/core/bitstreams /b96b361a-a806-5567-8e8a-b14392e11fa0/content.

Comparison of Landscape Survey Data in SEI 2021 and SEI 2024

Introduction

This appendix compares the landscape data findings included in *The State of Economic Inclusion Report 2021* (SEI) and *The State of Economic Inclusion Report 2024*. The data that underpin the findings were collected in Landscape Surveys 2020 and 2023, respectively. Therefore, data referred to in the report under 2021 were collected in 2020, and data referred to under 2024 were collected in 2023.

Broadly, the data from SEI 2024 indicate that the core characteristics and objectives of programs are like those captured in SEI 2021, with most programs providing more than four components in sequence over 12 to 36 months to support self-employment and productivity. Programs also continue to be delivered through engagement with multiple stakeholders. In the global footprint, programs are found in countries across income levels, but most programs are in Sub-Saharan Africa (SSA), as in 2021.

However, the data also highlight key shifts between SEI 2021 and SEI 2024. The number of economic inclusion programs and participants in these programs have increased significantly. In addition, a higher percentage of programs report that women's empowerment and climate resilience are their main objectives in SEI 2024. The data also highlight changes in program delivery. More programs reported using digital tools, particularly to provide components such as coaching, business capital, and training and to support grievance and redress mechanisms. There is also increased collaboration between institutions, with a higher proportion of programs using external agencies to deliver economic inclusion program components.

Reach of the Economic Inclusion Programs

SEI 2024 unveils a significant increase in the number of economic inclusion programs globally: 405 programs in 88 countries, compared to 219 programs in 75 countries in SEI 2021. The global coverage of these programs has also expanded, reaching more than 15 million households and 70 million individuals in 2023, compared to 9.8 million households and 45.8 million individuals in 2020.[1]

Distribution of Programs by Lead Institution

There has been an increase in the share of nongovernment-led programs, from 51 percent of programs in 2021 to 57 percent of programs in 2024 (refer to figure B.1). There has also been an increase in the proportion of participants nongovernment-led programs serve, from 13 percent in 2021 to 26 percent in 2024 (refer to figure B.2).

FIGURE B.1 **Distribution of Government-Led and Nongovernment-Led Economic Inclusion Programs**

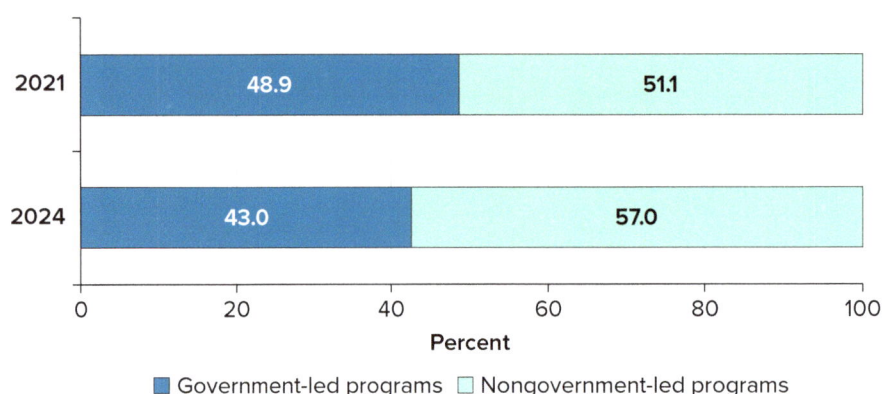

Source: Partnership for Economic Inclusion, World Bank.

Note: Figure shows the percentage of all programs (*N* = 405 in SEI 2024 and *N* = 219 in SEI 2021).

FIGURE B.2 **Distribution of Participants in Government-Led and Nongovernment-Led Programs**

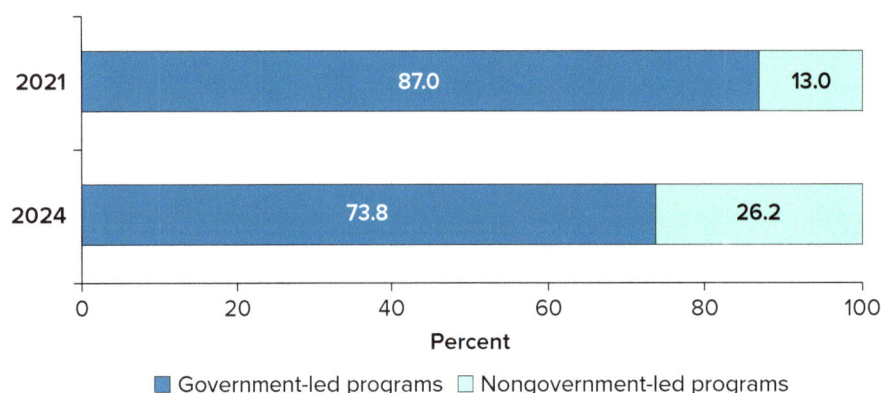

Source: Partnership for Economic Inclusion, World Bank.

Note: Figure shows the percentage of total participants (*N* = 15,323,059 in SEI 2024 and *N* = 9,773,043 in SEI 2021).

This shift may be the result of new programs emerging and the sustained scale-up of nongovernment-led programs since 2021. However, government-led programs continue to serve the majority of participants (refer to figure B.2).

Regional Distribution of Programs

The distribution of programs across regions in SEI 2024 is similar to SEI 2021 (refer to figure B.3). However, the distribution of participants across regions has changed, with a higher proportion of participants in SSA in 2024 than in 2021 (75 percent compared to 59 percent). This change is due to both the increase in the number of programs and the expansion of existing programs in the region. The data also indicate that participants from South Asia have decreased from 32 percent in 2021 to 17.3 percent in 2024 (refer to figure B.4).

FIGURE B.3   **Distribution of Economic Inclusion Programs, by Region**

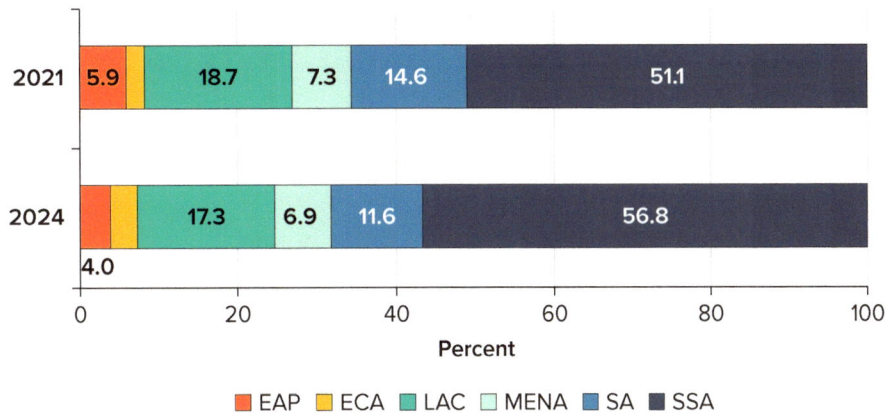

Source: Partnership for Economic Inclusion, World Bank.

Note: EAP = East Asia and Pacific; ECA = Europe and Central Asia; LAC = Latin America and the Caribbean; MENA = Middle East and North Africa; SA = South Asia; SSA = Sub-Saharan Africa. Percentage of all programs (*N* = 405 in SEI 2024 and *N* = 219 in SEI 2021).

FIGURE B.4   **Distribution of Participants in Economic Inclusion Programs, by Region**

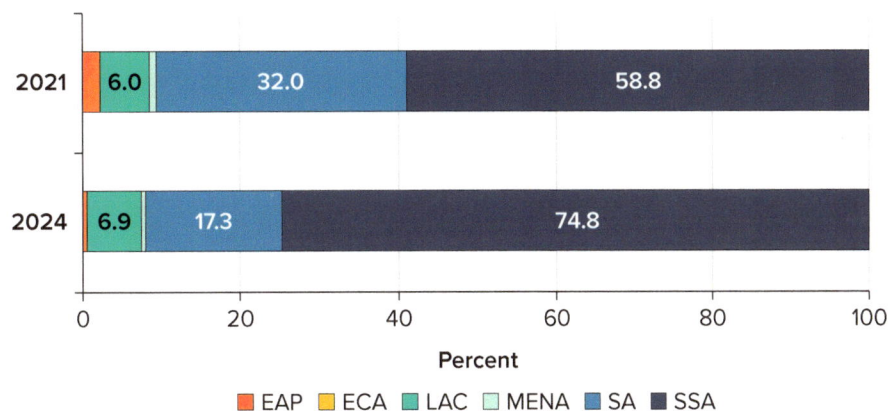

Source: Partnership for Economic Inclusion, World Bank.

Note: EAP = East Asia and Pacific; ECA = Europe and Central Asia; LAC = Latin America and the Caribbean; MENA = Middle East and North Africa; SA = South Asia; SSA = Sub-Saharan Africa. Data on the number of participants in SEI 2024 is missing for 72 programs, most of which were in the last phases of preparation before actual delivery of support for participants began. Data on the number of participants from 2021 are missing for 18 programs. Percentage of total participants (*N* = 15,323,059 in SEI 2024 and *N* = 9,773,043 in SEI 2021).

Distribution of Programs by Context

Economic inclusion programs operate in countries at different stages of development, such as low-income countries, middle-income countries, and high-income countries. While there has been no notable change in the distribution of programs across countries based on their stage of development, there has been a small increase in the proportion of programs that operate in upper-middle-income countries (from 16.4 percent in 2021 to 18.5 percent in 2024; refer to table B.1). There has also been a slight increase in the proportion of programs operating in contexts of fragility, conflict, and violence (31.5 percent in 2021 compared to 33.1 percent in 2024).

TABLE B.1   Percentage of All Programs with a Presence in Different Contexts

Country classification or context	SEI 2021	SEI 2024
Low-income country	37.4%	35.1%
Lower-middle-income country	42.9%	44.0%
Upper-middle-income country	16.4%	18.5%
High-income country	3.2%	2.5%
Fragility, conflict, and violence	31.5%	33.1%

Source: Partnership for Economic Inclusion, World Bank.

Note: Table shows the percentage of all programs (*N* = 405 in SEI 2024 and *N* = 219 in SEI 2021).

FIGURE B.5   Percentage of All Programs with a Presence in Rural, Urban, and Peri-Urban Areas

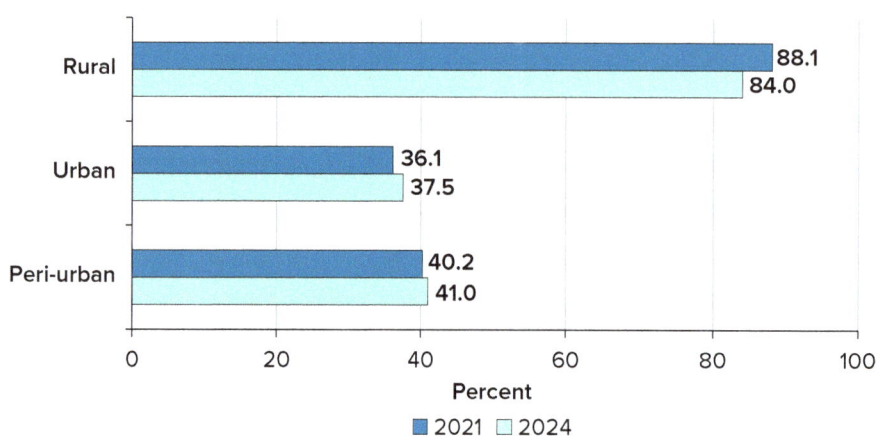

Source: Partnership for Economic Inclusion, World Bank.

Note: Figure shows the percentage of all programs (*N* = 405 in SEI 2024 and *N* = 219 in SEI 2021).

Most programs continue to operate in rural areas (over 80 percent), but in SEI 2024 a slightly higher percentage of programs operate in urban or peri-urban areas (refer to figure B.5). In SEI 2021, 54 percent of programs operated in urban or peri-urban areas, and in SEI 2024 this has increased to 57 percent of all programs. Some programs operate exclusively in urban or peri-urban areas, and this has also increased, from 12 percent of all programs exclusively operating in urban or peri-urban areas in 2021 to 16 percent in 2024.

Distribution of Programs by Coverage

The distribution of programs by their geographic coverage in SEI 2024 is similar to SEI 2021, with a slightly lower proportion of programs operating nationally (refer to figure B.6).

The distribution of programs based on the number of participants they serve shows that most government-led programs continue to serve at least 10,000 participants and most nongovernment-led programs serve less than 10,000 participants (refer to figure B.7).

FIGURE B.6   **Distribution of Programs by State, Regional, and National Presence**

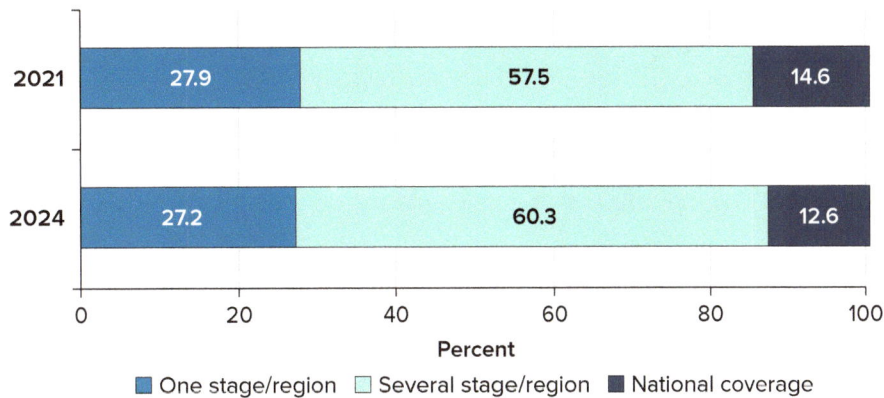

Source: Partnership for Economic Inclusion, World Bank.
Note: Figure shows the percentage of all programs (N = 405 in SEI 2024 and N = 219 in SEI 2021).

FIGURE B.7   **Distribution of Government-Led and Nongovernment-Led Programs, by Number of Current Direct Participants**

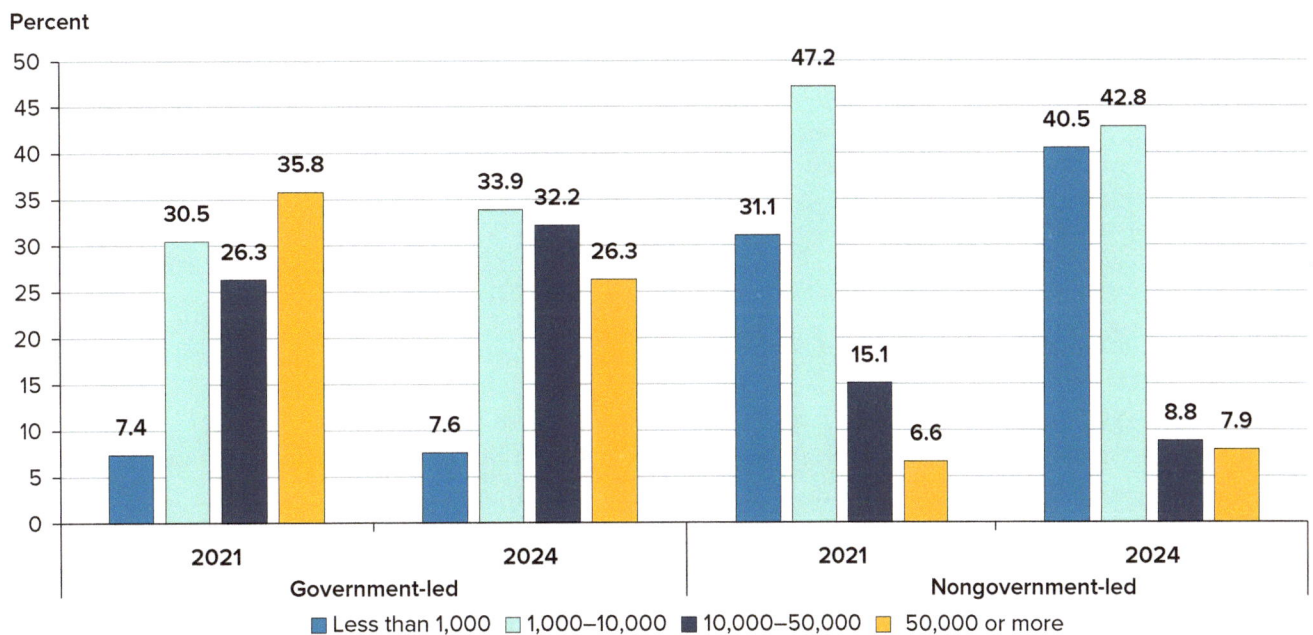

Source: Partnership for Economic Inclusion, World Bank.
Note: Figure shows the percentage of government- and nongovernment-led programs with coverage data (N_1 = 118 and N_2 = 215 in SEI 2024 and N_1 = 95 and N_2 = 106 in SEI 2021, respectively).

There is an increase in the percentage of programs that reach less than 1 percent of people living below the national poverty line (refer to figure B.8, panel a), as well as an increase in the distribution of countries by their coverage of all participants in a country as a share of the population living below the national poverty line (refer to figure B.8, panel b). While the absolute number of people engaged in these programs has increased by over 50 percent, coverage continues to be small relative to the number of people living in poverty.

FIGURE B.8   **Distribution of Program Coverage as a Share of the Population Living below the National Poverty Line**

a. Individual programs

Percent

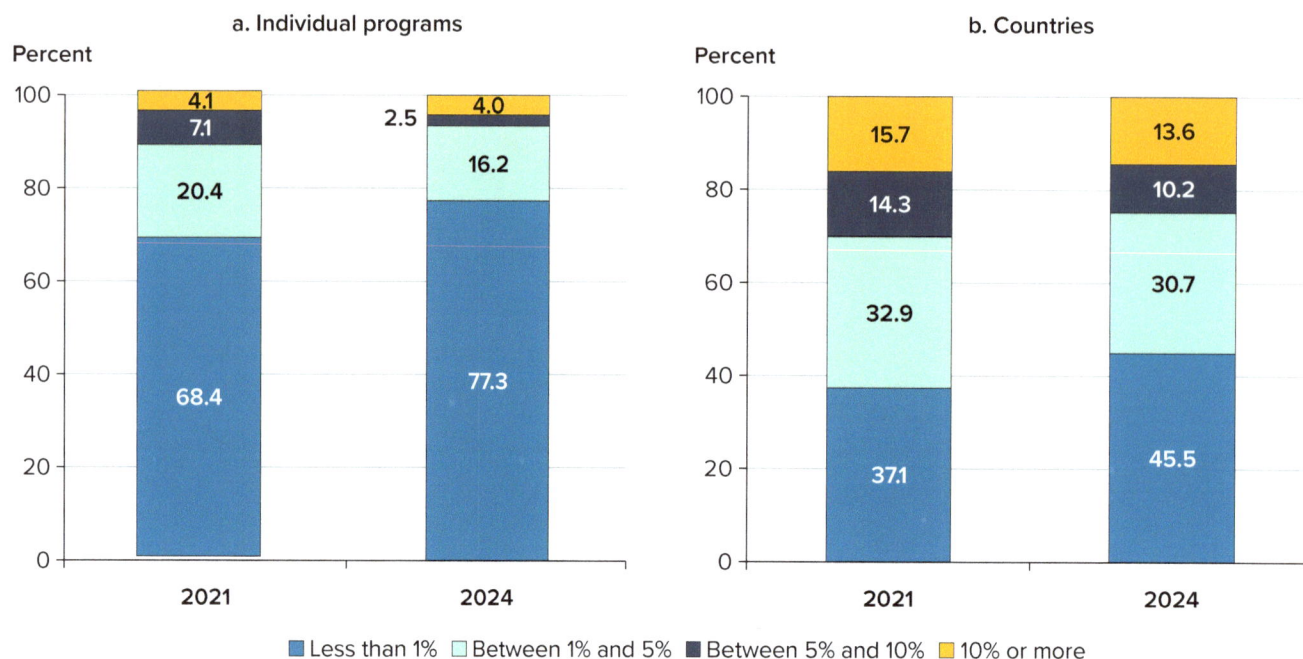

b. Countries

Percent

Less than 1%   Between 1% and 5%   Between 5% and 10%   10% or more

Source: Partnership for Economic Inclusion, World Bank.

Note: The analysis is based on 196 programs in SEI 2021 and 322 programs in SEI 2024 (those providing data on the number of participants that operate in countries with available poverty data). Panel a shows percentage of programs, and panel b provides aggregated data at the country level. The number of countries with coverage and poverty data is 88 in SEI 2024 and 70 in SEI 2021. The coverage ranges do not include the upper bound, for example, the range "Between 5% and 10%" goes from 5 percent to 9.99 percent.

Program Objectives

Most programs continue to focus on supporting self-employment opportunities broadly, with 84 percent of programs reporting self-employment, income diversification, or increased productivity as a main objective in both 2021 and 2024. However, there have been some key shifts in program objectives between 2021 and 2024 (refer to figure B.9). There has been an increase in the percentage of programs that seek to empower women from nearly 17 percent in 2021 to 33 percent in 2024, likely due to the growing recognition that to achieve economic inclusion for women, programs must address the unique barriers they face.

Similarly, more programs report climate resilience as an objective, increasing from 4.6 percent in 2021 to 20 percent in 2024. This may be due to the increasing focus on the interaction between economic inclusion and climate resilience and the rising concerns surrounding climate change. SEI 2024 also reflects an increase in the percentage of programs that report enhancing market access as their main objective, shifting from 10 percent in 2021 to 23.5 percent in 2024. This shift may be the result of increasing evidence on the importance of market linkages for supporting economic inclusion. In contrast, a lower proportion of programs focused on access to wage employment, decreasing from 18.7 percent in 2021 to 13.6 percent in 2024. This change may reflect weaker labor markets globally.

FIGURE B.9   **Main Program Objectives of Economic Inclusion Programs**

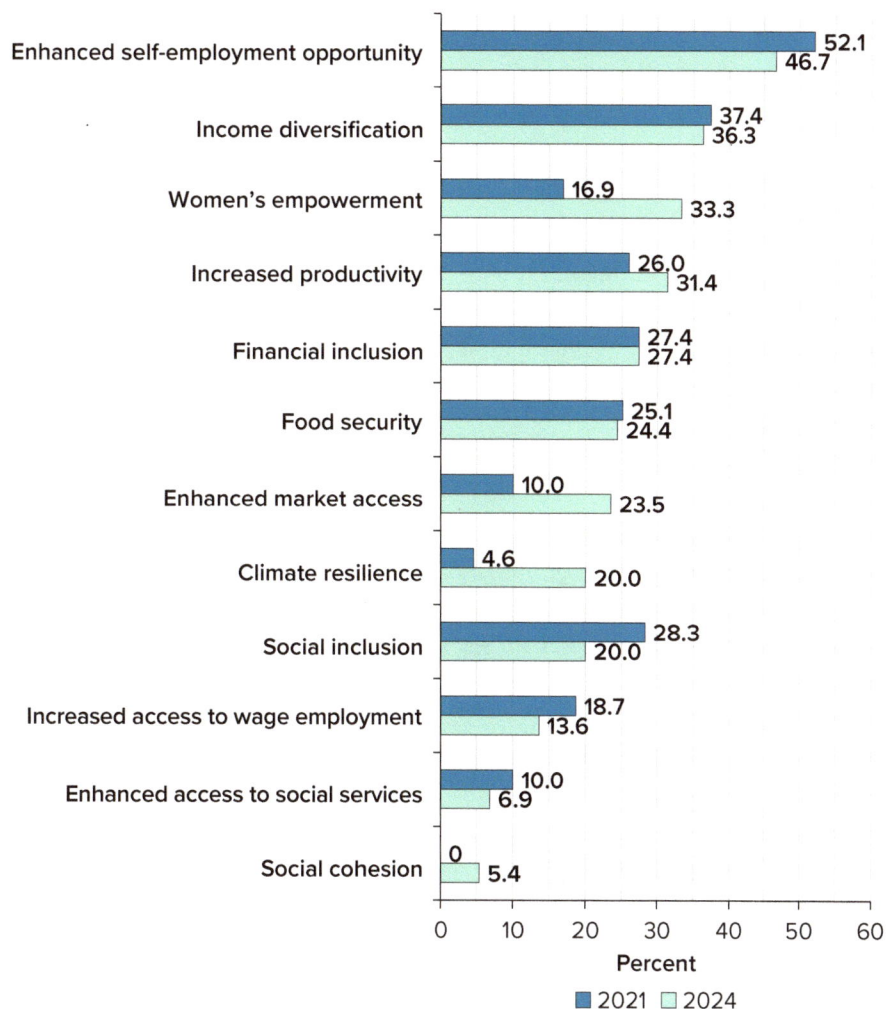

Objective	2021	2024
Enhanced self-employment opportunity	52.1	46.7
Income diversification	37.4	36.3
Women's empowerment	16.9	33.3
Increased productivity	26.0	31.4
Financial inclusion	27.4	27.4
Food security	25.1	24.4
Enhanced market access	10.0	23.5
Climate resilience	4.6	20.0
Social inclusion	28.3	20.0
Increased access to wage employment	18.7	13.6
Enhanced access to social services	10.0	6.9
Social cohesion	0	5.4

Percent

■ 2021   □ 2024

Source: Partnership for Economic Inclusion, World Bank.

Note: Figure shows the percentage of all programs (*N* = 405 in SEI 2024 and *N* = 219 in SEI 2021). Respondents could select up to three options. The option for "social cohesion" was not included in the 2020 survey. The 2020 survey included "environmental risk management" instead of "climate resilience"; therefore, these two datapoints are not fully comparable.

Target Populations and Targeting Methodologies

Economic inclusion programs are typically designed to reach specific population groups or poverty segments, such as the poor, extreme-poor, and ultra-poor populations, who face significant barriers to improving their economic circumstances. Many economic inclusion programs are also designed to serve specific demographic categories that may face additional challenges. For instance, programs often prioritize women, recognizing the unique barriers they encounter in accessing economic opportunities and resources.

To effectively reach these diverse groups, economic inclusion programs often use a mix of targeting methods. These can include geographical targeting, where programs focus on specific regions with high poverty rates, as well as community-based targeting, where local knowledge is used to identify the most vulnerable individuals. Some programs use categorical targeting, based on specific criteria such as age, gender, or disability status, while others may use means-testing or proxy indicators to identify eligible participants.

Target Populations

While the majority of economic inclusion programs continue to target the poor population, programs are increasingly targeting vulnerable populations whose vulnerability is not solely driven by their income. This trend can be seen in both government-led programs and nongovernment-led programs. Fewer programs reported targeting the extreme-poor population in 2024 compared to 2021 (refer to figure B.10). Similarly, fewer programs reported targeting either the extreme-poor or ultra-poor populations only, falling from 30 percent in 2021 to nearly 26 percent in 2024. In fact, 55 percent of programs reported targeting the poor population broadly in 2024 compared to almost 59 percent in 2021, while 19 percent reported not targeting by poverty level in 2024 compared to only 8 percent in 2021. This shift may be the result of the increased number of area-focused interventions that focus on communities, areas, or systems, and therefore tend to target participants more broadly.

FIGURE B.10 **Proportion of Programs, by Poverty Segments Targeted**

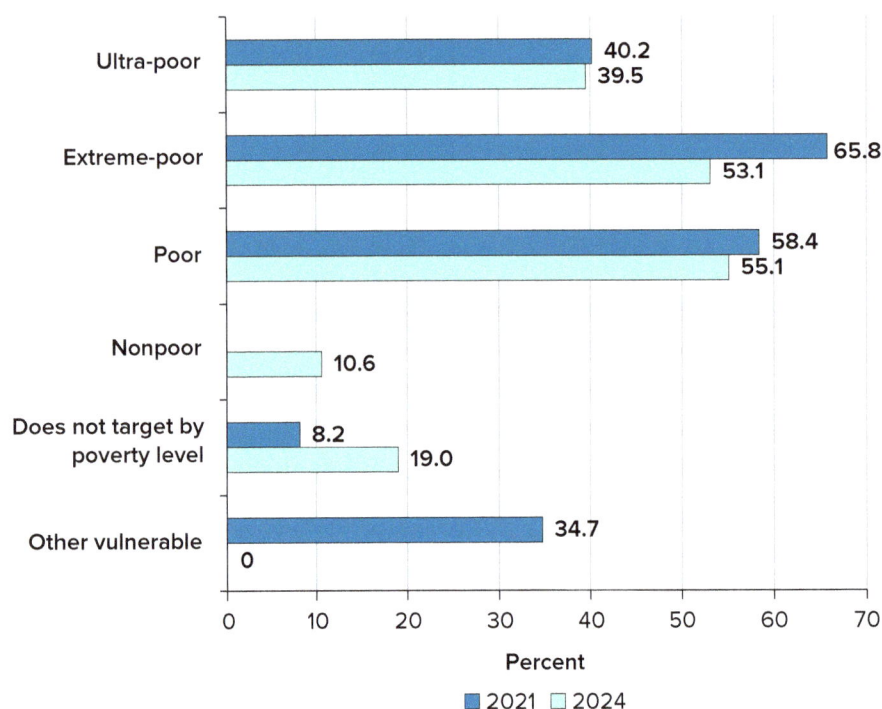

Source: Partnership for Economic Inclusion, World Bank.

Note: Figure shows the percentage of all programs (N = 405 in SEI 2024 and N = 219 in SEI 2021). Programs may target more than one poverty segment. The question in the 2023 survey and in 2020 had some differences. The option of "vulnerable" in the 2020 survey was replaced by "those above the poverty line" in the 2023 survey, and the option "none (the program does not target by poverty level)" was included. In the 2020 survey, there was a separate question on targeting methods that captured the proportion of programs that do not target by poverty level, and that has been used in this figure to report on the percentage of programs that do not target by poverty level.

FIGURE B.11 **Proportion of Programs, by Population Group Targeted**

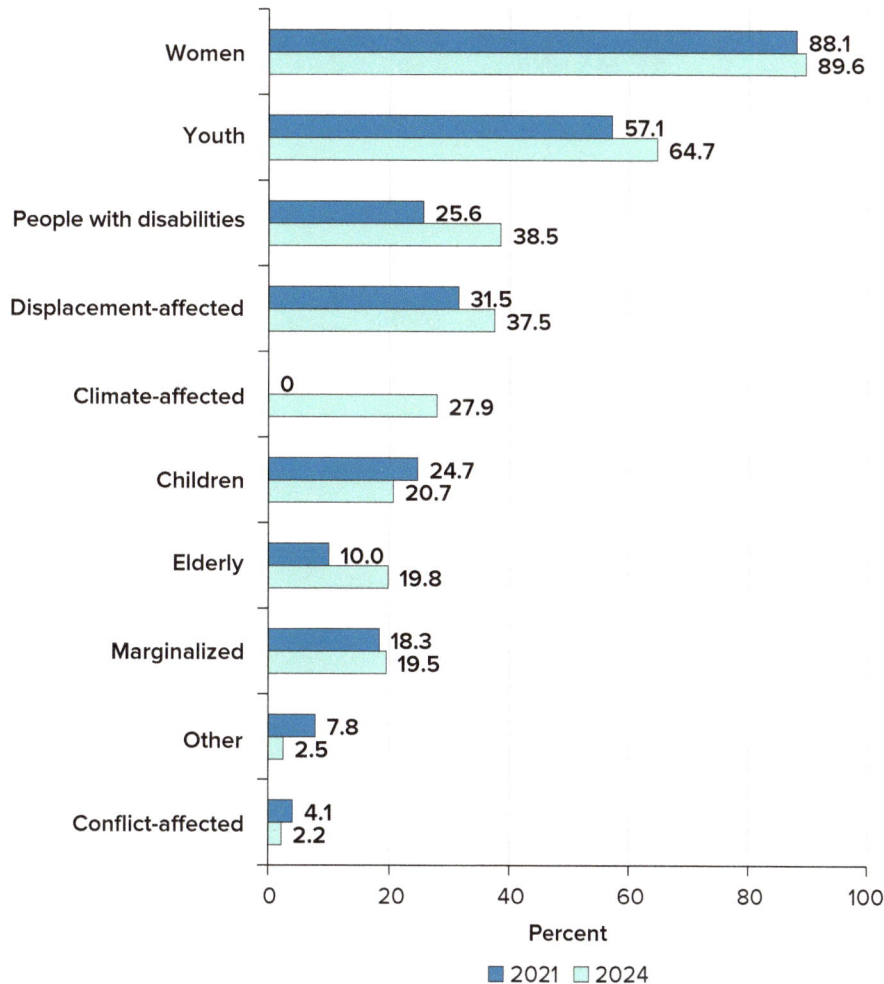

Source: Partnership for Economic Inclusion, World Bank.

Note: Figure shows the percentage of all programs (*N* = 405 in SEI 2024 and *N* = 219 in SEI 2021). Programs may target more than one poverty segment. The 2024 survey used the word "targeting" instead of "prioritizing" and included the option "people affected by climate change or environmental risks."

Programs continue to overwhelmingly target women (refer to figure B.11). SEI 2024 shows a higher proportion of programs targeting youth, the second priority group for economic inclusion programs. Similarly, more programs reported targeting the elderly population (nearly 20 percent compared to 10 percent), people with disabilities (39 percent compared to 26 percent), and displacement-affected populations (38 percent compared to 32 percent), suggesting shifts in program priorities in response to identified needs.

Targeting Methodologies

There has been an increase in the use of geographical targeting and categorical targeting and a decrease in proxy means-testing as a targeting method (refer to figure B.12). This change may be due to the increase in area-focused programs that typically target certain geographic areas or systems. The survey data also indicate a slight increase in the percentage of programs that leverage existing government registries to identify participants, from 33 percent in 2021 to 38 percent in 2024.

FIGURE B.12   **Proportion of Programs, by Targeting Methodologies**

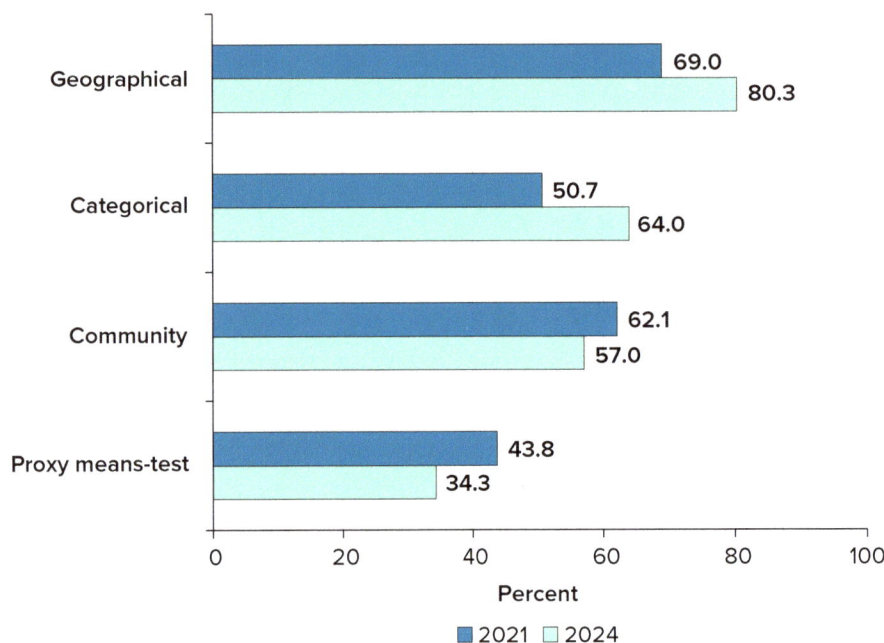

Source: Partnership for Economic Inclusion, World Bank.

Note: Figure shows the percentage of all programs in SEI 2024 (*N* = 405) and SEI 2021 (*N* = 219).

Program Components

Most economic inclusion programs provide an integrated package of interventions, rather than one or two stand-alone interventions, because their design is based on the recognition that the poorest and most vulnerable people face multiple constraints.

Number and Type of Core Components

The distribution of programs based on the number of components they provide has seen no significant shift between 2021 and 2024 (refer to figure B.13). Similarly, the core components provided by programs remained consistent between 2021 and 2024 (refer to figure B.14). The most notable difference was that, in 2024, a lower proportion of programs reported providing transfers (54 percent) compared to 2021 (68 percent). This decline in the provision of transfers appears to be driven by programs that target the poor broadly (71 percent to 58 percent) and programs that do not target by poverty level (28 percent to 17 percent). Most of programs that target either the extreme-poor or ultra-poor populations exclusively continue providing transfers (71 percent in 2021 and 73 percent in 2024).

FIGURE B.13   Distribution of Programs, by Number of Components

Percent

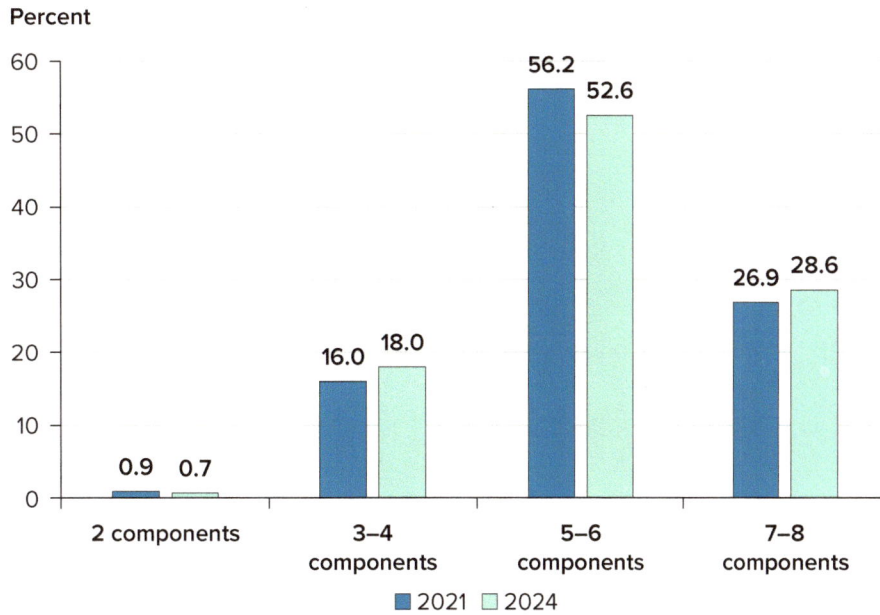

	2 components	3–4 components	5–6 components	7–8 components
2021	0.9	16.0	56.2	26.9
2024	0.7	18.0	52.6	28.6

■ 2021 □ 2024

Source: Partnership for Economic Inclusion, World Bank.

Note: Figure shows the percentage of all programs (*N* = 405 in SEI 2024 and *N* = 219 in SEI 2021).

FIGURE B.14   Proportion of Programs, by Their Components

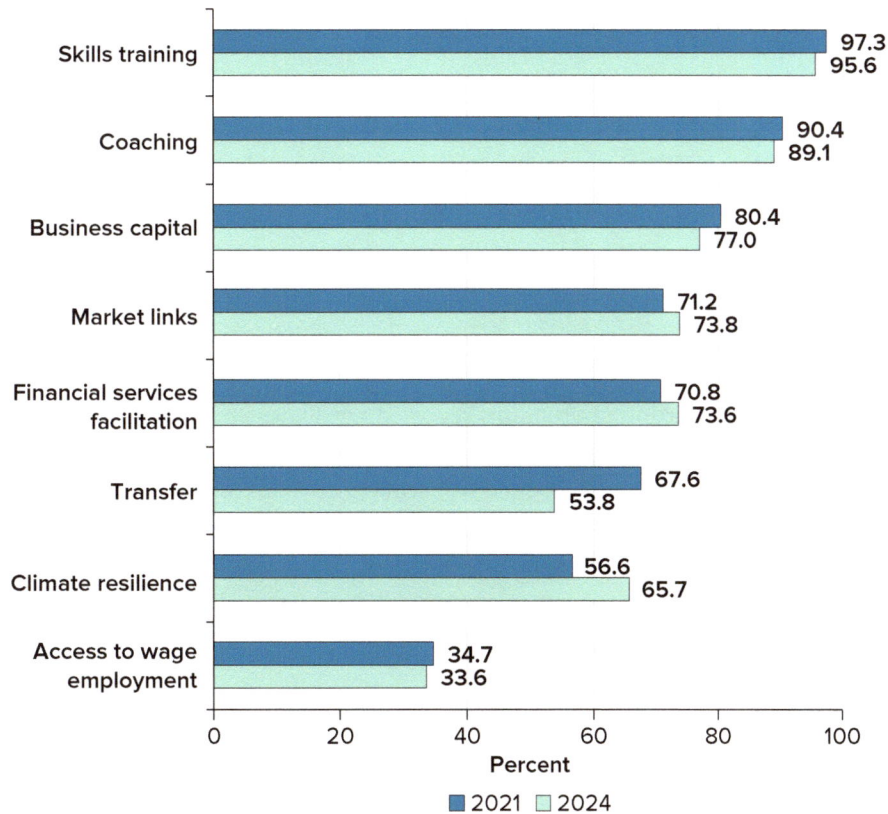

	2021	2024
Skills training	97.3	95.6
Coaching	90.4	89.1
Business capital	80.4	77.0
Market links	71.2	73.8
Financial services facilitation	70.8	73.6
Transfer	67.6	53.8
Climate resilience	56.6	65.7
Access to wage employment	34.7	33.6

Percent

■ 2021 □ 2024

Source: Partnership for Economic Inclusion, World Bank.

Note: Figure shows the percentage of all programs (*N* = 405 in SEI 2024 and *N* = 219 in SEI 2021). The 2020 survey referred to "sustainable natural resources management and/or climate change adaptation" instead of "climate resilience."

FIGURE B.15   **Distribution of Programs, by Duration of Interventions**

Percent

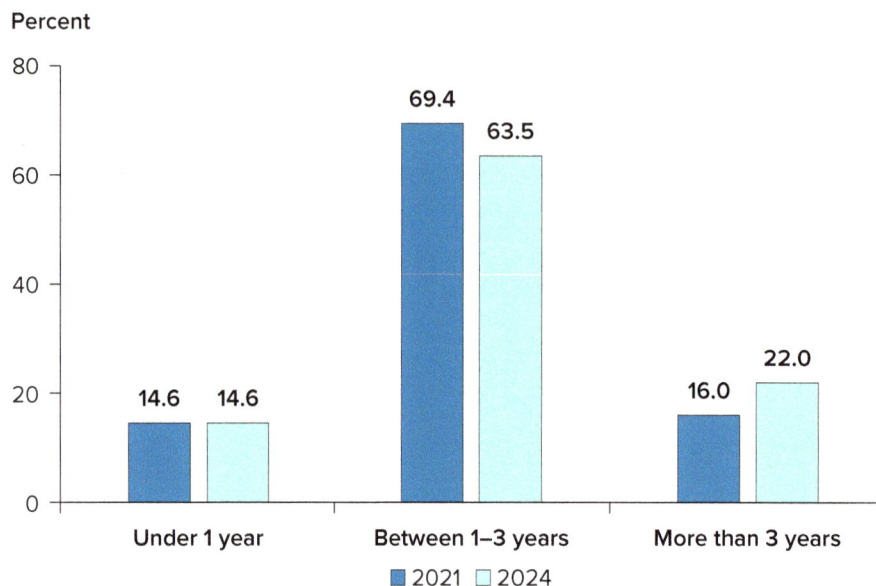

Source: Partnership for Economic Inclusion, World Bank.

Note: Figure shows the percentage of all programs (*N* = 405 in SEI 2024 and *N* = 219 in SEI 2021).

Duration of Program Interventions

In 2024, a higher proportion of programs reported supporting participants for more than 3 years (refer to figure B.15). This increase reflects that more programs in SEI 2024 than in SEI 2021 were built on agricultural and environmental interventions, which tend to be of longer duration than other programs.

Sequencing of Components

In 2024, a higher proportion of programs reported not sequencing the delivery of their components (24 percent) compared to 2021 (16 percent) (refer to figure B.16). This decline in programs delivering components in sequence is driven by the rise of area-focused programs that tend to target the vulnerable more broadly. The majority of programs that focus exclusively on the extreme-poor or ultra-poor populations, however, continue to deliver their components in sequence (92 percent in 2021 and 94 percent in 2024).

FIGURE B.16   Distribution of Programs, by Sequencing of Components

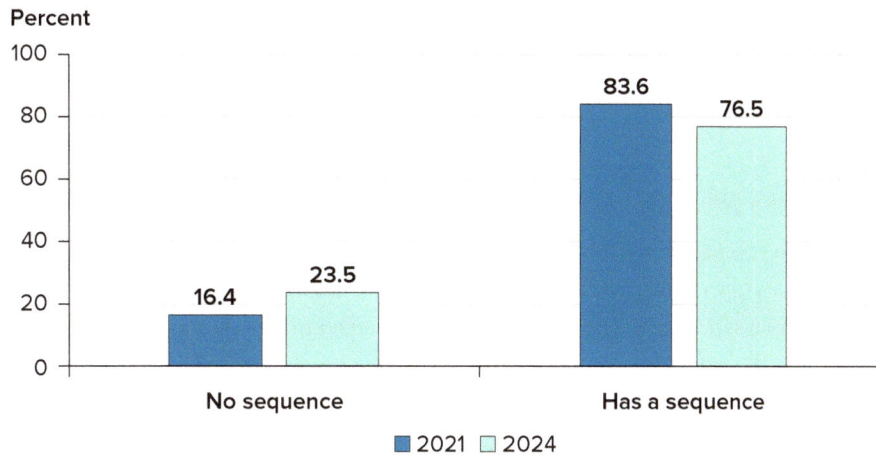

Source: Partnership for Economic Inclusion, World Bank.

Note: Figure shows the percentage of all programs (N = 405 in SEI 2024 and N = 219 in SEI 2021).

FIGURE B.17   Proportion of Programs That Scaled Up along Core Dimensions

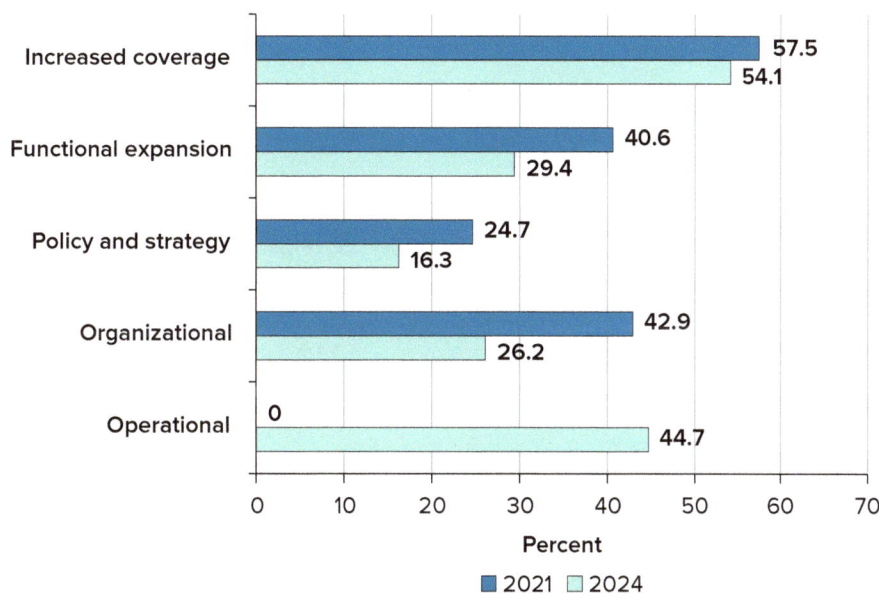

Source: Partnership for Economic Inclusion, World Bank.

Note: Figure shows the percentage of all programs (N = 405 in SEI 2024 and N = 219 in SEI 2021). In 2023, "Operational" scale-up was calculated using responses to questions on how programs adapted to COVID-19, specifically, if they said they either leveraged digital technologies to deliver the program or made other changes to deliver the program. Because no such question was asked in the 2020 survey, an equivalent "Operational" scale-up could not be calculated.

Scale-Up

In 2021, three-fourths of programs reported scaling up along at least one core dimension in the 2 years before the survey, while 65 percent of programs did so in 2024. In 2024, a lower proportion of programs reported having scaled up on each of the core dimensions than in 2021. For example, in 2021, 43 percent of programs expanded organizational capacity compared to 26 percent in 2024 (refer to figure B.17).

Use of Digital Tools

There has been an increase in the proportion of programs that use digital tools, rising from 89 percent in 2021 to 93 percent in 2024. This uptake is, in part, due to COVID-19. In 2024, 34 percent of programs reported leveraging digital tools for program delivery in response to COVID-19. These data also align with the global trend of using more technology.

This increase in the use of technology is seen across all program activities (refer to figure B.18). Most notably, the proportion of programs using digital tools to provide components has risen from 28 percent to nearly 49 percent, and the proportion of programs using them to support grievance or redress mechanisms has risen from 27 percent to 42 percent.

FIGURE B.18   **Proportion of Programs That Use Digital Tools to Support Specific Activities**

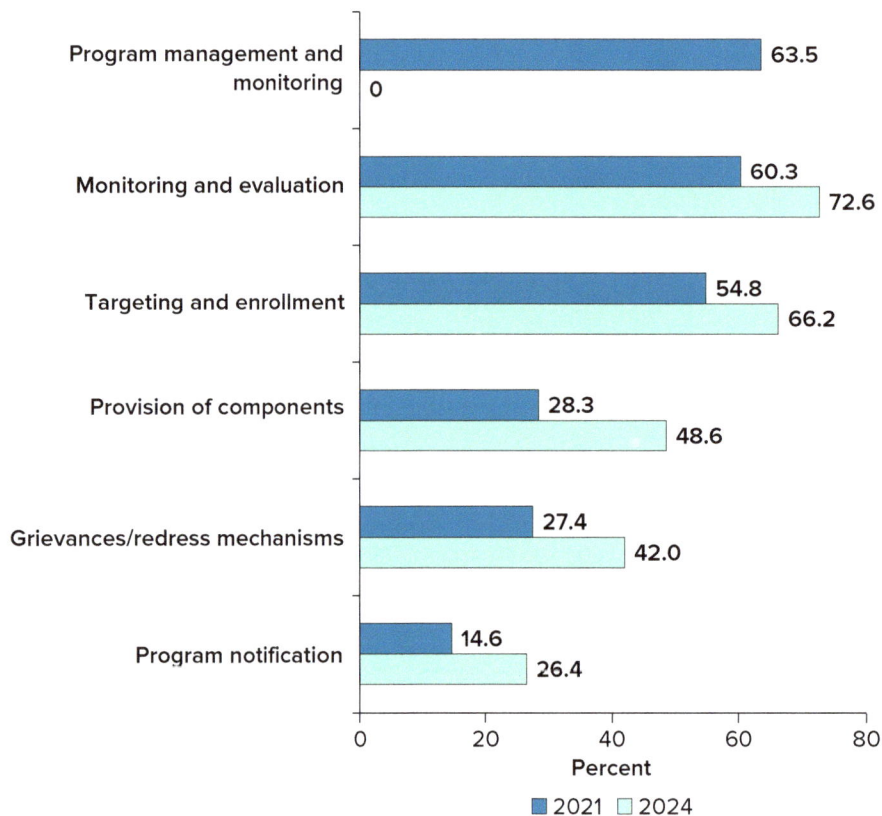

Source: Partnership for Economic Inclusion, World Bank.

Note: Figure shows the percentage of all programs (*N* = 405 in SEI 2024 and *N* = 219 in SEI 2021). The 2023 survey referred to "targeting and enrollment" and "provision of economic inclusion program components," while the 2020 survey only said "enrollment" and "provision of components, respectively." The 2020 survey also separated monitoring and evaluation by "beneficiary monitoring" and "program management and monitoring." "Beneficiary monitoring" from the 2020 survey has been analyzed alongside "program management and monitoring" from the 2023 survey.

FIGURE B.19   **Proportion of Programs That Use Digital Tools to Provide Components**

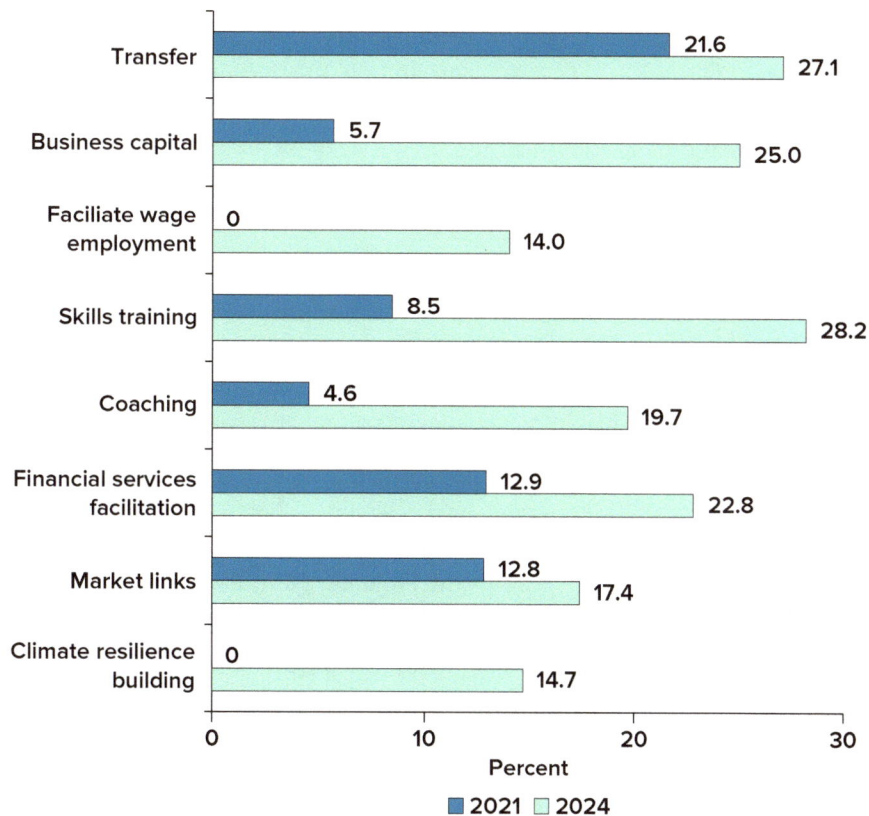

Transfer	2021: 21.6, 2024: 27.1
Business capital	2021: 5.7, 2024: 25.0
Faciliate wage employment	2021: 0, 2024: 14.0
Skills training	2021: 8.5, 2024: 28.2
Coaching	2021: 4.6, 2024: 19.7
Financial services facilitation	2021: 12.9, 2024: 22.8
Market links	2021: 12.8, 2024: 17.4
Climate resilience building	2021: 0, 2024: 14.7

Percent

■ 2021 □ 2024

Source: Partnership for Economic Inclusion, World Bank.

Note: Figure shows the percentage of programs providing each of the components as part of the economic inclusion package. Refer to figure B.14 for more information. The option "access to market information" in the 2020 survey has been analyzed under "market links" and the options "digital savings accounts" and "other digital financial services" from the 2020 survey have been analyzed under "financial services facilitation" in this figure. The 2020 survey did not include "climate resilience building" and "facilitate wage employment" in the question on digital delivery of program components.

This rise in the use of technology to provide components has taken place for the delivery of every main component, particularly in the delivery of coaching (from 4.5 percent to 19.7 percent), business capital (5.7 percent to 25 percent), and skills training (8.5 percent to 28.2 percent) (refer to figure B.19).

Institutional Arrangements

Institutional arrangements and the involvement of external agencies can vary significantly across economic inclusion programs, reflecting the diverse contexts and needs of different countries and communities. These variations are shaped by factors such as the political environment, the capacity of local institutions, the availability of resources, and the specific objectives of programs.

Financing of Programs

A range of institutions, either the lead or external institutions, support the financing of programs (refer to figure B.20). Governments and the World Bank continue to be the two main institutions financing programs.[2] However, the percentage of programs funded by nongovernmental organizations has also seen a steep increase in SEI 2024.

Role of Lead Agencies

There are limited changes in the roles of lead agencies (refer to figure B.21), but it seems the lead agency takes on roles in a lower proportion of programs in 2024 compared to 2021, across several roles. This difference suggests a higher reliance on external agencies to implement economic inclusion programs, as shown in the next section.

FIGURE B.20   Distribution of Programs, by Financing Organization

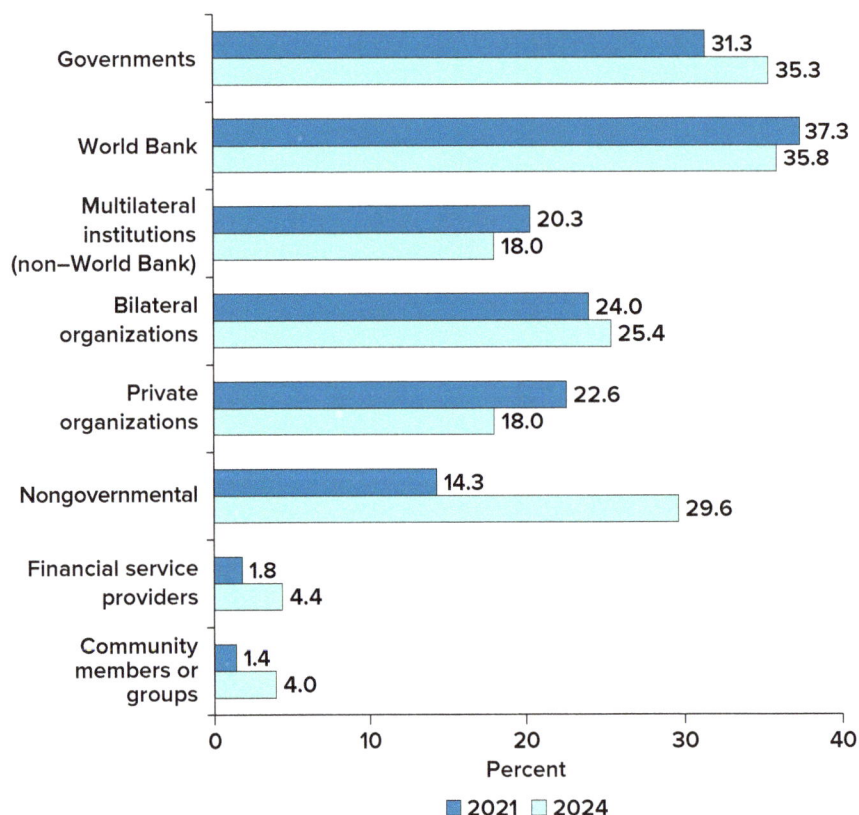

Source: Partnership for Economic Inclusion, World Bank.

Note: Data on financing institutions are missing for two programs in the SEI 2021. Figure shows the percentage of programs (*N* = 405 in SEI 2024 and *N* = 217 in SEI 2021).

FIGURE B.21   Proportion of Programs in Which the Lead Agency Takes on Specific Roles

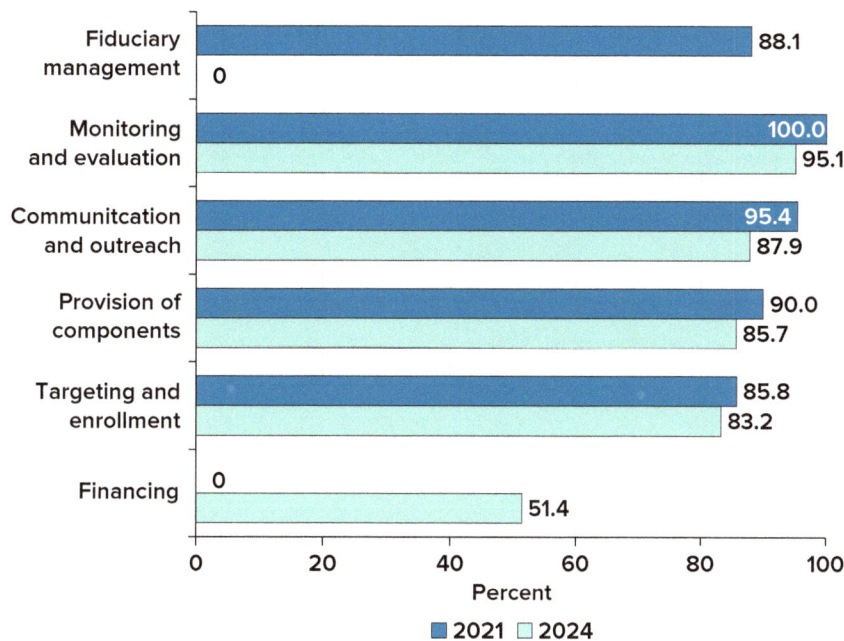

Source: Partnership for Economic Inclusion, World Bank.

Note: Figure shows the percentage of all programs (*N* = 405 in SEI 2024 and *N* = 219 in SEI 2021). "Financing" was not an option in the 2020 survey, and "fiduciary management" was not an option in the 2023 survey. In 2020, "program monitoring and evaluation" and "beneficiary monitoring" were separate options, and in 2023, there was only the option of "program monitoring and evaluation." These responses have been analyzed under "monitoring and evaluation" in this figure.

Role of External Agencies

Lead organizations often engage service delivery providers to support program implementation. In 2021, 78 percent of programs relied on partners for the provision of program components. This issue saw a slight increase to 82 percent in 2024. There has been a substantial increase in the proportion of programs that depend on financial service providers, private organizations, and community members to deliver components (refer to figure B.22). This trend highlights the increasing collaboration between different institutions to deliver economic inclusion programs.

FIGURE B.22   Proportion of Programs with an External Agency Involved in the Delivery of Components

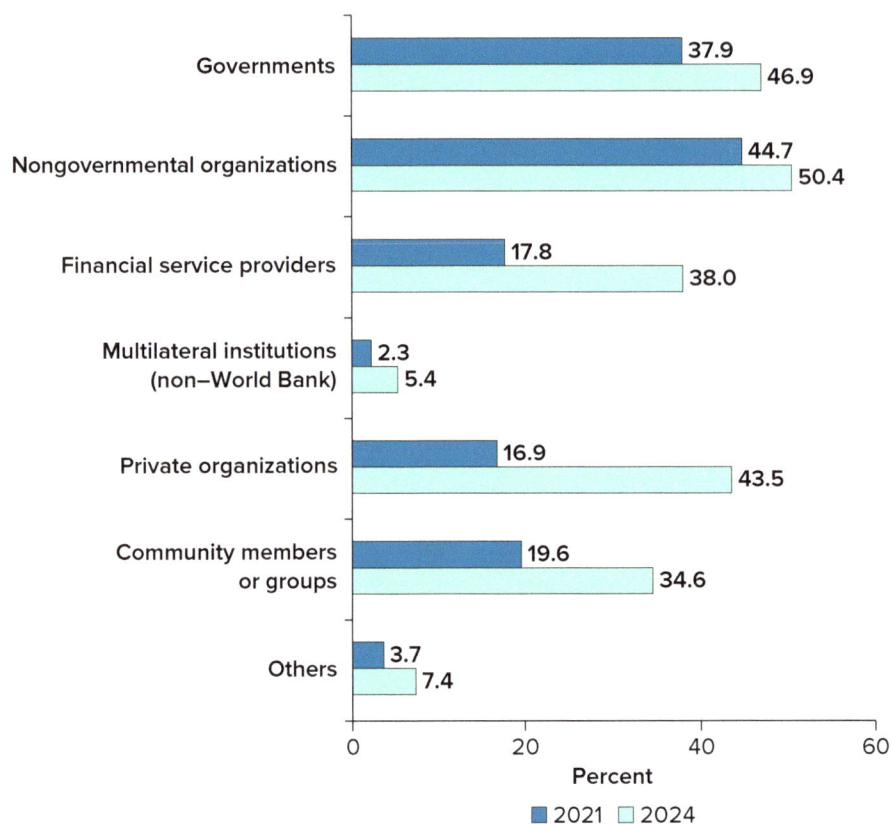

Source: Partnership for Economic Inclusion, World Bank.

Note: Figure shows the percentage of all programs (*N* = 405 in SEI 2024 and *N* = 219 in SEI 2021).

Notes

1. As mentioned in chapter 2, data checks performed during the Landscape Survey 2023 revealed that the coverage data reported in 2020 on the Satat Jeevikoparjan Yojana (SJY) program, led by India's Bihar Rural Livelihoods Promotion Society (BRLPS), included participants of various programs implemented by BRLPS. Figures have been corrected to only include the number of participants in the SJY program.
2. As noted in appendix A, the Landscape Survey may not have captured all programs funded by other multilateral organizations, and, as such, the sample is biased toward World Bank–financed projects.

Economic Inclusion Programs Surveyed Globally

This appendix provides key data points for country, program start date, lead implementing agency, and current and cumulative coverage of the 405 programs that participated in the World Bank's Partnership for Economic Inclusion Landscape Survey 2023 (refer to Table C.1). The data collected from these programs is summarized in the full report, offering insights into the design and implementation of these initiatives.

TABLE C.1   Economic Inclusion Programs Included in the Global Survey

Program	Economy	Year program began	Lead implementing agency or agencies	Type of lead implementing agency	Current participants (direct)	Cumulative participants (direct)
Stronger Women, Stronger Nations Program	Afghanistan	2002	Women for Women International	Nongovernment	3,310	130,226
Ultra-Poor Graduation Programme: Tailoring Reintegration in Afghanistan's Capital–Kabul (TRACK)	Afghanistan	2022	BRAC Afghanistan	Nongovernment	400	400
Kwenda Program, supported by the World Bank's Angola Strengthening the National Social Protection System Project	Angola	2020	Local Development Institute under the Ministry for Territorial Administration	Government	25,324	25,324
The Smallholder Agricultural Transformation Project	Angola	2023	Ministry of Agriculture and Forest	Government	—	—
Climate Intelligent and Inclusive Agri-food Systems Project	Argentina	2022	General Directorate of Sectoral and Special Programs and Projects, under the Secretariat of Development Planning and Federal Competitiveness	Government	—	—
Promoting Better Jobs through Integrated Labor and Skills (FOMENTAR) Program	Argentina	2022	Ministry of Labor, Employment and Social Security	Government	200,000	200,000
Sustainable Recovery of Landscapes and Livelihoods in Argentina Project	Argentina	2022	National Parks Administration	Government	1,093	1,093
Promoting Social Inclusion and Self-Reliant Livelihood Activities	Armenia	2020	Armenian Association of Social Workers	Nongovernment	307	307
Wage Employment Facilitation Program	Aruba	2022	HIAS Aruba	Nongovernment	281	281
Climate-Smart Agriculture and Water Management Project	Bangladesh	2021	Bangladesh Water Development Board, Department of Agricultural Extension, and Department of Fisheries	Government	—	—
Economic Recovery of the Climate Migrants and New Poor Living in Climate Vulnerable Urban Low-Income Settlements	Bangladesh	2022	BRAC	Nongovernment	802	802

(Table continues next page)

TABLE C.1 Economic Inclusion Programs Included in the Global Survey *(continued)*

Program	Economy	Year program began	Lead implementing agency or agencies	Type of lead implementing agency	Current participants (direct)	Cumulative participants (direct)
Enhancing Resilience of Coastal Communities and Improving Income of Extreme Poor Households in Khulna District	Bangladesh	2021	Shushilan	Nongovernment	5,725	5,725
Gender Inclusive Pathways out of Poverty (GPOP) for Vulnerable Households in Cox's Bazar Project	Bangladesh	2018	World Vision Bangladesh	Nongovernment	2,880	2,880
Integrated Development Program (IDP)	Bangladesh	2013	BRAC	Nongovernment	54,300	54,300
Last Mile Rural Distribution	Bangladesh	2013	JITA Bangladesh, with support from CARE International Social Ventures	Nongovernment	—	—
Recovery and Advancement of Informal Sector Employment	Bangladesh	2021	PKSF	Government	40,000	43,455
Resilience, Entrepreneurship, and Livelihood Improvement (RELI) Project	Bangladesh	2021	Social Development Foundation	Government	804,000	804,000
Returnee Migrants Reintegration Program	Bangladesh	2018	BRAC	Nongovernment	284	7,284
Skills Development Program (STAR and PROMISE)	Bangladesh	2012	BRAC	Nongovernment	17,193	220,056
Strengthening Women's Ability for Productive New Opportunities (SWAPNO) Project	Bangladesh	2015	Local Government Division, with technical support of the UNDP	Government	12,492	12,492
Sustainable Coastal and Marine Fisheries Project	Bangladesh	2018	Department of Fisheries	Government	125,500	125,500
Sustainable Microenterprise and Resilient Transformation (SMART)	Bangladesh	2023	PKSF	Government	—	—
Ultra Poor Graduation (UPG) Program	Bangladesh	2002	BRAC	Nongovernment	70,000	2,312,477

(Table continues next page)

TABLE C.1 Economic Inclusion Programs Included in the Global Survey (*continued*)

Program	Economy	Year program began	Lead implementing agency or agencies	Type of lead implementing agency	Current participants (direct)	Cumulative participants (direct)
Urban Green Graduation–Dhaka	Bangladesh	2023	Concern Worldwide	Nongovernment	—	—
Climate Resilient and Sustainable Agriculture Project	Belize	2022	Belize Social Investment Fund	Government	—	—
Agricultural Competitiveness and Export Diversification Project	Benin	2020	Ministry of Agriculture, Livestock, and Fisheries	Government	18,000	18,000
Gazetted Forests Management Project	Benin	2019	General Directorate of Water and Forests and Hunting	Government	4,500	33,738
The Azoli Program, supported by the World Bank's Youth Inclusion Project	Benin	2021	National Employment Agency	Government	4,335	6,043
Food Security and Agriculture Productivity Project	Bhutan	2017	Ministry of Agriculture and Livestock	Government	11,938	11,938
Internal Voluntary Relocation through Employment Based Modality	Brazil	2018	Brazilian Army	Government	3,680	11,815
Program Prosper Family (Programa Prospera Família)	Brazil	2023	Office for Social Development of the State of São Paulo	Government	7,500	18,000
Agrifood Program for Integrated Resilience and Economic Development of the Sahel (Pro-ARIDES)	Burkina Faso	2021	SNV Burkina Faso, with consortium partners CARE International–Netherlands, Wageningen University & Research, and The Royal Tropical Institute	Nongovernment	63,525	63,525
Communal Climate Action and Landscape Management Project	Burkina Faso	2023	Ministry of Ecological Transition and Environment	Government	—	—
Graduation Project for the Autonomy and Dignity of Displaced Persons (GADICH)	Burkina Faso	2022	Action pour la Promotion des Initiatives Locales	Nongovernment	3,000	3,000
Inclusive Livelihood Activities for Women and People with Disabilities in Ouargaye	Burkina Faso	2018	OCADES Tenkodogo	Nongovernment	197	197
Regional Sahel Pastoralism Support Project II (PRAPS–2)	Burkina Faso	2022	Ministry of Agriculture, Animal and Fisheries Resources	Government	—	—

(Table continues next page)

TABLE C.1 Economic Inclusion Programs Included in the Global Survey (*continued*)

Program	Economy	Year program began	Lead implementing agency or agencies	Type of lead implementing agency	Current participants (direct)	Cumulative participants (direct)
Social Safety Net Project	Burkina Faso	2014	Ministry of National Solidarity and Humanitarian Action	Government	6,606	23,606
Supporting Host Communities and Internally-displaced Persons to Facilitate Sustainable Transition Towards Inclusive Solutions (SHIFT)	Burkina Faso	2021	DRC	Nongovernment	1,217	1,217
Support for Self-sufficiency and Support for the Development of Resilience	Burkina Faso	2022	Veterinarian Sans Frontieres Belgium	Nongovernment	2,000	3,000
Valorization of Agro-Pastoral Potential in the Eastern Region of Burkina Faso Program (VALPAPE)	Burkina Faso	2023	Caritas Suisse	Nongovernment	3,000	3,000
Cash for Jobs Project	Burundi	2021	Ministry of National Solidarity, Human Rights, Social Affairs and Gender	Government	—	—
Green Graduation	Burundi	2023	Concern Worldwide Burundi	Nongovernment	—	—
Integrated Community Development Project	Burundi	2020	Ministry of Interior	Government	1,260	1,260
Landscape Restoration and Resilience Project	Burundi	2018	Ministry of Environment, Agriculture, and Livestock	Government	17,580	88,535
Refugee Protection, Health and Livelihoods Project	Burundi	2020	AVSI Foundation Burundi	Nongovernment	780	780
Human Capital Project	Cabo Verde	2022	Ministry of Family and Social Inclusion	Government	—	—
Social Inclusion Project	Cabo Verde	2018	Ministry of Family and Social Inclusion	Government	1,867	1,867
Livelihood Enhancement and Association of the Poor (LEAP) Project	Cambodia	2017	Ministry of Interior	Government	—	11,312

(Table continues next page)

TABLE C.1 Economic Inclusion Programs Included in the Global Survey (*continued*)

Program	Economy	Year program began	Lead implementing agency or agencies	Type of lead implementing agency	Current participants (direct)	Cumulative participants (direct)
Contributing to Durable Solutions and Social Cohesion amongst Conflict-affected people in the North West, South West and Littoral regions of Cameroon	Cameroon	2022	NRC	Nongovernment	1,490	1,490
Economic Inclusion of Youth Program, supported by the World Bank's Adaptive Safety Nets and Economic Inclusion Project	Cameroon	2022	Ministry of Economy, Planning, and Territorial Administration	Government	—	—
Emergency Project to Combat the Food Crisis in Cameroon	Cameroon	2022	Ministry of Agriculture and Rural Development	Government	—	—
Lake Chad Region Recovery and Development Project	Cameroon	2021	Ministry of Economy, Planning, and Regional Development	Government	7,127	7,127
Strengthening the Resilience, Self-reliance, and Socio-economic Inclusion of Central Africa Republic's Refugees and Host Community Households Living in Extreme Poverty	Cameroon	2022	DRC	Nongovernment	950	2,150
Climate Resilient Agriculture and Productivity Enhancement Project	Chad	2018	Ministry of Agriculture, Irrigation and Agricultural Equipment	Government	476,000	476,000
Green Graduation	Chad	2023	Concern Worldwide	Nongovernment	600	600
Local Development and Adaptation Project	Chad	2020	Ministry of Environment, Fisheries, and Sustainable Development	Government	—	—
Project to Support the Strengthening of Food and Nutritional Security of Vulnerable Populations in the Province of Wadi Fira in Eastern Chad	Chad	2020	CARE International	Nongovernment	11,732	11,732
Regional Sahel Pastoralism Support Project II (PRAPS–2)	Chad	2022	Ministry of Livestock and Animal Production	Government	—	—
Support to Women Entrepreneurs	Chile	2020	World Vision International	Nongovernment	99	1,100

(Table continues next page)

TABLE C.1 **Economic Inclusion Programs Included in the Global Survey (***continued***)**

Program	Economy	Year program began	Lead implementing agency or agencies	Type of lead implementing agency	Current participants (direct)	Cumulative participants (direct)
Closing Gaps: Financial Inclusion for All in Colombia	Colombia	2022	Humanity & Inclusion	Nongovernment	150	150
Conectad@s–Colombia	Colombia	2023	Fundación Capital	Nongovernment	500	500
Entrepreneurship School with Gender Lens	Colombia	2021	HIAS Colombia	Nongovernment	82	132
Entrepreneurship School with Gender Lens 2.0	Colombia	2023	HIAS Colombia	Nongovernment	20	20
Families in Their Land	Colombia	2011	Prosperidad Social	Government	3,828	155,416
IRACA Program	Colombia	2012	Prosperidad Social	Government	9,750	56,417
Local Integration and Livelihoods for Forcibly Displaced and Stateless Persons in Medellin	Colombia	2019	Coporación Ayuda Humanitaria	Nongovernment	450	480
Orinoquia Integrated Sustainable Landscapes	Colombia	2019	World Wildlife Fund Colombia	Nongovernment	—	—
Pathways of Opportunities, an Ultra Poverty Graduation Model	Colombia	2022	Opportunity International's Asociación General Para Asesorar Pequeñas Empresas	Nongovernment	250	250
Social Cohesion and Livelihoods Empowerment (SCALE) for Youth-led Durable Solutions	Cross-border: Colombia and Ecuador	2022	NRC	Nongovernment	110	110
She Feeds the World	Colombia	2023	CARE International Colombia	Nongovernment	2,000	2,000
VenEsperanza	Colombia	2019	Mercy Corps	Nongovernment	60,798	477,425
Socio-economic Recovery Activity (ARSE), supported by the World Bank's Productive Safety Net Program	Comoros	2021	Ministry of Health, Solidarity, Social Protection and Gender Promotion	Government	10,290	10,290

(Table continues next page)

TABLE C.1 Economic Inclusion Programs Included in the Global Survey (*continued*)

Program	Economy	Year program began	Lead implementing agency or agencies	Type of lead implementing agency	Current participants (direct)	Cumulative participants (direct)
AFTER–Early Recovery with Crisis-Affected Communities	Congo, Dem. Rep.	2020	Concern Worldwide	Nongovernment	2,154	2,154
Chronic Humanitarian Crisis (CHC) Stream	Congo, Dem. Rep.	2023	Social Action for the Promotion of the Left Behind	Nongovernment	400	400
Eastern Recovery Project (STEP)	Congo, Dem. Rep.	2014	Social Fund of the Democratic Republic of Congo	Government	23,469	167,680
Forest Dependent Communities Support Project	Congo, Dem. Rep.	2016	Caritas Internationalis ARITAS	Nongovernment	30,000	30,000
Green Graduation	Congo, Dem. Rep.	2023	Concern Worldwide	Nongovernment	350	350
Humanitarian Assistance to Conflict-Affected Households in Eastern Democratic Republic of Congo	Congo, Dem. Rep.	2022	Concern Worldwide	Nongovernment	740	740
Multi-sectoral Humanitarian Response to Displaced and Host Populations Affected by the Conflict in Ituri and North Kivu Provinces	Congo, Dem. Rep.	2022	Airtel Money	Nongovernment	250	750
National Agricultural Development Program	Congo, Dem. Rep.	2022	Ministry of Agriculture	Government	—	—
Partnership for the Development of the Eastern Congo (P–DEC)	Congo, Dem. Rep.	2021	Mercy Corps	Nongovernment	4,525	7,157
Stronger Women, Stronger Nations Program	Congo, Dem. Rep.	2004	Women for Women International	Nongovernment	5,679	110,419
Sustainable Livelihoods in the Lomako Reserve: A Conservation and Micro Enterprise Development Partnership	Congo, Dem. Rep.	2021	African Wildlife Foundation	Nongovernment	216	780

(Table continues next page)

TABLE C.1   Economic Inclusion Programs Included in the Global Survey *(continued)*

Program	Economy	Year program began	Lead implementing agency or agencies	Type of lead implementing agency	Current participants (direct)	Cumulative participants (direct)
Sustainable Livelihoods in the Okapi Wildlife Reserve	Congo, Dem. Rep.	2021	WCS	Nongovernment	600	600
LISUNGI Safety Nets System Project	Congo, Rep.	2014	Ministry of Social Affairs and Humanitarian Action	Government	13,078	31,752
Northern Congo Agroforestry Project	Congo, Rep.	2022	Ministry of Forest Economy	Government	—	—
Skills for Development and Employability Project	Congo, Rep.	2013	Ministry of Technical and Professional Education	Government	3,500	13,000
Support to Indigenous Peoples and Local Communities for Sustainable Resources Management	Congo, Rep.	2021	CIPIVIE	Nongovernment	—	—
Sustainable Livelihoods in the Nouable-Ndoki National Park	Congo, Rep.	2022	WCS	Nongovernment	300	300
Agribusiness Methodology	Costa Rica	2021	HIAS Costa Rica	Nongovernment	19	25
Graduation Model Approach	Costa Rica	2021	HIAS Costa Rica	Nongovernment	130	150
Human Talent Consultancy	Costa Rica	2021	HIAS Costa Rica	Nongovernment	130	147
Livelihoods and Economic Inclusion Program for Refugees	Costa Rica	2023	Women's Foundation, Omar Dengo Foundation	Nongovernment	3,500	9,000
Sustainable Fisheries Development Project	Costa Rica	2020	Costa Rica Fisheries Institute	Government	—	—
Inclusive Pinar del Río: Economic Inclusion and Empowerment of People with Disabilities and Their Families	Cuba	2022	Provincial Labor Directorate	Government	449	449
Forest Investment Project (Phase 2)	Côte d'Ivoire	2022	Ministry of Water and Forests	Government	—	—
Gulf of Guinea Northern Regions Social Cohesion Project	Côte d'Ivoire	2022	Cashew and Cotton Council	Government	962	962
National Productive Cash Transfer Program	Côte d'Ivoire	2015	Safety Net Coordination Office, under the Ministry of Solidarity and Fight against Poverty	Government	100,000	227,000

(Table continues next page)

TABLE C.1 Economic Inclusion Programs Included in the Global Survey (continued)

Program	Economy	Year program began	Lead implementing agency or agencies	Type of lead implementing agency	Current participants (direct)	Cumulative participants (direct)
PROSPER III: Thriving Cocoa Communities	Côte d'Ivoire	2022	CARE International Cote D'Ivoire/Guinea	Nongovernment	9,796	9,796
Women for Change Regional Expansion	Côte d'Ivoire	2020	Ministry of National Education and Literacy and Ministry of Women, Family and Children	Government	28,571	28,571
Youth Employment and Skills Development Project Phase 3	Côte d'Ivoire	2022	Employment Programs Coordination Office, Ministry of Technical and Vocational Training and Apprenticeship	Government	—	—
Development Response to Displacement Impacts Project (DRDIP) in the Horn of Africa	Djibouti	2016	Djibouti Social Development Agency	Government	1,243	1,243
Integrated Cash Transfer and Human Capital Project	Djibouti	2021	Ministry of Social Affairs and Solidarity	Government	2,000	4,000
Social Protection Emergency Crisis Response Project	Djibouti	2022	Ministry of Social Affairs and Solidarity	Government	4,000	4,000
Leveraging Eco-Tourism for Biodiversity Protection in Dominica	Dominica	2023	Ministry of Environment Rural Modernization and Kalinago Upliftment	Government	—	—
Improve Yourself, SUPERATE, Economic Inclusion Component, supported by the World Bank's Integrated Social Protection Inclusion and Resilience Project	Dominican Republic	2022	SUPERATE Program	Government	—	30,756
Integrated Landscape Management in Dominican Republic Watersheds Project	Dominican Republic	2021	Ministry of Environment and Natural Resources	Government	—	—
Agribusiness Project	Ecuador	2017	HIAS Ecuador	Nongovernment	50	215
Entrepreneurship School	Ecuador	2016	HIAS Ecuador	Nongovernment	272	3,487
Entrepreneurship School 2.0	Ecuador	2021	HIAS Ecuador	Nongovernment	70	270
Entrepreneurship School with Gender Lens	Ecuador	2016	HIAS Ecuador	Nongovernment	143	667

(Table continues next page)

TABLE C.1 Economic Inclusion Programs Included in the Global Survey *(continued)*

Program	Economy	Year program began	Lead implementing agency or agencies	Type of lead implementing agency	Current participants (direct)	Cumulative participants (direct)
Graduation Model Approach and Socio-Economic Support Program	Ecuador	2016	HIAS Ecuador	Nongovernment	300	5,729
Human Development Credit, supported by World Bank's Social Safety Net Project	Ecuador	2007	Ministry of Economic and Social Inclusion	Government	36,015	681,722
Human Talent Consultancy Services	Ecuador	2016	HIAS Ecuador	Nongovernment	233	7,471
Territorial Economic Empowerment for the Indigenous, Afro-Ecuadorians and Montubian Peoples and Nationalities (TEEIPAM) Project	Ecuador	2022	National Institute of Popular and Solidarity Economy	Government	—	—
FORSA Program, supported by the World Bank's Strengthening Social Safety Net Project	Egypt, Arab Rep.	2019	Ministry of Social Solidarity	Government	35,861	35,861
Self-reliance, Economic Empowerment, and Inclusion of Refugees and Asylum Seekers	Egypt, Arab Rep.	2023	CRS, Caritas Internationalis, and Refuge Egypt	Nongovernment	629	1,016
Advancing Women Enterprises	Ethiopia	2021	CARE International Ethiopia	Nongovernment	3,000	3,000
De-risking, Inclusion and Value Enhancement of Pastoral Economies in the Horn of Africa (DRIVE)	Ethiopia	2022	ZEP-RE (PTA Reinsurance Company)	Nongovernment	15,000	21,000
Delivering Resilient Enterprises and Market Systems (DREAMS) for Refugees	Ethiopia	2023	Village Enterprise	Nongovernment	1,200	1,200
Desert Locust Crises Response and Resilience Building Project	Ethiopia	2021	LWF Ethiopia	Nongovernment	4,085	4,085
Development Response to Displacement Impacts Project, Phase Two (DRDIP II)	Ethiopia	2022	Ministry of Agriculture	Government	19,908	183,293

(Table continues next page)

TABLE C.1   Economic Inclusion Programs Included in the Global Survey (*continued*)

Program	Economy	Year program began	Lead implementing agency or agencies	Type of lead implementing agency	Current participants (direct)	Cumulative participants (direct)
Entrepreneurship and Market Inclusion for the Transformation (EMIT) of Livelihoods of Extreme Poor in Borana	Ethiopia	2022	Caritas Switzerland	Nongovernment	3,000	3,000
Feed the Future Ethiopia—Livelihoods for Resilience Activity (L4R)	Ethiopia	2016	CARE International Ethiopia	Nongovernment	97,124	128,280
Feed the Future Resilience in a Pastoral Areas (RIPA South)	Ethiopia	2020	GOAL Ethiopia, Global Communities, and International Development Enterprise	Nongovernment	53,500	53,500
Green Rural Entrepreneur Access Project (REAP) Ethiopia	Ethiopia	2022	Caritas Switzerland	Nongovernment	2,100	2,100
Livelihood Improvement Program for Women and Youth (LIWAY)	Ethiopia	2017	SNV	Nongovernment	26,277	77,894
Livestock and Fishery Sector Development Project	Ethiopia	2018	Ministry of Agriculture	Government	201,664	201,664
Lowlands Livelihood Resilience Project	Ethiopia	2019	Ministry of Irrigation and Lowlands	Government	32,878	32,878
Resilience and Evidence-based Graduation of Extreme Poor Households	Ethiopia	2023	Concern Worldwide	Nongovernment	5,400	5,400
Resilience in Pastoral Areas (RIPA–North)	Ethiopia	2020	Mercy Corps	Nongovernment	145,213	145,213
Resilient Landscapes and Livelihoods Project	Ethiopia	2019	Ministry of Agriculture	Government	100,936	173,326
Rural Productive Safety Net Program Phase 5 (PSNP5)	Ethiopia	2021	Food Security Coordination Directorate, Ministry of Agriculture	Government	42,874	42,874
Second Agricultural Growth Project	Ethiopia	2015	Ministry of Agriculture	Government	2,348,576	2,500,000
Semien Gondar Resilience Project	Ethiopia	2021	Concern Worldwide and Helvetas Swiss Intercooperation	Nongovernment	6,350	6,350
Sprinklers irrigation	Ethiopia	2018	LWF	Nongovernment	100	100

(Table continues next page)

TABLE C.1   Economic Inclusion Programs Included in the Global Survey (*continued*)

Program	Economy	Year program began	Lead implementing agency or agencies	Type of lead implementing agency	Current participants (direct)	Cumulative participants (direct)
Urban Productive Safety Net and Jobs Project (UPSNJP)	Ethiopia	2020	Ministry of Urban Development and Infrastructure, Ministry of Labor and Skills, Ministry of Women and Social Affairs, and Refugee and Returnee Agency	Government	1,440,472	1,440,472
Women Empowerment through Gender Transformative Market Opportunities (WEGO)	Ethiopia	2021	CARE International Ethiopia	Nongovernment	6,400	6,400
Skills Development and Employability Project	Gabon	2016	Ministry of Technical and Vocational Education	Government	7,259	7,259
Empowerment, Resilience, Transformation and Development (ERTAD) Project	Georgia	2023	World Vision Germany, World Vision Georgia Foundation, and DRC	Nongovernment	—	—
Complementary Livelihood and Asset Support Scheme, supported by the World Bank's Productive Safety Net Project	Ghana	2019	Ministry of Local Government, Decentralization and Rural Development	Government	8,000	29,000
Landscape Restoration and Small-Scale Mining Project	Ghana	2022	Environmental Protection Agency, under the Ministry of Environment, Science, Technology and Innovation and the Ministry of Lands and Natural Resources	Government	16,011	16,011
PROSPER III Project—Improving Food Security and Gender Equality	Ghana	2022	CARE International in Ghana	Nongovernment	18,491	18,491
Transforming the Vaccine Delivery System for Chicken and Goats in Ghana	Ghana	2019	CARE International in Ghana	Nongovernment	3,710	3,925
Women for Change (W4C) Project	Ghana	2020	CARE International in Ghana	Nongovernment	12,805	12,805
YOUStart Program	Ghana	2022	Ministry of Finance	Government	—	—

(Table continues next page)

TABLE C.1 Economic Inclusion Programs Included in the Global Survey (*continued*)

Program	Economy	Year program began	Lead implementing agency or agencies	Type of lead implementing agency	Current participants (direct)	Cumulative participants (direct)
From Local Power	Guatemala	2019	Trickle Up	Nongovernment	1,050	3,043
Green Corps: Generating Integration Opportunities for People with International Protection Needs	Guatemala	2023	Foundation for Ecodevelopment and Conservation	Nongovernment	25	150
Guatemala Dedicated Grant Mechanism for Indigenous Peoples and Local Communities	Guatemala	2021	Sotzil Association	Nongovernment	2,418	2,418
Livelihoods Generation Support	Guatemala	2023	World Vision Guatemala and Children's Shelter	Nongovernment	215	215
Nafa Program, supported by the World Bank's Emergency Response and Nafa Program Support Project	Guinea	2021	National Agency for Economic and Social Inclusion	Government	—	—
Entrepreneurship School with Gender Lens	Guyana	2023	HIAS Guyana	Nongovernment	53	95
Changing The Way We Care (CTWWC)	Haiti	2021	CRS	Nongovernment	70	70
Pathway to a Better Life	Haiti	2007	Fonkoze	Nongovernment	3,350	9,300
Pathway to a Better Life	Haiti	2022	Fonkoze	Nongovernment	1,700	1,700
Raising Up Again	Haiti	2021	Fonkoze	Nongovernment	4,700	4,700
Temporary Social Safety Net and Skills for Young People	Haiti	2019	Social and Economic Fund	Government	28,000	28,000
Empowerment through Protection, Develops Enduring Resilience (EMPODER)	Honduras	2022	HIAS Honduras	Nongovernment	108	108
Improving the Livelihoods of Miskito Indigenous Peoples in La Moskitia	Honduras	2019	Fundación Ayuda en Acción	Nongovernment	1,200	1,200
Prosperous Futures	Honduras	2022	CARE International Honduras	Nongovernment	500	500
Building Climate Smart Integrated Agriculture for Smallholder Farmers in Damoh, Madhya Pradesh	India	2021	CARE International India Solutions for Sustainable Development	Nongovernment	9,000	9,000

(Table continues next page)

TABLE C.1   Economic Inclusion Programs Included in the Global Survey (*continued*)

Program	Economy	Year program began	Lead implementing agency or agencies	Type of lead implementing agency	Current participants (direct)	Cumulative participants (direct)
Chhattisgarh Inclusive, Rural and Accelerated Agriculture Growth Project (CHIRAAG)	India	2021	Department of Agriculture Development and Farmer Welfare and Biotechnology, State of Chhattisgarh	Government	1,160	1,160
Climate Smart Agriculture for Tribal Women Farmers	India	2023	Tapananda Rural Development Society	Nongovernment	150	150
Economic Empowerment of Ultrapoor Persons with Disabilities	India	2022	Sightsavers India	Nongovernment	1,000	1,000
Empowering Smallholder Farmers through Promotion of Sustainable Agriculture and Water Harvesting and Conservation Methods in Bathinda, Punjab	India	2021	CARE International India Solutions for Sustainable Development	Nongovernment	9,000	9,000
Empowering Smallholder Farmers through Strengthening Agri and Allied Clusters in Chhota Udepur, Gujarat	India	2021	CARE International India Solutions for Sustainable Development	Nongovernment	6,000	6,000
Farmer Field and Business School	India	2022	CARE International India Solutions for Sustainable Development	Nongovernment	8,000	8,000
Fisheries Sector COVID-19 Recovery Project	India	2023	Department of Fisheries, Ministry of Fisheries, Animal Husbandry and Dairying	Government	—	—
Meghalaya Community-Led Landscapes Management Project	India	2018	Meghalaya Basin Development Agency	Government	30,000	150,000
Mobile Connections to Promote Women's Economic Empowerment	India	2016	Trickle Up India Foundation	Nongovernment	2,800	2,800
Partnering to Scale Up Graduation with Jharkhand State Livelihood Promotion Society	India	2015	Jharkhand State Livelihood Promotion Society	Government	18,100	23,100
Satat Jeevikoparjan Yojana (SJY) program	India	2018	Bihar Rural Livelihood Promotion Society (JEEViKA), Government of Bihar	Government	155,000	155,000

(Table continues next page)

TABLE C.1 Economic Inclusion Programs Included in the Global Survey (*continued*)

Program	Economy	Year program began	Lead implementing agency or agencies	Type of lead implementing agency	Current participants (direct)	Cumulative participants (direct)
State of Maharashtra's Agriculture and Rural Transformation Project	India	2019	Department of Agriculture, Government of Maharashtra	Government	180,000	180,000
Tamil Nadu Rural Transformation Project	India	2017	Tamil Nadu Rural Transformation Society	Government	432,191	432,191
Targeting the Hardcore Poor (THP)	India	2006	Bandhan Konnagar	Nongovernment	65,000	125,000
Tejaswini: Socioeconomic Empowerment of Adolescent Girls and Young Women in Jharkhand	India	2016	Jharkhand Women Development Society, under the Department of Women, Child Development and Social Services	Government	30,000	30,000
Ultra-Poor Market Access (UPMA)	India	2021	Trickle Up	Nongovernment	1,016	1,016
Zoe Empowers	India	2009	Zoe India	Nongovernment	2,971	8,021
Zoe Empowers	India	2021	Jeevanadh Charitable Trust	Nongovernment	2,260	2,611
Agriculture Value Chain Development Project (I-CARE)	Indonesia	2022	Ministry of Agriculture	Government	—	—
Archipelago Economic Hero Program (PENA)	Indonesia	2022	Ministry of Social Affairs	Government	4,766	4,766
Mangroves for Coastal Resilience Project	Indonesia	2022	Ministry of Environment and Forestry	Government	—	—
Ocean for Prosperity	Indonesia	2023	Ministry of Marine Affairs and Fisheries	Government	—	—
Strengthening Rights and Economies of Adat and Local Communities	Indonesia	2017	Samdhana Institute	Nongovernment	8,805	8,805
Achieving Socio-Economic Stability of Returnees, Host Community, and Internally Displaced People in Iraq 2 (ASET Phase 2)	Iraq	2022	AVSI Foundation	Nongovernment	297	1,099
Community-led Economic Recovery and Resilience Initiatives in Ninewa	Iraq	2022	DRC	Nongovernment	250	250

(Table continues next page)

TABLE C.1   Economic Inclusion Programs Included in the Global Survey *(continued)*

Program	Economy	Year program began	Lead implementing agency or agencies	Type of lead implementing agency	Current participants (direct)	Cumulative participants (direct)
Economic Inclusion Pilot, under the Promoting and Protecting Human Capital Project	Iraq	2023	Ministry of Labor and Social Affairs	Government	—	—
Improving Conditions for Self-reliance and Durable Solutions for Displacement-affected Communities in Dohuk and Salah Al-Din Governorates	Iraq	2022	NRC	Nongovernment	586	586
Stronger Women Stronger Nations Program	Iraq	2003	Women for Women International	Nongovernment	4,433	24,314
Human Talent Consultancy Services (Wage Employment Facilitation)	Israel	2022	HIAS	Nongovernment	100	100
Jordan Youth, Technology and Jobs	Jordan	2020	Ministry of Digital Economy and Entrepreneurship	Government	6,500	15,000
Resilient Youth Socially and Economically Empowered (RYSE) Project	Jordan	2021	DRC	Nongovernment	556	1,011
AgriFin Digital Farmer 2 (ADF 2) Program	Kenya	2021	Mercy Corps Kenya	Nongovernment	1,356,089	1,356,089
Can Asset Transfer or Asset Protection Policies Alter Poverty Dynamics in Northern Kenya? A Randomized Controlled Trial	Kenya	2017	BOMA	Nongovernment	2,100	2,100
Changing the Way We Care (CTWWC) Initiative	Kenya	2018	CRS–Kenya	Nongovernment	2,830	2,830
De-risking, Inclusion, and Value Enhancement of Pastoral Economies in the Horn of Africa	Kenya	2022	ZEP–RE (PTA Reinsurance Company)	Nongovernment	30,000	30,000

(Table continues next page)

TABLE C.1 Economic Inclusion Programs Included in the Global Survey (continued)

Program	Economy	Year program began	Lead implementing agency or agencies	Type of lead implementing agency	Current participants (direct)	Cumulative participants (direct)
Development Response to Displacement Impacts Project (DRDIP)	Kenya	2017	State Department for the Development of Arid and Semi-Arid Lands (ASALs) in the Ministry of East African Community, Regional Development and ASALs	Government	59,501	64,701
Economic Inclusion as Pathway to Self-reliance	Kenya	2023	NRC	Nongovernment	—	—
Emergency Locust Response Project	Kenya	2020	Ministry of Agriculture and Livestock Development	Government	70,000	70,000
Feed the Future Kenya Livestock Market Systems	Kenya	2017	Mercy Corps	Nongovernment	2,000	65,867
Graduation Model Approach	Kenya	2021	HIAS Kenya	Nongovernment	200	267
Girls Improving Resilience through Livelihoods + Health (GIRL–H)	Kenya	2020	Mercy Corps	Nongovernment	2,225	27,659
Global Labor Program-Inclusive Futures	Kenya	2021	Sightsavers	Nongovernment	190	190
Human Talent Consultancy Services (Wage Employment Facilitation)	Kenya	2021	HIAS Kenya	Nongovernment	40	53
Inbusiness Program	Kenya	2022	Light for the World	Nongovernment	655	2,431
Kenya Core Programming	Kenya	2010	Village Enterprise	Nongovernment	3,603	105,700
Kenya Social and Economic Inclusion Project (KSEIP)	Kenya	2020	Department of Social Development in the Ministry of Labour and Social Protection	Government	7,100	7,100
Kenya Youth Employment and Opportunities Project	Kenya	2016	State Department for Youth Sports and Arts	Government	4,750	137,000
Let's Go Together	Kenya	2022	AVSI Foundation	Nongovernment	250	250
Livelihoods for Inclusion and Transformation (LIFT) Northern Kenya (an adapted climate-focused graduation program)	Kenya	2022	BOMA	Nongovernment	10,950	10,950

(Table continues next page)

TABLE C.1 Economic Inclusion Programs Included in the Global Survey *(continued)*

Program	Economy	Year program began	Lead implementing agency or agencies	Type of lead implementing agency	Current participants (direct)	Cumulative participants (direct)
Marine Fisheries and Socio-Economic Development Project	Kenya	2022	State Department for Fisheries, Aquaculture and the Blue Economy, under the Ministry of Agriculture, Livestock, Fisheries and Irrigation	Government	2,200	2,200
National Agricultural and Rural Inclusive Growth Project	Kenya	2017	Ministry of Agriculture and Livestock Development	Government	528,000	528,000
National Agriculture Value Chain Development Project	Kenya	2022	Ministry of Agriculture and Livestock Development	Government	5,000	6,000
NAWIRI–Rural Entrepreneur Access Project (REAP) for Nutrition	Kenya	2019	Mercy Corps	Nongovernment	8,700	12,000
Nutrition in Arid and Semi-Arid Lands within Integrated Resilience Institutions (NAWIRI) Project	Kenya	2020	Village Enterprise	Nongovernment	10,009	10,600
Rural Entrepreneur Access Project (REAP)	Kenya	2018	BOMA	Nongovernment	20,000	42,489
Strengthening Capacity of Religious Women in Early Childhood Development (SCORE ECD)	Cross-border: Kenya, Ghana, Malawi, and Zambia	2014	Association of Sisterhoods of Kenya, Zambian Association of Sisterhoods, Association of Women Religious in Malawi, and Association of Consecrated Women in Eastern and Central Africa	Nongovernment	9,879	9,879
Sustainable Entrepreneurship and Economic Development (SEED) program	Kenya	2021	BOMA	Nongovernment	2,400	2,400
Tumikia Mtoto Project	Kenya	2022	AVSI Foundation	Nongovernment	7,976	7,976
Village Enterprise Days for Girls Collaboration	Kenya	2020	Village Enterprise	Nongovernment	702	2,728
Women Economic Empowerment through Climate Smart Agriculture (WEE–CSA)	Kenya	2021	Village Enterprise	Nongovernment	910	910
Zoe Empowers	Kenya	2007	Zoe Empowers Kenya	Nongovernment	13,570	48,518

(Table continues next page)

TABLE C.1 Economic Inclusion Programs Included in the Global Survey (*continued*)

Program	Economy	Year program began	Lead implementing agency or agencies	Type of lead implementing agency	Current participants (direct)	Cumulative participants (direct)
Strong Women, Stronger Nations Program	Kosovo	1999	Women for Women Kosova	Nongovernment	328	35,005
National Development Program, supported by the World Bank's Regional Economic Development Project	Kyrgyz Republic	2021	Community Development and Investment Agency	Government	6,000	60,000
Lao Landscapes and Livelihoods Project	Lao PDR	2021	Department of Forestry at the Ministry of Agriculture and Forestry	Government	5,000	5,000
Bolstering Agriculture Systems' Ability to Invest, Nourish, and Employ	Lebanon	2021	CARE International; Mercy Corps; Berytech; Georges N. Frem Foundation; Lebanese Organization for Study and Training; and Al Majmoua	Nongovernment	3,395	3,395
CHASE Youth Empowerment Program	Lebanon	2022	DRC	Nongovernment	120	120
Sustainable Social Protection and Livelihood Solutions for Severely Vulnerable Households	Lebanon	2020	Save the Children	Nongovernment	1,200	1,200
Liberia Forest Program	Liberia	2016	Forestry Development Agency	Government	15,206	15,206
Rural Economic Transformation Project	Liberia	2021	Ministry of Agriculture	Government	22,385	22,385
Small Enterprise Development Program	Liberia	2023	CRS	Nongovernment	150	400
Support for Small Businesses (SSB) Program, supported by the World Bank's Recovery of Economic Activity for Liberian Informal Sector Employment project	Liberia	2016	Liberia Agency for Community Empowerment (LACE)	Government	1,280	4,569
Zoe Empowers	Liberia	2014	Zoe Empowers Liberia	Nongovernment	4,152	10,722
Drought Response Program in the South of Madagascar	Madagascar	2016	Development Intervention Fund under the Prime Minister's office	Government	70,000	70,000
Social Safety Net Project	Madagascar	2015	Development Intervention Fund under the Prime Minister's office	Government	127,763	204,682

(Table continues next page)

TABLE C.1   Economic Inclusion Programs Included in the Global Survey (*continued*)

Program	Economy	Year program began	Lead implementing agency or agencies	Type of lead implementing agency	Current participants (direct)	Cumulative participants (direct)
Support to Resilient Livelihoods in the South of Madagascar	Madagascar	2021	Ministry of Interior and Decentralization	Government	—	—
Graduation of Families from Dependence to Dignity	Malawi	2019	World Relief	Nongovernment	2,500	4,430
Improving Self-reliance and Livelihoods for People of Concern and Host Communities	Malawi	2019	Churches Action in Relief and Development	Nongovernment	863	1,748
Integrated Support for Orphans, Vulnerable Children and Youth Project	Malawi	2020	CRS	Nongovernment	4,000	4,700
Raising Assets and Income for a Sustainable Environment (RAISE) Project	Malawi	2021	Concern Worldwide	Nongovernment	62,974	86,475
Resilient Economic Development (RED) Gains Project	Malawi	2019	Save the Children	Nongovernment	2,250	4,091
Social Support for Resilient Livelihoods Project	Malawi	2020	Community Savings and Investment Promotion Cooperative Union Limited	Nongovernment	345,742	345,742
Titukulane Resilience Food Security Activity	Malawi	2019	CARE International	Nongovernment	—	233,482
Usiwa Watha Ultra-Poor Graduation Program	Malawi	2021	Opportunity International Malawi	Nongovernment	320	320
Yamba Malawi's Childhoods & Livelihoods Program	Malawi	2017	Yamba Malawi	Nongovernment	815	1,500
Yamba Malawi FARMSE project in Chikwawa, Nsanje, and Phalombe Districts	Malawi	2023	Yamba Malawi	Nongovernment	2,500	2,500
Zoe Empowers	Malawi	2013	Zoe Ministry Malawi	Nongovernment	5,558	17,649

(Table continues next page)

TABLE C.1   Economic Inclusion Programs Included in the Global Survey (*continued*)

Program	Economy	Year program began	Lead implementing agency or agencies	Type of lead implementing agency	Current participants (direct)	Cumulative participants (direct)
Albarka Resilience Food Security Activity (RFSA)	Mali	2020	Save the Children	Nongovernment	95,959	148,387
Drylands Development Project	Mali	2018	Ministry of Rural Development	Government	22,325	22,325
Emergency Safety Nets Program	Mali	2013	Technical Unit for the Management of Social Safety Nets and Technical Unit for the Unified Social Registry	Government	20,000	31,000
Feed the Future Mali Sugu Yiriwa in the Delta zone	Mali	2021	CARE International Mali, in consortium with Amassa Afrique Verte et Amprode Sahel	Nongovernment	31,331	46,340
Regional Sahel Pastoralism Support Project II (PRAPS–2)	Mali	2022	Ministry in charge of Livestock	Government	—	—
Agriculture Development and Innovation Support Project	Mauritania	2023	Ministry of Agriculture	Government	—	—
Re-certification and development of an exit strategy for Tekavoul, supported by the World Bank's Social Safety Net System Project II	Mauritania	2020	General Delegation of Taazour	Government	3,388	5,388
Regional Sahel Pastoralism Support Project II (PRAPS–2)	Mauritania	2022	National Institute for the Promotion of Technical and Vocational Training, under the Ministry of Employment	Government	4,000	4,000
Dedicated Grant Mechanism for Indigenous People and Local Communities	Mexico	2017	Rainforest Alliance	Nongovernment	3,850	3,850
Impulsa Tu Rumbo Program	Mexico	2022	Secretary of Social Protection and Opportunities under the Secretariat of Equality and Inclusion, Government of Nuevo Leon	Government	14,000	14,000
Local Integration Program	Mexico	2016	UNHCR Mexico	Nongovernment	3,200	33,200
Second Chance Education	Mexico	2019	Prosociedad	Nongovernment	133	133
Sowing Life Program (SLP)	Mexico	2019	Federal Secretary of Welfare	Government	450,038	450,038

(Table continues next page)

TABLE C.1 Economic Inclusion Programs Included in the Global Survey *(continued)*

Program	Economy	Year program began	Lead implementing agency or agencies	Type of lead implementing agency	Current participants (direct)	Cumulative participants (direct)
Strength, Unity, Empowerment, Resilience for Women in Extreme Poverty	Mexico	2022	Trickle Up	Nongovernment	3,623	3,623
Strengthening Entrepreneurship in Productive Forest Landscapes	Mexico	2018	National Forestry Commission	Government	23,443	172,668
Support for the Social Reintegration Youth at Risk Program	Mexico	2022	Youth Directorate under the Secretary of Human Rights, State of Jalisco	Nongovernment	21	41
Entrepreneurship-focused Socioemotional Skills for the Most Vulnerable Youth in Rural Mongolia	Mongolia	2019	Save the Children Japan in Mongolia	Nongovernment	6,114	6,114
Micro-entrepreneurship Support Program	Mongolia	2019	Ministry of Labour and Social Protection of Mongolia	Government	1,090	1,090
Morocco Green Generation Program-for-Results	Morocco	2020	Directorate of Strategy and Statistics, under the Ministry of Agriculture, Fisheries, Rural Development, Water and Forestry	Government	550	550
Support of the Economic Inclusion of Youth	Morocco	2019	Ministry of Economic Inclusion, Small Businesses, Employment and Skills, with Regional Authorities	Government	4,000	12,000
Emprega Program, supported by the World Bank's Harnessing the Demographic Dividend Project	Mozambique	2020	National Youth Institute, under the State Secretariat for Youth and Employment	Government	3,612	3,612
Forest Investment Project	Mozambique	2017	Ministry of Agriculture and Rural Development	Government	28,916	28,916
Mozambique Conservation Areas for Biodiversity and Development—Phase 2	Mozambique	2018	National Fund for Sustainable Development	Government	5,033	5,033
Northern Mozambique Rural Resilience Project	Mozambique	2021	National Sustainable Development Fund, under the Ministry of Agriculture and Rural Development	Government	26,429	26,429

(Table continues next page)

TABLE C.1   Economic Inclusion Programs Included in the Global Survey (*continued*)

Program	Economy	Year program began	Lead implementing agency or agencies	Type of lead implementing agency	Current participants (direct)	Cumulative participants (direct)
Package of Economic Acceleration Measures (PAE), supported by the World Bank's Access to Finance & Economic Opportunities Project–Mais Oportunidades	Mozambique	2023	Zambezi Valley Development Agency	Government	—	—
Rural Enterprise Finance Project (REFP)	Mozambique	2021	Fundación Capital	Nongovernment	4,897	4,897
Sustainable Rural Economy Program	Mozambique	2021	National Fund for Sustainable Development	Government	65,000	65,000
Zoe Empowers	Mozambique	2022	Mozambique United Methodist Church	Nongovernment	747	747
Community Forestry	Nepal	2021	REDD Implementation Centre, under the Ministry of Forests and Environment	Government	—	—
Forests for Prosperity Project	Nepal	2021	REDD Implementation Centre, under the Ministry of Forests and Environment	Government	81,667	81,667
Hurricanes Eta and Iota Emergency Response Project	Nicaragua	2021	United Nations Office for Project Services	Nongovernment	360	1,720
Lake Chad Recovery and Development Project	Niger	2021	Executive Secretary for the Stabilization and Development Strategy for the Sahel, under the Prime Minister's Cabinet	Government	20,000	34,000
Niger Refugee and Host Communities Support Project	Niger	2019	Office of the Prime Minister of Niger	Government	—	76,545
Project to Strengthen the Resilience and Social Cohesion of Vulnerable Populations (RECOSA)	Cross-border: Niger and Burkina Faso	2019	Humanity and Inclusion	Nongovernment	7,000	7,000
Productive Support Component, under the Adaptive Safety Net Project II (PFSA II)	Niger	2019	Social Safety Nets Technical Management Unit	Government	—	—
Regional Sahel Pastoralism Support Project II (PRAPS–2)	Niger	2022	Ministry in Charge of Livestock	Government	—	—
Resilience Food Security Activity (RFSA)	Niger	2018	Save the Children	Nongovernment	194,852	194,852
USAID Hamzari Program	Niger	2018	CARE International Niger	Nongovernment	26,640	31,754

(Table continues next page)

TABLE C.1   Economic Inclusion Programs Included in the Global Survey (*continued*)

Program	Economy	Year program began	Lead implementing agency or agencies	Type of lead implementing agency	Current participants (direct)	Cumulative participants (direct)
Agro-Climatic Resilience in Semi-Arid Landscapes (ACReSAL) in Nigeria	Nigeria	2022	Federal Ministry of Environment, in collaboration with the Federal Ministry of Water Resources and the Federal Ministry of Agriculture and Rural Development	Government	—	—
Agro-Processing, Productivity Enhancement and Livelihood Improvement Support (APEALS) Project	Nigeria	2017	Federal Ministry of Agriculture and Rural Development	Government	55,864	55,864
COVID-19 Action Recovery and Economic Stimulus Program	Nigeria	2021	Federal CARES Support Unit, under the Federal Ministry of Finance, Budget and National Planning	Government	173,415	739,461
Feed the Future Nigeria Rural Resilience Activity (FTF–RRA)	Nigeria	2019	Mercy Corps	Nongovernment	133,029	154,219
Livestock Productivity and Resilience Support Project	Nigeria	2022	Federal Ministry of Agriculture and Rural Development	Government	—	—
National Social Safety Net Project	Nigeria	2016	Federal Ministry of Humanitarian Affairs Disaster Management and Social Development	Government	—	—
Nigeria For Women Project	Nigeria	2018	Ministry of Women Affairs (at the federal and state levels)	Government	406,805	406,805
Protection Safety Net for People of Concern in Northeast (BAY States)	Nigeria	2016	American University of Nigeria	Nongovernment	1,200	36,050
Stronger Women Stronger Nations program	Nigeria	2002	Women for Women International	Nongovernment	7,019	84,306
UNHCR Livelihood and Economic Inclusion Project for the Cameroonian Refugee Operation in Nigeria	Nigeria	2023	Cuso International, Mediatrix Development Foundation, and UNHCR	Nongovernment	450	7,693
Youth Employment and Social Support Operation (YESSO) Project	Nigeria	2013	Federal Operations Coordinating Unit, supervised by the National Social Safety Net Coordinating Office in the Ministry of Humanitarian Affairs, Disaster Management and Social Development	Government	486,904	486,904

(Table continues next page)

TABLE C.1 Economic Inclusion Programs Included in the Global Survey (*continued*)

Program	Economy	Year program began	Lead implementing agency or agencies	Type of lead implementing agency	Current participants (direct)	Cumulative participants (direct)
Community Support Program (CASA-1000)	Pakistan	2020	Planning and Development Department of the Provincial Government of Khyber Pakhtunkhwa	Government	50,000	50,000
Dairy Development Programme (DDP)	Pakistan	2021	PPAF	Nongovernment	2,765	2,796
Growth for Rural Advancement and Sustainable Progress (GRASP)	Pakistan	2021	International Trade Centre	Nongovernment	6,478	13,730
Interest Free Loan Program (Phase 2)	Pakistan	2021	PPAF	Nongovernment	133,354	173,550
National Poverty Graduation Program (NPGP)	Pakistan	2017	Ministry of Poverty Alleviation & Social Safety	Government	220,000	220,000
Punjab Human Capital Investment Project	Pakistan	2020	Punjab Social Protection Authority	Government	47,024	47,024
Revitalizing Youth Enterprise (RYE) Program (Phase 2)	Pakistan	2022	PPAF	Nongovernment	200	224
Development of Territorial Networks	Panama	2020	Ministry of Social Development	Government	2,055	2,055
Entrepreneurship School	Panama	2021	HIAS	Nongovernment	100	400
Entrepreneurship School 2.0	Panama	2022	Banesco and HIAS	Nongovernment	111	111
Entrepreneur Godfather (Padrino Empresario) Program	Panama	1986	Ministry of Social Development	Government	200	28,000
Social Cohesion Program	Panama	2019	Ministry of Social Development	Government	1,000	4,500
Talent without Borders	Panama	2021	HIAS, with support of the UNHCR	Nongovernment	70	114
Agriculture Commercialization and Diversification Project	Papua New Guinea	2020	Department of Agriculture and Livestock, the Cocoa Board of Papua New Guinea, and the Coffee Industry Corporation	Government	—	—
Program Tenonderã	Paraguay	2014	Ministry of Social Development	Government	5,000	69,908
Graduation Model Approach (GMA)	Peru	2020	HIAS	Nongovernment	135	670
Haku Wiñay/Noa Jayatai program	Peru	2014	Cooperation Fund for Social Development, under the Ministry of Development and Social Inclusion	Government	148,800	353,566

(Table continues next page)

TABLE C.1   Economic Inclusion Programs Included in the Global Survey (*continued*)

Program	Economy	Year program began	Lead implementing agency or agencies	Type of lead implementing agency	Current participants (direct)	Cumulative participants (direct)
Human Talent Consultancy Services (Wage Employment Facilitation)	Peru	2021	HIAS	Nongovernment	1,367	4,382
National Solidarity Assistance Program Pensión 65	Peru	2011	Ministry of Development and Social Inclusion	Government	17,726	17,726
Prevail	Philippines	2014	ICM	Nongovernment	2,773	5,915
Thrive Together: Empowering Young People with Disabilities	Philippines	2021	Humanity and Inclusion	Nongovernment	172	172
Transform	Philippines	2009	ICM	Nongovernment	41,456	320,000
Area Program (AP)	Rwanda	2020	World Vision Rwanda	Nongovernment	4,079	5,079
Developing Human Capital	Rwanda	2022	World Relief Rwanda	Nongovernment	9,050	9,050
Graduation Project	Rwanda	2021	Caritas Archdiocese of Kigali	Nongovernment	460	460
Graduation Pilot Pathways to Economic Inclusion and Self-reliance of the Refugees and Their Host Communities	Rwanda	2020	Caritas Rwanda	Nongovernment	1,143	2,958
Green Graduation	Rwanda	2023	Concern Worldwide	Nongovernment	2,100	2,100
Inclusive Nutrition and Early Childhood Development (INECD)	Rwanda	2021	CRS	Nongovernment	218,043	264,285
Poverty Alleviating Coalition (PAC) Project	Rwanda	2021	World Vision International	Nongovernment	2,921	3,000
Poverty Graduation Program	Rwanda	2021	Village Enterprise Rwanda	Nongovernment	5,058	7,671
Rwanda Priority Skills for Growth Program	Rwanda	2017	Ministry of Education	Government	3,548	54,054
Social Economic Inclusion of Refugees and Host Communities in Rwanda Project	Rwanda	2019	Five districts hosting refugee camps, Development Bank of Rwanda, and Rwanda Transport Development Agency	Government	116,628	116,628

(Table continues next page)

TABLE C.1 Economic Inclusion Programs Included in the Global Survey (*continued*)

Program	Economy	Year program began	Lead implementing agency or agencies	Type of lead implementing agency	Current participants (direct)	Cumulative participants (direct)
Stronger Women, Stronger Nations Program	Rwanda	1997	Women for Women Rwanda	Nongovernment	703	79,973
Sustainable Livelihoods Enhancement Scheme	Rwanda	2017	Local Administrative Entities Development Agency	Government	141,539	447,247
Volcanoes Community Resilience Project	Rwanda	2021	Ministry of Environment	Government	—	—
Zoe Empowers	Rwanda	2007	Zoe Empowers Rwanda	Nongovernment	11,513	45,623
Casamance Economic Development Project	Senegal	2022	Ministry of Territorial Communities, Development and Land Management	Government	—	—
Natural Resources Management Project	Senegal	2022	Ministry of Sustainable Development and Ecological Transition and Ministry of Fisheries and Marine Economy	Government	—	—
Regional Sahel Pastoralism Support Project II (PRAPS–2)	Senegal	2022	Ministry of Livestock and Animal Production	Government	—	—
Yook Koom Koom Program, supported by the World Bank's Adaptive Safety Net Project	Senegal	2014	General Delegation to Social Protection and National Solidarity	Government	45,000	60,000
Serbia Competitive Agriculture Project	Serbia	2019	Ministry of Agriculture, Forestry, and Water Management of Serbia	Government	1,349	1,349
Developing Neighborhood Entrepreneurs, Accelerating Argo-Businesses and Gender Inclusion in Transforming the Local Economy	Sierra Leone	2023	Gender Impact and Women in Entrepreneurship Initiative	Nongovernment	115	115
Agriculture and Rural Transformation Project	Solomon Islands	2022	Ministry of Agriculture and Livestock	Government	—	—
Pacific Islands Regional Oceanscape Program—Second Phase for Economic Resilience	Solomon Islands	2022	Ministry of Fisheries and Marine Resources	Government	—	—

(Table continues next page)

TABLE C.1 Economic Inclusion Programs Included in the Global Survey (*continued*)

Program	Economy	Year program began	Lead implementing agency or agencies	Type of lead implementing agency	Current participants (direct)	Cumulative participants (direct)
Building Pathways Out of Poverty for Ultra-Poor IDPs and Vulnerable Host Communities in Baidoa	Somalia	2021	World Vision Somalia	Nongovernment	5,000	5,000
Climate Resilient and Environmentally Sustainable Solutions Somalia/Somaliland (CRESS)	Somalia	2023	Concern Worldwide	Nongovernment	—	—
De-risking, Inclusion and Value Enhancement of Pastoral Economies in the Horn of Africa (DRIVE)	Somalia	2022	ZEP–RE (PTA Reinsurance Company)	Nongovernment	1,787	1,787
Regional Livestock Program	Somalia	2023	Mercy Corps	Nongovernment	—	—
Social Transfers for Vulnerable People (SAGAL) Project	Somalia	2020	Concern Worldwide	Nongovernment	2,321	2,321
Supporting Climate Adaptation and Durable Solutions for Displacement-Affected Communities in Afgoye District	Somalia	2023	Concern Worldwide	Nongovernment	—	—
Complementary Action for Resilience Building Project	South Sudan	2021	NRC	Nongovernment	4,650	4,650
Economic Inclusion as Pathway to Self-Reliance	South Sudan	2023	NRC	Nongovernment	—	—
Improving the Quality of Education in a Safe, Food-Secure, Inclusive, and Protective Environment, for Crisis-Affected Children and Youth in South Sudan	South Sudan	2020	NRC	Nongovernment	790	5,000
Resilience through Agriculture in South Sudan (RASS) Activity	South Sudan	2021	DAI Global, LLC; CARE International; International Fertilizer Development Center; and Waterfield Design Group	Nongovernment	8,000	10,500

(Table continues next page)

TABLE C.1 Economic Inclusion Programs Included in the Global Survey *(continued)*

Program	Economy	Year program began	Lead implementing agency or agencies	Type of lead implementing agency	Current participants (direct)	Cumulative participants (direct)
Resilient Agricultural Livelihoods Project	South Sudan	2021	Ministry of Agriculture and Food Security	Government	15,500	15,500
Stronger Women, Stronger Nations Program	South Sudan	2013	Women for Women International	Nongovernment	2,400	21,098
Women's Social and Economic Empowerment Project	South Sudan	2021	Ministry of Gender Child and Social Welfare	Government	—	—
Socio-Economic Empowerment for Graduation out of Poverty	Sri Lanka	2022	Department of Samurdhi Development	Government	—	—
Productive Safety Net, under the Social Safety Nets Project	Sudan	2016	Ministry of Labor and Social Development	Government	1,000	1,000
RESTORE III Project	Syrian Arab Republic	2021	GOAL Global/Goal Syria	Nongovernment	400	400
RESILAND CA+ Program: Resilient Landscapes Restoration Project	Tajikistan	2022	Committee of Environmental Protection	Government	—	—
Disability Inclusive Graduation Program	Tanzania	2022	BRAC Maendeleo Tanzania	Nongovernment	1,050	1,050
Integrated Program for Local Area Development	Tanzania	2021	President's Office–Finance and Planning, Zanzibar	Government	—	—
Productive Social Safety Net Program	Tanzania	2012	Tanzania Social Action Fund	Government	313,411	716,327
Savings and Credit Groups for Food Security and Ecosystem Sustainability	Tanzania	2021	CARE International–World Wildlife Fund Alliance	Nongovernment	8,132	8,132
Zoe Empowers	Tanzania	2019	Zoe Africa Tanzania	Nongovernment	3,090	3,831
Safety Nets and Basic Services Project	Togo	2022	National Agency for Support to Grassroots Development	Government	10,589	10,589
Integrated Landscapes Management in Lagging Regions Project	Tunisia	2017	Ministry of Agriculture, Water Resources, and Fisheries	Government	300	400
Social and Solidarity Economic Integration in the Hills of Kairouan Project	Tunisia	2021	Kairouan Regional Agricultural Development Commission	Government	540	540
Support to Economic Recovery and Job Creation in the Agri-Food Sector and Rural North West	Tunisia	2021	Microfinanza SRL	Nongovernment	52	52

(Table continues next page)

TABLE C.1　Economic Inclusion Programs Included in the Global Survey (continued)

Program	Economy	Year program began	Lead implementing agency or agencies	Type of lead implementing agency	Current participants (direct)	Cumulative participants (direct)
Support to Economic Recovery and Job Creation in the Agri-Food Sector and Rural South	Tunisia	2021	ENDA Inter-Arabe	Nongovernment	41	41
Support to Economic Recovery and Job Creation in the Agri-Food Sector and Rural Space	Tunisia	2021	Tunisian Union of Social Solidarity	Nongovernment	88	88
Youth Economic Inclusion Project	Tunisia	2017	Ministry of Employment and Professional Training	Government	—	—
Agricultural Employment for Refugees and Turkish Citizens through Enhanced Market Linkages (FESAS)	Türkiye	2020	Agricultural Credit Cooperatives of Türkiye	Nongovernment	4,500	4,500
Development of Businesses and Entrepreneurship for Syrians under Temporary Protection and Turkish Citizens Project	Türkiye	2017	Small and Medium Enterprises Development Organization	Government	254	254
Formal Employment Creation Project	Türkiye	2020	Türkiye Development and Investment Bank	Nongovernment	—	—
Forest and Village Relations (ORKOY) Program	Türkiye	1974	Directorate General of Forestry	Government	11,127	526,797
Scaling-up Farmers Field Business Schools (FFBS)	Türkiye	2022	CARE International	Nongovernment	—	—
A Model for Sustainable Peace/ Security and Development	Uganda	1999	Uganda Peace Foundation	Nongovernment	650	7,026

(Table continues next page)

TABLE C.1 Economic Inclusion Programs Included in the Global Survey (*continued*)

Program	Economy	Year program began	Lead implementing agency or agencies	Type of lead implementing agency	Current participants (direct)	Cumulative participants (direct)
Building Pathways Out of Poverty	Uganda	2023	Raising the Village	Nongovernment	45,063	133,070
Building Self-Reliance and Resilience in West Nile	Uganda	2022	DRC	Nongovernment	800	800
Climate Smart Agricultural Transformation Project	Uganda	2022	Ministry of Agriculture, Animal Industry, and Fisheries	Government	—	—
Delivering Resilient Enterprises and Market Systems (DREAMS) for Refugees	Uganda	2022	Village Enterprise	Nongovernment	3,600	3,600
Development Response to Displacement Impacts Project	Uganda	2016	Office of the Prime Minister	Government	26,703	26,703
Early Childhood and Graduation Programing in Humanitarian Settings—Ultra Poor Graduation (UPG)	Uganda	2022	BRAC Uganda	Nongovernment	700	700
Enyua Community Afforestation Program	Uganda	2019	National Forest Authority	Government	540	540
Generating Growth Opportunities and Productivity for Women Enterprises Project	Uganda	2023	Ministry of Gender, Labour and Social Development and the Private Sector Foundation	Government	—	—
Graduating to Resilience program	Uganda	2017	AVSI Foundation	Nongovernment	7,051	13,680
Inclusive Market-based Development for Smallholder Farmers in Northern Uganda	Uganda	2020	CARE International Uganda	Nongovernment	68,250	68,250
National Uganda Social Action Fund Program	Uganda	2015	Office of the Prime Minister	Government	100,100	132,838
Poverty Alleviation and Removal of Kibale Snares (PARKS) Project	Uganda	2021	Village Enterprise	Nongovernment	1,240	1,840
Prevention of Street Children Graduation (PSGP) Project	Uganda	2020	Agency for Accelerated Regional Development	Nongovernment	450	450
Sustainable Market-Inclusive Livelihood Pathways to Self-reliance	Uganda	2022	AVSI Foundation	Nongovernment	7,042	7,042

(Table continues next page)

TABLE C.1   Economic Inclusion Programs Included in the Global Survey *(continued)*

Program	Economy	Year program began	Lead implementing agency or agencies	Type of lead implementing agency	Current participants (direct)	Cumulative participants (direct)
Village Enterprise Core Uganda	Uganda	1988	Village Enterprise	Nongovernment	12,230	123,798
Young Africa Works in Uganda: Markets for Youth Program	Uganda	2020	GOAL Global	Nongovernment	24,800	105,802
Youth Engine Project	Uganda	2021	GOAL Uganda	Nongovernment	900	1,350
Enhancing Economic Opportunities for Rural Women	Uzbekistan	2022	Women's Committee under the Ministry of Employment and Poverty Reduction	Government	748	748
Entrepreneurship Support through Business Start-up Subsidies	Uzbekistan	2019	Ministry of Employment and Poverty Reduction	Government	5,000	10,079
RESILAND CA+ Program: Resilient Landscapes Restoration Project	Uzbekistan	2023	International Relations and Ecotourism Development	Government	—	—
She Feeds the World	Viet Nam	2022	CARE international in Vietnam	Nongovernment	1,200	1,200
Increasing Resilience and Improving Socioeconomic Conditions at Al Mina Port	West Bank and Gaza	2022	NRC	Nongovernment	—	—
Palestinian Heritage Trail: Increased Economic Opportunities and Improved Livelihood for Fragile Communities Project	West Bank and Gaza	2022	Palestinian Heritage Trail	Nongovernment	60	60
The Gaza Emergency Cash for Work and Self-Employment Support Project	West Bank and Gaza	2018	NGO Development Center	Nongovernment	—	6,100
Supporting Women's Livelihoods Component under the Girls' Education and Women's Empowerment and Livelihoods Project	Zambia	2015	Ministry of Community Development and Social Services	Government	20,649	116,891
The Ultra-Poor Graduation Model: Securing Durable Solutions for Persons of Concern and Their Hosts	Zambia	2021	World Vision Zambia	Nongovernment	1,200	1,200

(Table continues next page)

TABLE C.1   Economic Inclusion Programs Included in the Global Survey (*continued*)

Program	Economy	Year program began	Lead implementing agency or agencies	Type of lead implementing agency	Current participants (direct)	Cumulative participants (direct)
Transforming Landscapes for Resilience and Development (TRALARD) Project	Zambia	2019	Ministry of Green Economy and Environment	Government	28,965	28,965
Insect Farming Project	Zimbabwe	2022	World Vision Zimbabwe	Nongovernment	60	60
Scaling Up Irrigation in Tongogara Refuge Camp	Zimbabwe	2022	UNHCR	Nongovernment	435	435
Zoe Empowers	Zimbabwe	2011	Zoe Empowers Zimbabwe	Nongovernment	5,933	23,154

Source: Table original for this report.

Note: BRAC = Bangladesh Rural Advancement Committee; CRS = Catholic Relief Services; DRC = Danish Refugee Council; ICM = International Care Ministries; IDPs = internally displaced persons; LWF = Lutheran World Federation; Fonkoze = Fondasyon Kole Zepòl; IDPS = internally displaced persons; NGO = nongovernmental organization; NRC = Norwegian Refugee Council; PPAF = Pakistan Poverty Alleviation Fund; PKSF = Palli Karma-Sahayak Foundation; UNDP = United Nations Development Programme; UNHCR = United Nations High Commissioner for Refugees; WCS = Wildlife Conservation Society.

Glossary

agency The capacity of individuals to act independently and to make their own free choices.

cash plus The combination of cash transfers or other safety net programs (for example, public works) with additional interventions. These diverse complementary interventions can include financial literacy training, social and behavioral change communication, or links to external services such as health insurance. This integrated approach of adding complementary components to cash transfers is what constitutes "cash plus."

community structure A community-based entity that can be mobilized within the purview of a program intervention or, if existing, be utilized by a program intervention. Examples include informal community savings and credit groups, local governance groups, formalized producer organizations, demographic groups (women's cooperatives, youth groups), or activity groups (for example, sports, religious, or other interests).

convergence or program convergence When the components of two or more existing, discrete programs serve the same group of beneficiaries.

cost-effectiveness A measure used to evaluate the efficiency of an intervention, program, or investment by comparing its costs to its outcomes or benefits. A program or intervention is considered cost-effective when the benefits outweigh the costs.

coverage The total number of beneficiaries reached by a program or a combination of programs relative to the total population.

coverage equivalent The total number of beneficiaries reached by a program or combination of programs relative to specific poverty measures. This report considers three measures: the national poverty line, the extreme poverty line, and the Multidimensional Poverty Index.

delivery system The system used to implement social protection and labor benefits and services. This system includes the implementation phases and processes along the delivery chain, the main actors (people and institutions), and the enabling factors (communications, information systems, and technology).

economic inclusion The gradual integration of individuals and households into broader economic and community development processes. Integration is achieved by addressing the multiple constraints or structural barriers faced by poor people at different levels: the household (for example, human and physical capacity), the community (social norms), the local economy (access to markets and services), and formal institutions (access to political and administrative structures). Throughout the report, these constraints are viewed as simultaneous and often nonseparable, most intensively affecting extreme-poor and vulnerable groups. The term *economic inclusion* is sometimes used interchangeably with the term *productive inclusion*.

economic inclusion program Bundles of coordinated, multidimensional interventions that support individuals, households, and communities to sustainably increase their incomes and assets. Economic inclusion programs are also known as *productive inclusion programs.*

- **area-focused programs** These programs have broader objectives associated with community-, region-, market-, or system-level interventions. They typically include people living in one or more poverty categories and deliver two or more components. Utilizing a "pull" strategy, these programs enroll people broadly and aim to engage those living in extreme poverty within the community, region, market, or other systems that the program seeks to change.

- **climate-resilient economic inclusion (CREI) programs** A subset of economic inclusion programs that enhance the medium- to long-term climate resilience of poor and vulnerable individuals and communities.

- **household-focused programs** These programs directly target households and use a multidimensional set of interventions to provide a "big push." This approach helps households build assets, increase income, gain knowledge, and develop the confidence needed to access services and engage in broader systems, including previously inaccessible market systems.

extreme-poor Refer to **poverty level.**

fragility, conflict, and violence (FCV) The World Bank Group classification of countries with high institutional and social fragility and of countries affected by violent conflict.

functional scale-up Increasing the scope of an activity, where initially a program starts with a single focus but then layers or links additional multisectoral interventions.

green jobs Decent jobs that contribute to preserving or restoring the environment. These jobs can be found in traditional sectors, such as manufacturing and construction, or in new and emerging green sectors, such as renewable energy and energy efficiency.

green transition A shift toward an economic model that is not based on fossil fuels and overconsumption of natural resources. The concept contains societal actions that seek to mitigate climate change (by reducing greenhouse gas emissions concentration) and adapt to it while acknowledging ecological and environmental degradation caused by other factors, such as overconsumption.

just transition Originally rooted in the US labor movement in the 1970s, the term has been reinterpreted within environmental and climate justice communities and incorporated into the Paris Agreement. It refers to a set of principles, processes, and practices aimed at ensuring that no people, places, sectors, countries, or regions are left behind in the transition from a high-carbon to a low-carbon economy. The term emphasizes the need for targeted and proactive measures from governments, international organizations, and other authorities to minimize the negative impacts of economy-wide transitions while maximizing benefits for those disproportionately affected.

nature-based solution (NBS) An action aimed at protecting, sustainably managing, and restoring natural and modified ecosystems, providing simultaneous benefits to both people and nature.

nongovernmental organization (NGO) A group that is neither part of a government nor a conventional profit-maximizing business. Although some NGOs may accept funding from governments or collaborate with government agencies, an NGO is by definition not a government entity. Their work often focuses on humanitarian or environmental causes.

opportunity The capacity of households in economic inclusion programs to capture and capitalize on investments that improve livelihoods and build human capital and one that they would otherwise miss.

poverty level

- **poor** Persons whose consumption is below the national poverty line, as defined by the government, or those who, because of their personal or community characteristics, face barriers in accessing opportunities to earn sustainable livelihoods and have elevated risks of being or staying in poverty or being socially marginalized.

- **extreme poor** Persons whose consumption is below the US$2.15 per day (at 2017 US$ purchasing power parity, PPP) and who can work on a sustained basis. Also defined as the bottom 50 percent of the poor population in a country or those unable to meet basic needs.

- **ultra poor** Persons whose consumption is below US$1.08 per day (at 2017 US$, PPP). Also defined as those experiencing the severest forms of deprivation such as being persistently hungry or lacking sources of income.

- **other vulnerable** Other groups that do not meet any of the previous criteria such as those living just above the poverty line or groups marginalized irrespective of their poverty level.

- **near poor** Persons whose consumption is marginally above the poverty line but remain vulnerable to falling into poverty due to economic shocks, health emergencies, job loss, or other adverse events.

purchasing power parity (PPP) The number of units of a country's currency required to buy the same amount of goods and services in the domestic market as a US dollar would buy in the United States.

resilience The strengthened ability of a household to manage risk and respond to and cope with sudden shocks that are likely to overwhelm them.

scale-up or *scale* The process by which a program is established, expanded, or adapted under real-world conditions into broader national policy and programming. This process often builds on the success of programs shown to be effective on a small scale or under controlled conditions. It may also be driven without prior piloting and testing, often in response to a political decision or directive. The process is not just about coverage—the number of beneficiaries served by the program in relation to the total population of the country—but also about quality—the quality of impact and sustainability of coverage, as well as processes of change and adaptation. Therefore, economic inclusion at scale considers the programmatic and institutional mechanics required to embed programs at the national level through large-scale antipoverty programs, led by governments with clear alignment with national strategies, partnership development, and underlying political economy considerations.

self-help program A savings-and-credit group consisting of women and men who meet regularly to undertake financial savings and internal loans from the group's common funds. Self-help groups can be federated, with each group represented in a federation structure that can serve as a platform for economic inclusion, linking the poorest to the formal banking system and enabling a range of services, including insurance, credit counseling, sound financial practice orientation, as well as digital and mobile banking.

social protection Social protection and labor systems help poor and vulnerable people cope with crises and shocks, find jobs, invest in the health and education of their children, and protect the aging population.

social safety net or *safety net* Noncontributory transfer programs that target in some manner poor individuals and those vulnerable to poverty and shocks. Social safety nets can include cash, in-kind transfers, social pensions, public works, and school feeding programs aimed at poor and vulnerable households. It is analogous to the US term *welfare* and the European term *social assistance*.

www.ingramcontent.com/pod-product-compliance
Lightning Source LLC
Chambersburg PA
CBHW050906210326
41597CB00002B/43